WOODCARVING TOOLS, MATERIALS & EQUIPMENT

VOLUME 2

WOODCARVING TOOLS, MATERIALS & EQUIPMENT

NEW EDITION

VOLUME 2

C H R I S P Y E

GUILD OF MASTER CRAFTSMAN PUBLICATIONS LTD

First edition published 1994 by
Guild of Master Craftsman Publications Ltd
Castle Place, 166 High Street,
Lewes, East Sussex BN7 1XU

Reprinted 1996, 1997, 2000

This new edition in two volumes 2002, both reprinted 2003

This volume, Volume 2, reprinted in 2007

Text © Christopher J. Pye 1994, 2002
© in the Work GMC Publications 2002
Principal photography by Chris Skarbon,
© GMC Publications 2002;
other photography as listed on page 170
Line drawings © Christopher J. Pye 1994, 2002,
except where otherwise stated

ISBN-13: 978-1-86108-201-5 (Volume 1)
ISBN-10: 1-86108-201-0 (Volume 1)

ISBN-13: 978-1-86108-202-2 (Volume 2)
ISBN-10: 1-86108-202-9 (Volume 2)

ISBN-10: 0-946819-49-1 (First Edition)
ISBN-13: 978-0-946819-49-2 (First Edition)

A catalogue record for this book is available from the British Library.

Managing Editor: Gerrie Purcell
Production Manager: Jim Bulley
Editor: Stephen Haynes
Designer: Ian Hunt Design
Cover Designer: Danny McBride
Cover photograph by Anthony Bailey, © GMC Publications 2002
Set in Goudy and Trajan

Colour origination by Viscan Graphics (Singapore)
Printed and bound in China by Hing Yip Printing Co Ltd

Gino Masero's hands

CONTENTS OF VOLUME 2

OUTLINE OF VOLUME 1

MEASUREMENTS

Although care has been taken to ensure that the metric measurements are true and accurate, they are only conversions from imperial; they have been rounded up or down to the nearest whole millimetre, or to the nearest convenient equivalent in cases where the imperial measurements themselves are only approximate.

ACKNOWLEDGEMENTS

When I cast my mind, like a net, over all the people who have, in whatever way, contributed to this book, I soon realized that my gratitude must extend more widely than I have room to record. In fact there seems no end to those who have influenced me.

For example, I would include the makers of every carving I have ever gazed at, their patrons and tool-makers. Then there are those who have taught me, whose workshops I have visited, and who have shared their experience with me. And the authors of books and articles I have read, some long dead but whose thoughts I have taken as my own. And the carvers whose names appear as watery shadows on the handles of many of my tools, but of whom I know little or nothing at all. And students, whose names I have forgotten, who made me think about what I was telling them and why – and who caused me to write the original sheets on which this book is based. I want to acknowledge my debt to all these.

Foremost among them all must come the indefatigable Gino Masero, who oversaw my initial attempts at sharpening, and witnessed the first time I laid a cutting edge into a piece of limewood. His spirited friendship was a source of great joy, and I dedicate this book to him – an inadequate gesture of appreciation.

In the genesis of the book itself I am particularly grateful to my editor, Liz Inman, whose encouragement and enthusiasm really made the book possible.

In its preparation I took up the time of many people who freely gave me information, ideas and advice, and sometimes the tools and equipment themselves to try out: Tony Walker of Robert Sorby Ltd; Bill Tilbrook of Tilgear; John Tiranti of Alec Tiranti Ltd; Barry Martin of Henry Taylor Tools Ltd; Tony Iles of Ashley Iles (Edge Tools) Ltd; Charles Stirling of Bristol Design; Peter Peck of Record Tools; and Glynn Bilson of HTF Tools. I also thank Ray Gonzalez for the idea of numbering gouge handles to indicate particular circle arcs.

Coming closer to home, I would catch, as it were in a quick gather of the net, some of the many people who so generously gave their time to read through different parts and made helpful corrections and suggestions: Stephen Parr, Tony Walker, Candy Harrison and Ken Day. I would very much like to thank Gino Masero again for his efforts in this respect, as well as for the use of his drawings of the tilting portable bench. As for my good friend Phil Hutchins who, having no interest in carving whatsoever, took the role of an objective reader – his effort on my behalf can only be described as heroic. I am also very grateful to Phyllis van de Hoek who made life a lot easier by tirelessly photocopying the drawings.

And in my net, saving the loveliest catch till last, my wife Karin Vogel, who has put up with such a lot as I wrestled with several learning curves and has given me unstinting support in the background. I sincerely wish to thank her for her help and patience.

Since the first edition appeared, my mentor and friend Gino Masero has died, leaving only flashes of scaly lights in the mesh. It's a real pleasure to improve on what he started, and I am sorry he didn't have a chance to see this book in colour – he'd have loved it.

Many firms have given generous help in updating this book, both by making tools and equipment available and by freely giving advice and information. In particular I thank: Barry and Tony Iles of Ashley Iles (Edge Tools) Ltd; Alan Styles of Axminster Power Tool Centre; Geoff and Martin Brown of BriMarc Associates; Douglas Ballantyne of Carroll Tools Ltd; Nick Davidson of Craft Supplies Ltd; Clair Brewer of Bosch Ltd; Brenda Keely of Dremel UK; David Bennet of Falls Run Tools; Hegner UK; Rod Naylor; Dennis Abdy of Henry Taylor Tools Ltd; Richard Starkie of Starkie & Starkie; Mike Hancock of The Toolshop; and Wally Wilson of Veritas Tools Inc.

Special thanks to Stephen Haynes for his sharp eye and sedulous, but caring, editing; Chris Skarbon for his sympathetic photography; and Ian Hunt and Danny McBride, the book and cover designers.

That loveliest catch just grows more so.

HEALTH AND SAFETY

Notes on safety are found throughout this book. They are gathered together here for reference, with no apology for repetition. No claim is made for completeness, as full, or particular, circumstances cannot be accounted for.

The best safeguard against accidents is mindfulness. It is lack of concentration and forethought that causes most accidents. For example, putting your hand on the edge of a projecting gouge: what actually caused the accident was not the gouge, but the attitude that placed it dangerously in the first place. Lack of experience is also important. An effort should be made to understand and familiarize yourself with all tools and equipment before using them in earnest.

Safety lies in:

- being in control

- being aware of the dangers

- not being distracted

- not being over-confident

- gaining experience.

GENERAL SAFETY PRECAUTIONS

IN THE WORKSHOP

- Stand at the entrance to the workplace with a notepad and challenge yourself to think of all the ways you could be hurt in the space in front of you, including the tools and equipment.

- Keep a fully stocked first aid box easily accessible.

- Remember that there are even more possibilities for accidents when children and visitors enter the workplace.

- All electric wires should be installed, earthed and covered properly.

- Store and arrange tools and equipment safely, securely and conveniently.

- A fire alarm and extinguisher should always be installed.

- The carver's environment tends to be dry and contain inflammable wood chips, finishing agents, etc. Never leave a naked flame unattended. No smoking is the best advice. If you need to use a source of heat, first make sure it is safe.

- Bag up and remove dust and debris regularly, especially any rags used for finishing.

- Use and store solvents, glues, turpentine, spirit- and oil-based stains, as well as all other finishes, in well-ventilated areas. Keep containers closed when not in use, and keep them away from children, heat and naked flames.

- Make sure that where you walk is free from the danger of sharp edges and corners, things to bump into and wires to trip over. See that you can easily and safely work around your bench, and that wood chips and dust on the floor do not make it slippery.

- Sharp tools left clamped in vices with their tangs or edges exposed, or projecting in the air over the bench, are dangerous.

- Long hair, etc. should be tied back, and loose clothing (cuffs and ties) and jewellery (necklaces and rings) should be kept away from the moving parts of machines, and in general out of the sphere of activity.

ELECTRIC TOOLS AND EQUIPMENT

- Always follow the manufacturer's instructions and recommendations.

- Familiarize yourself with any tool or piece of equipment before using it.

- Safety guards, rests, etc. should be properly adjusted and used.

- Keep hands and fingers well clear of moving parts – remember that accidents happen quickly, sometimes before you have noticed anything wrong. Never reach over or across machines.

- Double-check everything, including the locking of chucks, the table, or any fence before starting the machine.

- Face or eye protection is always advisable. Grit and sparks are quite capable of penetrating the eyeball; chips of wood can fly off; and it is possible for a cutter or burr to break.

- Keep face masks and eye and ear protection easily to hand – and put them on before using the equipment.

- Fix work securely before drilling, power-shaping, and so on.

- Keep wiring from machines and electrical hand tools neatly out of the way, not trailing over the floor or work surfaces.

- Always sharpen, or change, a blade or cutter with the machine isolated – that is, with the plug pulled out.

- Do not drip water from the cooling jar over motors, electrical connections or plugs.

- Use a cutter or other accessories for a high-speed shaft at or below its maximum rated speed. Used above the speed for which it is designed, the cutter could fly apart, bend or otherwise be damaged.

- Never use a bent or damaged cutter or burr, or one that vibrates or chatters, in a high-speed flexible shaft – throw these away. Never force or pressure these accessories.

SAFETY PRECAUTIONS FOR WOODCARVERS

Again, many of these points occur in context in this book and should be studied there.

- Always hold work securely to a stable bench or surface.

- Do not lay carving tools down with their edges projecting, or close to where your hands are working.

- Keep your tools sharp and clean. Blunt tools require more force – sharp ones are less dangerous.

- Keep both hands, and all fingers, behind the cutting edge at all times.

- Never cut, or exert pressure, towards any part of the body.

- A tough glove is recommended when rasps are being used. A fingerless glove will protect the heels of the hands when working on wood with rough or sharp edges.

- Take particular care when using the benchstrop, especially on the forward stroke.

- Both hands should be on the carving tool, with the blade hand resting on the wood. The only exceptions to this are during mallet work and when using specific one-handed carving techniques.

- If using one hand to hold the work and the other to manipulate the chisel, use the thumb of the work-holding hand as a pivot or guide to control the cutting – never cut towards the work-holding hand.

- In vigorous mallet work, especially with very hard, brittle or old and dry woods, eye protection is advisable.

- Never try to catch a falling carving tool. Carve in footwear strong enough to protect the feet from such an event.

- When sanding, use a dust mask; never blow; and protect your eyes.

There are two other conditions which can affect carvers, besides the obvious family of accidents:

HAND AND WRIST DAMAGE

Hand and wrist damage caused by thumping tool handles with the palm of the hand is mentioned in the section on using mallets (Volume 2, Chapter 1). The damage can be permanent, so it is sensible to avoid the risk by using a mallet instead.

REPETITIVE STRAIN INJURY

RSI is felt as a burning sensation in the wrist or elbow joints of those prone to it, possibly accompanied by redness and swelling. It is commonly known as 'tennis elbow' or condylitis. The condition is caused by mechanical stress on a tendon attachment, especially through holding or repeating the same tense position of the joint for long periods of time. Seek medical advice early; this is important for reasons of health insurance.

It can be a slow condition to clear up, and may be incapacitating in the long term. On the other hand, there are forearm straps which can remove strain from the elbow and help full recovery. Do not imagine that the problem has gone, just because you have taken painkillers. Besides removing the strain from the joint, you will need to find new techniques of working which eliminate, or at least reduce, strain. Fortunately there is plenty of scope for this in woodcarving.

FOREWORD TO THE FIRST EDITION

I first met Chris Pye in 1974, shortly after I had moved from London to Sussex. In my newly acquired rural workshop, sited among blossoming apple trees, we took stock of one another across a carving bench, and became friends. I was on the verge of possible retirement, while Chris was in the early stages of his career, but it has always seemed remarkable how a common interest in woodcarving can quickly bridge any age gap.

Although having an irrepressible sense of humour, he struck me as being a thoughtful and studious person, an adept carver and with the ability to express himself well on craft matters – a rare combination.

Since those days in the early 1970s he has taught carving and developed into a designer-craftsman of some stature. This has been borne out by the creation of a very successful carving and woodturning business in the south-west of England, which thrived despite the recession.

As a woodcarving instructor myself, over the years I have made a point of reading through many craft books and periodicals on the subject, but only at intervals did I find something of major interest that I could pass on to students. There seemed to be a certain lack of vital information published, and to some degree it troubled me.

To be taught by a caring expert is the best possible way of learning a craft, and Chris Pye is foremost in this, being blessed with friendliness as well as approachability, and a genuine interest in his students, talented and otherwise. For the amateur, who for one good reason or another has to go it alone, it can be conceded that with some ability, carving is not too onerous in the initial stage (after all, our palaeolithic ancestors did not do too badly carving bone and ivory figurines). But major and minor problems can soon arise, often leading to frustration and despair. Setbacks tend to occur when the student, naturally, wants to progress towards more ambitious work. Apart from the inevitable problems that stem from lack of technique, the most serious difficulties, I have found, arise from trying to carve with blunt tools, or even damaged ones. So it was a most welcome and splendid surprise when Chris sent to me the outline of his book on carving tools, materials and a whole range of equipment that traditional and modern carvers require for their work.

Even at the initial stage I was happily aware of a very closely researched and comprehensive source book, packed with information, and with sketches and photos galore. I believe that it is a most useful work, and can only anticipate that it will be widely read, so increasing student potential, as well as obtaining for them the maximum enjoyment that a truly great craft can offer.

Gino Masero
December 1993

FOREWORD TO THE NEW EDITION

By the middle of the twentieth century the craft of woodcarving in the English-speaking world had dwindled, largely because the use of traditional ornament and the making of accurate figure sculpture had fallen out of fashion. It was continued in a handful of workshops satisfying a limited market for architectural and furniture ornament, and in those involved in the restoration of cathedrals and other historic buildings. People like Gino Masero, who guided Chris Pye, and William Wheeler, who taught me, were among the few who were willing and able to pass on their skills to outsiders. For the most part, woodcarving became the preserve of the amateur and the folk carver. Most of the amateurs were self-taught, or were instructed by the self-taught. In many cases in their teaching and writing they passed on bad habits and were ignorant of the methods and standards of the earlier master carvers. In a book by one such, I once read that oak was too hard to carve; the writer thereby dismissed most of the woodcarving done in medieval Europe, including great works of ornament and sculpture. Most recommended the use of sandpaper as a remedy for a rough finish, even on carvings where the effect would be to reduce the forms to lifelessness while consuming inordinate time and effort.

Since first encountering the writings of Chris Pye about carving and the carver's tools, I have valued and respected his ideas. Like me, he sets the greatest store by the old and well-tried ways using hand tools, but when some new development arises he is willing to employ it, provided it produces the desired result and saves time.

We all know people who collect gadgets, every time hoping that the new acquisition will prove the carver's panacea, the one magic tool that will effortlessly turn them into brilliant carvers. In the real world this does not happen. There is no substitute for study through drawing and a sequence of planned exercises supervised by good teachers – in other words, for hard work. However, down the centuries carving tools have evolved, each new shape being a solution to a carver's problem. Mostly the carvers were aiming to save time, to produce clean work and to be able to carve more sophisticated shapes. By now, the number and variety of tools and ancillary equipment is so bewildering that a book such as this is invaluable both for the novice wondering what is needed to start and for the experienced carver wishing to extend his or her range.

This new edition is an enlarged and up-to-date version of a book that has already become a most useful reference work. It is all-embracing and accurate in its content, and full of intelligence and good sense. It may not be a magic gadget but, used intelligently, it will set you on the way to carving well.

Dick Onians
September 2001

PART I

THE WORKSHOP AND ITS EQUIPMENT

AIMS OF PART I

- To describe the main tools used by carvers, in addition to woodcarving tools proper

- To review the power tools and machines which are most likely to be useful to woodcarvers

- To describe some simple ways of changing the existing shapes of woodcarving tools in order to make them suitable for particular carving situations, and to indicate the possibilities for making entirely new tools

- To consider the many different strategies for holding carved work

- To advise on what makes a suitable, pleasant and safe working environment for carving

The main tools used by carvers, in addition to woodcarving tools proper

The mallet is perhaps the most obvious of the carver's ancillary tools, and deserves special consideration. But specialized carving tools also take their place, of course, in the wider context of working wood. It's hard to imagine a carver who doesn't have to use more conventional woodworking tools now and then, before, during or after carving. There are, too, other tools for shaping wood besides 'carving tools' in the narrow sense of the term. Knowing about these additional tools helps to extend the possibilities of what a carver can do, and Chapter 1 looks at the most useful of them.

The power tools and machines which are most likely to be useful to woodcarvers

Woodcarving is all about removing mass: taking off wood you don't want and leaving what you do. Commonly, before the laying on of chisels there is a lot of waste wood to come away; and even during carving there are often areas that can be quickly and more conveniently 'wasted' by other means. Power tools and machines come into their own at these times, as well as for texturing and finishing in the later stages.

Chapter 2 looks at the principal types available to the carver, with notes on how and when they can help, and – possibly more importantly – the times when they won't.

Changing the existing shapes of woodcarving tools and making new ones

It comes as a surprise to many carvers how readily carving tools can be made or altered to suit a particular requirement. No busy carver has the time to reinvent the wheel and make carving tools that are readily available to buy, but I have found the satisfying ability to shape and make tools useful indeed on occasion. Many carvers are a little afraid of the metalworking aspects of carving tools. Chapter 3 demystifies the basics of tool shaping and tempering so that you can approach them with confidence.

Different strategies for holding carved work

How a carving is held – safely, flexibly and to the best carving advantage – really can make the difference between success and failure, between heartache and backache. Chapter 4 will help you become aware of some of the principal alternatives for holding your work, and will encourage you to build up a repertoire of options from which you can improvise if need be.

A suitable, pleasant and safe working environment for carving

It often surprises me how little thought is given by students to their carving environment – how carving is often relegated to damp cellars or cold garages. I believe that the workplace contributes enormously to successful and enjoyable woodcarving; it should be both an attractive haven and a help to you in your efforts. Chapter 5 looks at this neglected aspect of carving, and suggests ways to make the workplace work to support the carving process.

A detail of the lobster carving shown complete in Fig 7.18

CHAPTER ONE

ACCESSORY TOOLS

AIMS

- To describe the main tools used by carvers, in addition to woodcarving tools proper

- To give a few notes on their use and their place in the woodcarving process

The tools which carvers and sculptors use to achieve the effects they want, to experiment and explore, are many and varied. The tools and equipment discussed in this chapter are commonly used; some are so common that no more than a few notes, in passing, need be given.

As with woodcarving tools:

- Buy them as you need them.

- Buy the best quality you can afford.

- Use them safely.

- Care for them and store them correctly.

MALLETS

Mallets are used in woodcarving for the heavier, roughing-out stages and for setting in, especially in hard woods where handwork is inefficient or too stressful. The word *mallet* is a diminutive of *maul*, a heavy wooden hammer used for splitting logs. Both come through the French from the Latin *malleus*, meaning 'a hammer'.

Mallets can leave bold work that looks well at a distance, besides being a forerunner to finishing by hand – and indeed some carvers do most of their work with a mallet for the boldness, simplicity and flair that mallet work can give (Figs 1.1–1.4). Carvers

Fig 1.1 *An acanthus moulding in oak. The stab marks left by setting in with a mallet can be seen in the ground*

Fig 1.2 *A detail from the Tudor façade in Abbey Dore Church, Herefordshire. The mallet work needed to carve the hard oak can clearly be seen*

Fig 1.4 *A detail of Fig 1.3, showing the surface texture straight from the chisel*

Fig 1.3 *A face from Abbey Dore; note the bold, crisp and simple lines*

tend to collect a variety of mallets of different sizes and weights for different jobs (Fig 1.5).

SHAPES

Woodcarvers' mallets are round, not square. There are definite reasons why this shape is preferred by carvers, and several factors that make a good mallet shape.

The earliest known mallets, from ancient Egypt, were made quite naturally from branches of heavy wood, waisted to form a handle (Fig 1.6). Square billets of wood, again with an integral handle, are shown in Roman paintings being used for mortising, as they still are today. Both round- and square-headed mallets have a very long history, continuing up to the present time (Fig 1.7), and each has its own place. But why the different shapes?

In chopping out a woodworking joint, say a mortise, the flat side of the chisel cuts its own guiding jig (see Volume 1, page 137). To keep the face of the joint true, the chisel needs to be struck squarely so the force goes straight along the blade (Fig 1.8). Hence the need for the square, flat face of the mallet.

A carving gouge, on the other hand, is struck from all sorts of directions, as it can be presented to the

Fig 1.5 *A collection of carving mallets. Left to right:* lignum vitae, nylon, lignum vitae, annealed iron *(two examples),* beech

wood at an infinite number of angles. In this case the force is transmitted tangentially (Fig 1.9). The mallet does not have to be aligned in the exact way a square-faced one must be; therefore a round mallet, which always presents a similar face to the tool handle, can be used, and the carver can strike with confidence without ever looking away from the carving.

As well as being round in cross section, the heads of both square and round mallets are also slightly tapered towards the handle (Figs 1.10 and 1.11). In both cases the blow pivots from the elbow. The tapering head of the mallet allows the face to strike the handle of a cutting tool more squarely – at least in this one direction. In the case of the carving mallet, a slight belly at the striking point also helps to strengthen this part against wear and tear.

Fig 1.7 *Mallets have been used for thousands of years*

Fig 1.6 *The earliest mallets were made from a waisted log of hardwood* (a). *Passing a handle through the log* (b) *made another early type of mallet which had the advantage of striking with the end grain*

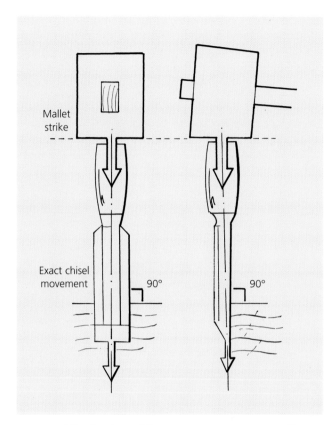

Fig 1.8 *The flat face of the joiner's or carpenter's mallet must be lined up squarely to the chisel if it is not to deflect the handle*

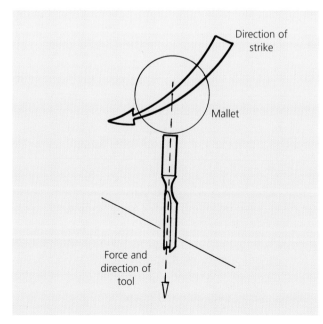

Fig 1.9 *The force of the round woodcarving mallet, striking from an infinite number of directions, passes at a tangent down the tool*

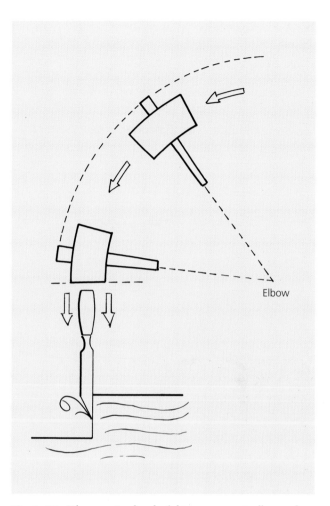

Fig 1.10 *The tapering head of this carpentry mallet works with the swing from the elbow to give a directed strike*

Fig 1.11 *A round carving mallet should also be tapered so as to reflect the swing from the elbow and strike the tool handle squarely*

Some other features contribute to a good mallet shape – bear these in mind if ever you make one:

- The handle should be comfortable, with nothing prominent to cause soreness or even blistering (Fig 1.12). A mallet can be used for long periods of work and you may not notice the effect until

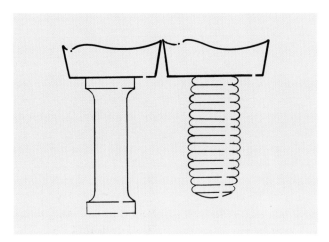

Fig 1.12 *Although they may look attractive, ridges on mallet handles can make the hand sore with prolonged use*

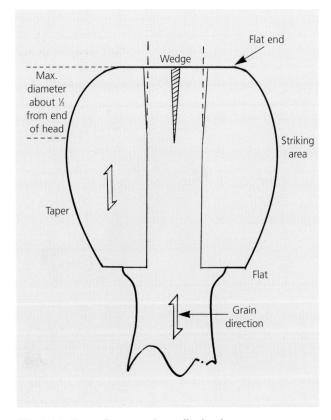

Fig 1.13 *Some features of a mallet head*

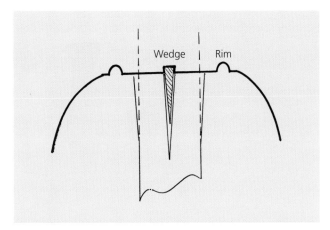

Fig 1.14 *If the wedge is left proud, it can be driven further in if the handle shrinks; the mallet still sits upright on the bench, thanks to the raised rim*

you put it down. Too fat a shape can make the hands ache; too thin feels a little weak and uncertain.

- The handle should be firmly wedged into the head of the mallet. A very important point is that the hole for the handle needs to taper out a little at the far end so that the wedged spigot of the handle becomes locked and immovable (Fig 1.13). Indeed, you have to drill the handle out should you ever need to replace it. If the hole is not tapered, the head can loosen, even despite the wedge – although this is less likely with smaller mallets, which are used more delicately. A flat top to the mallet head permits it to sit upright on the bench and not roll around.

- A nicety is to form a rim around the top of the mallet, leaving the wedge proud to begin with; the wedge can then be tapped in further if the handle shrinks (Fig 1.14).

MATERIALS

Mallets with a separate handle are relatively recent, probably stemming from the time when newly discovered dense woods, such as lignum vitae, could be exploited for their weight and size ratios. 'Lignum' is one of the best woods to use; the diameter of most other woods must be considerably larger to get a similar weight. However, almost any hardwood will make a mallet: for example, beech, elm or even fruitwoods (Table 1.1).

Mallets can be made of other materials, including:

- nylon (originally developed for stonecarving)

- mild steel (these need metal ferrules on the struck end of the carving-tool handle)

- lead-iron alloy (as in **dummy mallets**, again used in stonecarving)

- brass.

The use of metal gives a smaller size to the mallet for a given weight – and it will never wear out. The surface of a wooden mallet tends to be alternately end grain and side grain. The side grain will bruise and feather away after a while, far more than the end grain, giving an uneven shape to the mallet. In this context it is worth mentioning Lignostone mallets, made from beech veneers, compressed under enormous pressure with resin glue to result in a virtually indestructible surface consisting entirely of end grain (Fig 1.15).

Fig 1.15 A Lignostone mallet, made from compressed beech veneers. This one has a ridge on the handle which might well cause soreness if used for an extensive period; rounding it over would be a major improvement

The balls or 'woods' used in the game of bowls were traditionally made of lignum vitae. These days they are mostly made from artificial materials which are not affected by the weather, and old bowls sometimes become available. These can be made into excellent mallets, consisting totally of lignum hardwood – not sapwood, in the way of most commercially sold mallets (Fig 1.16). The process is described on pages 10–12.

The nylon mallets, which are manufactured rather large, can easily be shaped, or reduced in size, on a lathe.

The best wood for the handle is a straight, close-grained bit of ash, hickory or hornbeam, although other woods such as box or yew work well.

WOOD	DENSITY (APPROX.)	
	lb per cubic foot	*kg per m³*
Apple	20–40	320–640
Yew	40	640
Beech	45	720
Plum	50	800
Hickory	53	850
Lignum vitae	80	1,280

Table 1.1 Some woods used for mallets. For a heavy mallet, use the densest wood you can to keep the size as compact as possible. Remember that other materials such as nylon and brass are occasionally used

Fig 1.16 A mallet made from lignum heartwood (left) is far more durable than one made from a branch, which is mainly sapwood. Almost all commercial lignum mallets are of the second type

SIZE AND WEIGHT

Commercially made mallets vary in weight from a lightweight 1lb (0.45kg) to a Herculean 5lb (2.25kg); the dimensions vary according to the material from which they are made. The physical build of the individual carver, as well as the size of the work and the hardness of the wood, will dictate which weight is most comfortable to work with.

It is a mistake for a newcomer to choose a heavier mallet, thinking the work will go quicker. It may well do to begin with, but for most people heavy blows are quickly tiring, as well as stressful on the wrists and elbows. The carving tools and handles must also be fit for heavy mallet work.

It is better to go for light- and medium-weight mallets to begin with – possibly 1lb (0.45kg) and 2lb (0.9kg). If you are not used to these weights, it is a good idea to heft the mallet first, rather than buying it blindly through the mail.

Notes on using mallets appear on pages 13–14.

MAKING A MALLET

For those with the ability, and access to a lathe, turning a mallet is a fairly straightforward process. Read through the following notes first, however, to make sure you have the tools. Before raising lignum vitae dust, protect yourself from it adequately.

If you are turning a bowls ball, the centre of the original lignum vitae tree lies underneath the metal caps on either end (Fig 1.17). Bore the hole for the handle here, down the centre. Hairline shakes in the wood can be ignored, as they do not affect the performance of the mallet. The head is bored first with a 1in (25mm) Forstner bit, and the shape turned around the hole using temporary plugs of wood.

TURNING THE MALLET HEAD

1. Using a slow speed, bore to about ¾in (20mm) from the other end. Tap a conical wooden plug into the hole, then reverse the wood and finish boring through to the first hole. You may find it helpful to form two flat facets on opposite sides of the ball first; this allows a clamp to be attached to hold the ball still during the boring operation (Fig 1.18).

2. Accurately tap in a second plug and mount the wood between centres. Rough the head down to a cylinder, which gives the maximum diameter of the mallet head (Fig 1.19).

3. Square off the ends of the cylinder and take them down to ½in (38mm) diameter with a parting tool, leaving only ¼in (6mm) of thickness to remove around the hole (Fig 1.20).

4. Using the long point of a skew chisel, reduce the length of the very ends by no more than

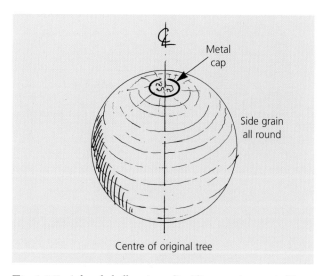

Fig 1.17 *A bowls ball or 'wood' of lignum vitae, suitable for turning into a mallet*

Fig 1.18 *If two flat faces are bandsawn on either side of the ball, a clamp can be attached to stop it rotating when being bored*

Fig 1.19 With the central hole plugged, the preliminary shaping of the mallet can be started

Fig 1.20 Starting to flatten the ends. The problem is how to finish up to the plug

¹⁄₁₆in (1.5mm) of wood at a time, scoring into the plug. Each time you have reduced the length of the head, wind in the tailstock and take up the slack that is produced. A cut, then a tightening up: in this way the plug is continuously worked into the hole and there is no danger of the work coming off the lathe. When the ends are completely shaved flat, take the work off the lathe and remove the plugs – a Stilson wrench or Mole grips may be useful here.

❺ Decide which is to be the handle end of the mallet, and make a hardwood spigot of a diameter that taps nicely into the hole at this end. The spigot should enter the hole to a

depth of about one third of the way into the ball. Lignum, although amazingly good at withstanding compression, will split more easily – so take care when inserting the spigot not to over-force it. Grip the spigot in a three-jaw scroll chuck. This should allow you to splay the end of the hole to accommodate the expanding wedge in the handle (Fig 1.21).

Fig 1.21 Reaming the hole to accommodate the wedge-splayed end of the handle

❻ Using a slow speed and light strokes with a straight-sided scraper, ream out the hole. An increase of diameter of ¹⁄₈in (3mm) at the exit – starting from a depth of about one third of the way in – is enough (Fig 1.22).

❼ Replace the plugs. Line up the mallet head on the lathe and give it its final shape with

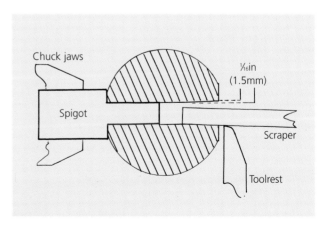

Fig 1.22 Carefully skim the hole to about one third of the way in

the skew chisel (Fig 1.23). Finish to at least 180 grit and polish with a coat or two of raw linseed oil. The head is now finished and can be put to one side.

Fig 1.23 *The final shape of the mallet head: bellied and slightly tapering*

TURNING THE HANDLE

❶ The handle (Fig 1.24) is turned as a normal bit of between-centres work. Make the spigot that goes through the head about ¼in (6mm) over length to begin with, and a snug fit. Undercut the shoulder slightly.

❷ Feel the handle for comfort; you can take it off the lathe and try it with the head on to get the right shape. Leave the waste material on the ends for the time being, and sand well. Burnishing the wood with shavings is the best finish, but it can be sealed with a coat of cellulose lacquer or shellac, finely cut back, if you prefer. Take care not to create a shiny, slippery surface.

Fig 1.24 *An assortment of handle shapes; comfort is very important*

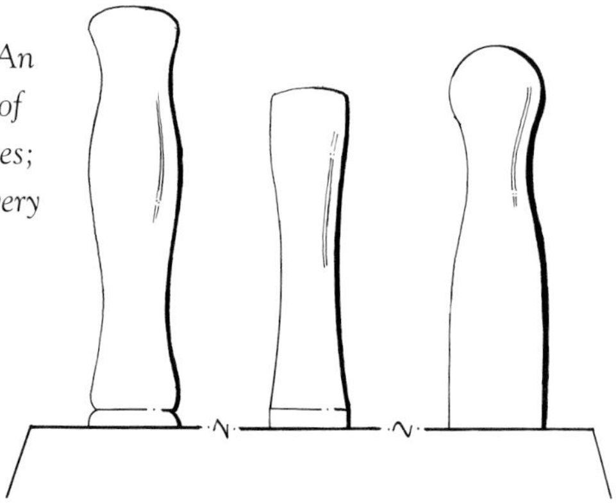

❸ Next, form the saw cut to take the wedge. Make a support so that the spigot of the handle can be offered to the bandsaw safely and accurately (Fig 1.25). Saw down the centre about two thirds of the way. A handsaw will also do.

❹ Make a long and slender wedge to go into the saw cut. Insert the spigot into the head, making sure the shoulder of the handle is flush against the underside. Standing the handle on end, drive the wedge home to lock the head on (Fig 1.26). Trim off the waste, the wedge and the spigot end with a small saw and chisel. Sand and seal as before.

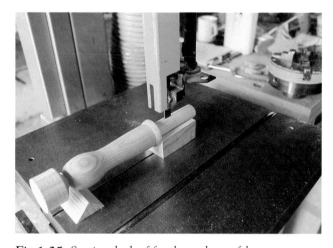

Fig 1.25 *Sawing the kerf for the wedge, safely*

Fig 1.26 *Driving the wedge home. It may be an idea to leave the mallet for a while in case the handle shrinks; then tap the wedge finally home, trimming it off so the mallet sits upright on the bench*

USING THE MALLET

Before using the mallet, it is worth removing as much wood as possible from the carving using the bandsaw or similar tool.

When a lot of mallet work is needed, as in large-scale sculpture, try to work in an even, rhythmic way. A regular pace will remove more wood, and be less tiring in the long run, than sporadic bursts of passion.

Keep the elbow of the mallet arm in – towards the body – as much as possible, and strike so as to include the shoulder (Fig 1.27). This achieves two things:

- The stress and fatigue on the elbow and arm are lessened, allowing the work to go on for longer.

- It is easier to put your weight behind the mallet blow, which increases the efficiency of the cutting enormously.

Try to have a sense of your feet in contact with the ground as you are using the mallet so that, braced in this way, the striking force travels forward into the handle of the gouge. The more your body is behind the mallet, the more efficient the cut will be.

Learn to use the mallet with either arm from the start, not just because this shares the work, but because it also avoids having to contort the body at awkward angles to make the necessary cuts to the carving. This is an especially valuable discipline for lettering work.

Do not try to remove too much wood at a time, or cut so deeply as to bury the carving tool.

The tighter the longitudinal curve of a carving tool, the less it should be hit with a mallet. The pressures delivered have to go somewhere, and they may go into breaking the tool.

Work in regular patterns across the surface to be removed. Traditional Japanese carving recognizes this way of working as producing beauty in its own right – carvings may be left in this stage as 'finished'.

Remember that a mallet has two weights, depending whether it is held by the handle or the head (Figs 1.28 and 1.29). Mallet work can be quite delicate, although perhaps not as controlled as handwork.

Besides the mallet, carvers have always propelled their gouges by striking them with the palm of the

Fig 1.28 The usual way to strike with a mallet: the extended thumb helps to guide the carving tool

Fig 1.29 Precise, light striking is possible if the mallet is held by the head

Fig 1.27 A good posture for using the mallet: the body to one side and the shoulder being used, rather than just the forearm and wrist

hand, perhaps building up quite considerable calluses over the years. While this is no doubt a useful technique for occasional, light work, there is a real danger of damaging the large numbers of nerves and tendons that pass through the wrist and palm – the carpal tunnel (Fig 1.30). The effect varies between individuals, but thickening here can give rise to a well-recognized, claw-like deformity of the hand – the surgical repair of which is often unsuccessful. If you must strike the handle with the palm, use the meaty bit at the base of the thumb or its equivalent on the other side, and avoid the centre. Do it lightly and infrequently. Better still, use the mallet.

Another possibility is a **palm mallet**; this is the proprietary term for a product marketed by Wood Carvers' Supply Inc. of Englewood, Florida, designed to protect this vulnerable area of the hand. The palm mallet is a leather-covered pad of shock-absorbing gel which soaks up pressure and impact. It is very effective, although still only for light work.

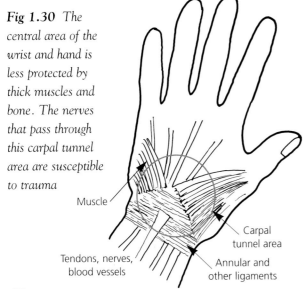

Fig 1.30 *The central area of the wrist and hand is less protected by thick muscles and bone. The nerves that pass through this carpal tunnel area are susceptible to trauma*

Muscle

Tendons, nerves, blood vessels

Carpal tunnel area

Annular and other ligaments

CARE

Mallets should reside – as all wood should – away from direct sources of heat. Very dry atmospheres may cause the wood to shrink. The mallet will recover if kept in a plastic bag with a damp cloth for a while. An occasional wipe with linseed oil will keep the wood sweet – though, unfortunately, this never works with the owner.

ABRADING TOOLS

Rasps, **files** and **rifflers** are bars of hardened steel with multiple teeth which remove wood as 'spoil', or coarse sawdust, rather than as chips or shavings. Buy the best-quality tools when you need them; poor-quality rasps and files quickly lose their cutting ability. There are so many variations, producing varied effects in different woods, that some experimenting may be necessary.

RASPS

Rasps, strictly speaking, have individually raised teeth, giving coarse, medium and fine cuts. The larger and coarser the teeth, the more quickly the wood is removed. An alternative type with strong, parallel cutting ridges is designed for shaping plastic and for car-body repair work. These work well on wood, giving a clean cut and a smooth finish (Fig 1.31)

The very best rasps and rifflers are handmade – hand-**stitched** – by Auriou in France. The slight irregularity of tooth position means an absence of the grooves that result from the rows of aligned teeth in a machine-stitched rasp, and a highly efficient cut (Fig 1.32). Particularly useful for flat surfaces in awkward places is the cranked Auriou rasp. Woodcarvers find themselves building up a range of shapes and sizes of rasp over the years, depending on their work.

Fig 1.31 *A selection of rasps: the largest is 2in (50mm) wide. The two on the left are intended for use on plastics, but are also effective on wood*

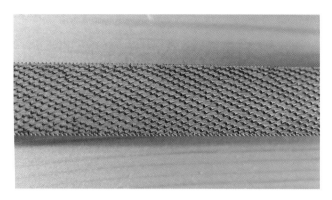

Fig 1.32 Close-up of the hand stitching of an Auriou rasp, showing the slightly irregular pattern which gives it its clean cut

The Japanese **saw rasp** is very unusual in that it is made of a lattice of hardened saw teeth, with large spaces for the swarf to fall away (Fig 1.33). This rasp is only to be had in one size. It has a very powerful, clean cut, one side coarse and the other fine.

Rasp blades are usually straight, with a flat, round or convex cross section; lengths vary from 8 to 12in (200 to 300mm). Farriers use particularly large rasps on horses' hooves, which work well on wood. Look also to suppliers of stonecarving tools.

FILES

Files differ from rasps in having fine ridges rather than individual teeth (Fig 1.34), producing a comparatively fine – sometimes extremely fine – cut, depending on the grade. They are very commonly used in metalwork, and are useful for producing an intermediary finish between that produced by rasps and that of sandpaper.

A **single-cut file** has a series of sharp ridges crossing the blade diagonally. The **double-cut file** has a second set of ridges crossing the first, producing diamond-shaped teeth; these files remove material quicker than the single-cut.

The size and spacing of the grooves determines the grade of file: *rough* is the coarsest, through *bastard*, *second-cut* and *smooth*, to *dead smooth*. Sometimes files are numbered according to a Swiss system, in which case 00 is the coarsest and 6 (or 06) the finest.

In cross section, files can be square, round, flat, half-round or triangular, each suitable for different purposes (Fig 1.35). The various lengths can be parallel or tapering (Fig 1.36).

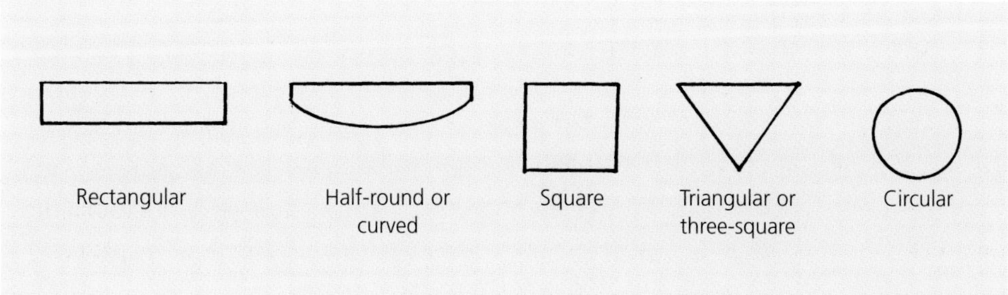

Fig 1.33 Close-up of the teeth of a Japanese saw rasp, which give it an extremely rapid, non-clogging cut

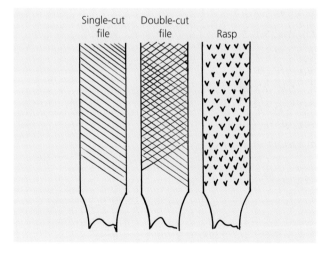

Fig 1.34 Files have ridges, while rasps have teeth

Rectangular   Half-round or curved   Square   Triangular or three-square   Circular

Fig 1.35 Files, rasps and rifflers can have a variety of basic cross sections

15

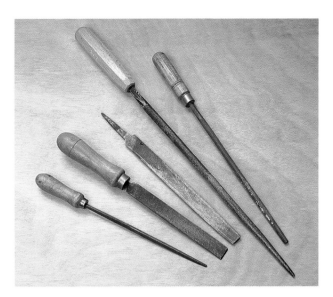

Fig 1.36 *Files: flat, round and triangular cross sections*

Small, round, tapering files are known as **rat-tail** or – smaller again – **mouse-tail** files. **Needle files** are slight, very fine versions of these files, often sold in sets and intended for precision metalwork. Needle rasps are also available.

Although files are common in tool shops, good selections will also be found in engineers' suppliers'. Look also at the files and rasps used for repairing vehicle bodywork and shaping plastic.

RIFFLERS

Rifflers are small paddle-like rasps, usually double-ended, with a narrow, metal handle in between (Fig 1.37). The lengths of these tools vary between 6in and 12in (10 and 300mm), but the cuts all tend to be similar – that is, medium.

The shape of the 'paddle' ends is very variable: straight, curved or angled; round, flat, triangular, convex or knife-like; parallel or tapered (Fig 1.38). The two ends may be different or the same. Different manufacturers will have their own idea of what is most useful, or marketable.

Possibly relating to the Old French *rifler*, meaning 'to scratch, strip or plunder', this bunch of assorted rasps can finish off corners and awkward areas which are inaccessible to carving tools. They can perform particularly useful functions in undercut and pierced work.

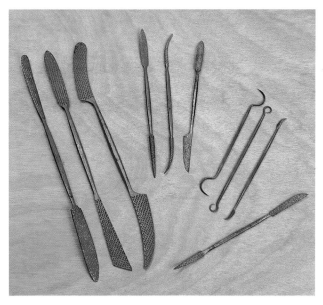

Fig 1.37 *Rifflers come in a great variety of shapes and sizes. The right-hand one has a coating of tungsten carbide particles*

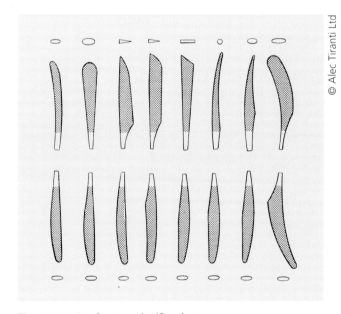

© Alec Tiranti Ltd

Fig 1.38 *A selection of riffler shapes*

MICROPLANES

Microplane is the registered name of the American firm Grace Engineering, whose UK distributor is Carroll Tools. Microplanes are made by a photo-chemical machining process out of stainless alloy (surgical) steel; they cannot rust, and resist clogging. Every tooth is indeed like a tiny, sharp plane (Fig 1.39), and they have a remarkable cutting ability.

Fig 1.39 *A close-up of the plane-like teeth which allow Microplanes to cut so fast and smoothly*

The teeth can be stropped with a hard leather and abrasive block, or rubbed on a fine oilstone to extend their working life.

Microplanes easily outperform that earlier replacement for the traditional rasp, the patented **Surform** or **shaper tool**. Stamped from sheet steel, this had hardened teeth to cut into the wood while the dust and shavings passed through holes in the blade to prevent clogging. I found that the teeth of the Surform skipped and skidded on the wood surface, dulled quickly, and tended to tear rather than cut; the tool was prone to rust, and still clogged when used on waxy woods.

The sizes and shapes of Microplanes are limited by the very nature of the blade, but a useful and continually extending range is to be had. Lengths include 8½in (216mm) and 3⅜in (85mm); available shapes are flat, round, half-round and square. Blades may be rigid or flexible. There is a size to fit Surform units, and another designed to be held in a standard 12in (305mm) hacksaw frame.

Children seem to find these tools very satisfying, but remember that they do have razor-sharp teeth. It would not be advisable to grip the blade itself unless you are wearing a thick leather glove.

Microplanes are lightweight, easy to use and remove wood quickly and efficiently; the resulting surface is smooth, with minimal marks. In many instances a Microplane will be a good substitute for a traditional rasp but, because of the limitation in shapes dictated by the nature of the Microplane

blade, rasps and rifflers will still be around for a long time.

TUNGSTEN CARBIDE

More and more, patented processes for attaching tungsten-carbide grit onto a flexible backing fibre are producing hard-wearing, rasp-like tools. The products themselves may be flexible or, when applied to hard plastic or an aluminium backing, shaped like true rasps or files.

There is usually a colour grading from coarse to fine cut. Although these tools, along with diamond-grit versions, are principally designed for metalwork, the coarsest versions will also abrade wood, rather like fine sandpaper.

USING ABRADING TOOLS

The function of rasps and files is more that of shaping than carving. They are not normally used for producing detail, but for reducing waste wood, rounding, refining, smoothing and exploring. It is always quickest to remove preliminary waste wood with a gouge and mallet.

It is easy to dismiss these tools as simple, or as expedients for those who cannot sharpen or use a carving tool properly – but very beautiful, refined and subtle forms can be made with these tools alone. They come into their own, prior to sanding, in the types of sculpture where very smooth planes are needed to show off the grain of the wood. Rasps start the process, followed by files and then sandpaper.

One end of a file or rasp will have a sharp tang for a handle, which is normally supplied separately. The handle needs a ferrule to prevent it splitting, and can be fitted as described for carving-tool handles (see Volume 1, pages 69–70). It is better to use a handle to prevent damaging the palm of your hand (Fig 1.40); if this is not possible, remove some of the tang on a grinding wheel.

Both hands are normally applied to a rasp. Binding the far end of a coarse rasp with tape, or wearing a tough glove, will protect your fingers from the metal teeth. This is also useful when you want to reverse the rasp and draw it towards you.

Fig 1.40 The tang of a rasp or file can be uncomfortably sharp to the palm; fit a simple handle for protection

When rasping or filing, strongly visualize the form beneath. As the tools are pushed forwards through their cut, send them around the contours of the shape that you are seeking, rather than producing a series of 'flats' (Fig 1.41). For a good result on the surface, make the rasp or file move sideways at the same time as moving it forwards. On internal curved surfaces, a half-round rasp or file stroked with this winding type of cut will avoid unwanted grooves forming (Figs 1.42 and 1.43).

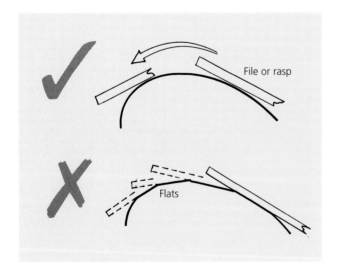

Fig 1.41 Move the rasp or file smoothly to follow the surface you are seeking

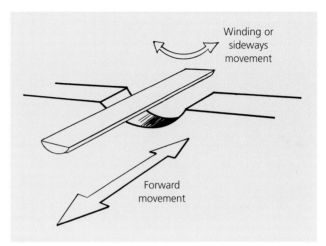

Fig 1.42 For internal curves, a combined action is best with the rasp or file

Fig 1.43 Winding the rasp through its cut is essential to achieve the smooth, unspoilt lines appropriate to this type of work. This rasp is one sold for car bodywork, and gives a very clean cut on wood

Sometimes, when carving in the conventional way, resorting to a rasp, file or riffler – before returning to the carving tools – can help to clarify larger forms and shapes.

CARE

The teeth of rasps and files do tend to clog with wood – especially those with a finer cut, or when working with resinous or moist material. The tools then become inefficient. Try coating them with chalk before using them on these sorts of wood. This does not apply to Microplanes, which allow the spoil to pass through the blade.

Fig 1.44 Regular use of a wire brush, and the smaller file card, will unclog the teeth of abrasive tools

A wire brush used across the teeth of a rasp will unclog them (Fig 1.44). Dried, resinous wood can be softened with paraffin oil (kerosene) before brushing, and it is also possible to dig around the teeth with a soft-metal point.

Files and tools with finer teeth need a **file card** – a special, short-bristled wire brush designed for the purpose. This brush is stroked across the teeth.

Files and rasps are often treated badly and thrown into boxes and damp corners. They really deserve better. Never use them as levers, as they are brittle and may snap; if used as hammers, the teeth may fly off. For similar reasons, store them carefully, perhaps in a rack to prevent their teeth from clashing together and blunting. The metal itself is susceptible to rust, which will affect the cutting edges and teeth by dulling them, so store them in a dry place.

Worn abrading tools are worth keeping, as they cut less voraciously than new ones.

SANDERS AND POWER FILES

For fast removal of stock and surface smoothing, sanding discs (on small angle grinders) and power files can be very useful.

The power file has a thin abrasive belt, about the size of a rasp. Both heavier and lighter-duty models are available, the latter being quite inexpensive and designed for home workshops. The main drawback of power files is the tremendous amount of fine dust that they generate. Their dust bags deal with only a limited amount of it; far better is to attach an industrial vacuum cleaner or other extractor in its place. Face masks are always necessary.

SANDPAPER

Whether a carving is sandpapered or not depends on the carver's intentions as well as the nature of the work. As sanding can be a tedious, unpleasant business, it is best to use other tools to get as close to the final surface as possible. Shaped scrapers (see pages 28–9) will flatten the surface, removing carving-tool and rasp marks.

Sandpaper comes in a variety of abrasives, backing papers and qualities. Flexible backing cloth is probably the most useful for carvers. The abrasive is graded between very coarse and extremely fine. In its manufacture the abrasive grit is sieved to ensure a uniform particle size: the more holes in the sieve, the finer the grit. The number marked on the back of the paper represents the number of holes in the sieve, so the higher the number, the finer the abrasive.

You need to work through the grades of paper to get the best result; the finer grades remove the scratch marks of the coarser grades. Always work *with* the grain, as working across the grain produces scratch marks, even the smallest of which will show up when the work is stained, oiled or waxed. It is better to sand with the fingers, sensitive to the surface beneath, rather than sanding blocks. Never be tempted to blow the dust away, as it may get in your eyes – a vacuum cleaner is a help here. After each sanding, dampen the wood slightly to raise the grain and, when it has dried, sand again.

CARPENTRY TOOLS

Tools which are found quite naturally in the kit of anyone working in wood also have a supporting place among carvers. Cutting away calculated amounts of waste wood with a saw, for example, will save a lot of time. As before, buy good-quality tools as they are needed.

HANDSAWS

This group of tools includes saws for cutting straight lines, cutting curves and enlarging holes.

For cutting straight lines

- **crosscut saws** for cutting *across* the grain

- **ripsaws** for cutting *with* the grain (Fig 1.45)

- **backsaws** (such as tenon saws or the 'gentleman's saw') for making fine cuts in either direction.

These saws come in varying degrees of coarseness, the cut being measured by the number of teeth per inch (**tpi**) – the lower the number, the coarser the cut. Disposable saws with hardened teeth (which cannot be sharpened) are tending to replace the conventional types that need sharpening (Fig 1.46). When they wear out, they can be recycled into scrapers, or used as surfaces for flattening sharpening stones (see Volume 1, pages 165–6).

All these saws are designed to cut in straight lines. First make a positive drawing cut with the saw to guide the subsequent cuts. Hold the handle with the index finger extended and cut rhythmically without jerking the forward pressure.

For cutting curves

- **bowsaws** (Fig 1.47)

- **coping saws**

- **fretsaws** (Fig 1.48).

Fig 1.47 *The bowsaw looks like something out of the ark – and may well be as old. The blade is held in position by removable pins so the saw can be used for pierced work*

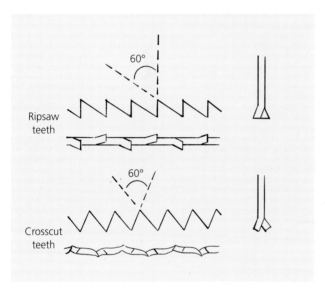

Fig 1.45 *You can distinguish a ripsaw (for cutting with the grain) from a crosscut saw (for cutting across the grain) by examining the teeth. Ripsaws have chisel-like points for paring between fibres; crosscuts have more knife-like teeth for cutting through them*

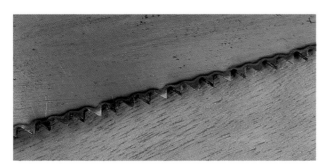

Fig 1.46 *A typical modern handsaw with 'hardpoint' teeth*

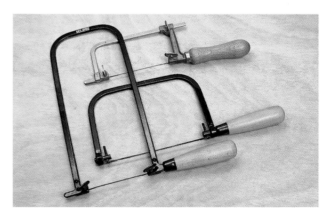

Fig 1.48 *Saws for curved work, all with detachable blades that will insert through holes pierced in a carving. The one with the deepest frame is the fretsaw; the smallest (the piercing saw) takes a thin fretsaw blade; the coping saw in the middle is the most useful one to have handy*

These saws have narrow, delicate, replaceable blades for cutting curves. The bowsaw, a really ancient tool, is the largest and coarsest. The fretsaw is the finest but has a great reach of cut. The blades themselves are usually of one coarseness and can be inserted through holes in the wood to cut internal curves; the blade can be turned in different directions to prevent the frame getting in the way. Make sure the blade is straight and not twisted along its length, and do not exert too much pressure. Twisting and pressure tend to snap the blade.

For enlarging holes

- **keyhole saw** or **padsaw** (Fig 1.49).

This is a narrow saw projecting from a handle, and is used, as its name suggests, for inserting into a preliminary hole and cutting a keyhole shape. From the carver's point of view, it can be used to enlarge holes without the reassembling necessary, for example, with a coping saw. Be gentle on the forward pressure to avoid kinking the blade.

PLANES

A carpenter's metal plane may be used for:

- dressing the surface of a panel of wood to reveal the grain

- smoothing the surface to make drawing on it easier

- joining pieces of wood.

Of the many varieties, the **smoothing plane** and the small, adjustable **block plane** are probably the most useful (Fig 1.50).

The cutting edge of a plane blade is sharpened so that it is slightly rounded, or 'nosed' (Fig 1.51), to prevent the corners digging in and to help merge cuts. When jointing the edge of a board, move the plane

Fig 1.50 *Smoothing (rear) and block planes*

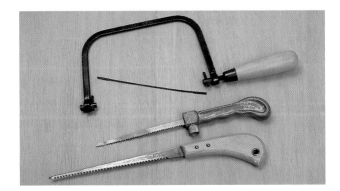

Fig 1.49 *Two versions of the keyhole saw; the bottom one is Japanese and cuts on the pull stroke. Above is the coping saw with blade detached*

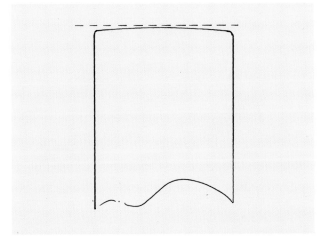

Fig 1.51 *A view of a plane blade, exaggerated slightly, to show the rounded corners and the slight curvature of the cutting edge*

across the wood so that the centre of the blade aligns with the part from which most wood needs to be removed; this allows you to level the edge without having to tilt the plane. To remove the shavings more easily when working hardwoods, move the **cap iron** (the backing plate screwed to the upper surface of the cutting blade on the larger planes) forwards to reveal no more than 1⁄16in (1.5mm) of blade; for softwoods, leave about 3⁄16in (5mm) showing. Sharpen keenly, and lay the plane on its side when not in use; store with the cutting edge retracted.

SPOKESHAVES

Spokeshaves will smooth large, curved areas – flattening off facets and shaping. Flat-faced spokeshaves are used for convex surfaces, and round-faced spokeshaves for concave ones (Fig 1.52). Those with the blade adjusted by screws are the most convenient.

Brass carving planes, with long handles and flat or curved blades, are a sort of one-handed spokeshave. Some carvers find them useful for finishing compound curves; personally, I've always had the nagging suspicion that they would perform better if they could be pulled rather than pushed – so do try them if possible before buying.

Like the plane, the cutting edge of a spokeshave is curved to give a slight prominence in the centre. A cleaner finish and an easier stroke are obtained if the cutting edge is presented at a skew to the direction of cut, to produce a slicing action. Try to feel into the curves you are making.

As the blades are quite small, holding them for sharpening can be a little awkward. Grip the blade in a block of wood kept especially for the purpose, jamming it into a deep saw cut, or hold it in a hand vice if you have one. Sharpen it just as keenly as a carving chisel.

HAND ROUTERS

Largely superseded by electrical routers, **hand routers** (Fig 1.53) may still have their place in levelling a background evenly – for example, between letters in relief work. The traditional wooden version is known as an **old woman's tooth**. The name *router* comes from the Anglo-Saxon *root* (as in 'rooting about'), meaning 'to dig or grub up'.

To work most efficiently, remove the bulk of the wood in the normal way and set in with gouge and mallet. A depth gauge made from wooden strips will be useful in this preliminary stage, which should end with about 1⁄8in (3mm) to spare. Finish to the required depth with the router – the blade of which should be properly sharp – working with the grain as far as possible. The surface may still need final grounding with flat (no. 3) gouges or scrapers to remove any tears left by the routing.

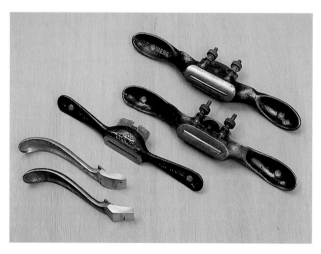

Fig 1.52 *A round-faced spokeshave (top) and two flat-faced ones. The small brass carving planes in the foreground have similar uses*

Fig 1.53 *The hand router, shown here in two sizes, is a cheap alternative for those who dislike the noise and speed of the electrical version, but need something for checking the level of a background*

OTHER TOOLS

The usual array of carpenters' tools includes hammers, screwdrivers, brace and bits, wheel brace (hand drill) and so on – all generally useful to a carver undertaking a variety of work. Although power drills have generally replaced the wheel brace, for example, it is sometimes simpler to pick up the hand tool from the side of the bench. And, again, the work may need a delicate and precise touch, such as only a slow, hand-controlled tool will give.

SPECIALIZED EDGE TOOLS

KNIVES

Very beautiful and complex carvings are created by knife work alone, and some carvers like to mix knives with their conventional carving tools – or at least have one or two knives handy.

Three very useful knives are always at hand in my workshop (Fig 1.54), dealing with a variety of background work as well as aspects of carving itself:

CRAFT KNIFE
There are two hanging to hand: the well-known Stanley type of knife and the smaller, first-class Veritas craft knife. Both have a variety of replaceable blades for cutting card for templates, small dowels and so on.

SLOYD KNIFE
This famous tool made by Frost of Sweden has a laminated blade, with a hard centre between two softer leaves. (I cannot bring myself to test it but, apparently, this arrangement allows it to be bent for scooping cuts.) I use it for larger-scale cutting and carpentry-like functions.

CARVING KNIVES
Besides the specialized ones listed below, a simple, very sharp and thin-bladed knife such as that made by Flexcut (Fig 1.55, second from left) is always on

Fig 1.54 Three useful types of workshop knives: the Stanley craft knife; long and short Frost sloyd knives; Veritas craft knife

Fig 1.55 Carving knives with fixed handles, including designs by Wayne Barton (left) and Flexcut (second left)

my bench among the carving tools, doubling as a skew chisel for jobs such as awkward undercutting and slicing in narrow, tight grooves.

Many types of knives are suitable, and available, for carving. All are straight-bladed, the names of the shapes varying according to both makers and users. There are, however, probably only five basic shapes to choose from (Fig 1.56). Some knives are angled and drawn towards the user to pare off shavings (Fig 1.57).

Safety considerations point to the danger of knives which fold, closing on the user's fingers. Locking knives, or knives with fixed blades, are much safer – especially for the beginner.

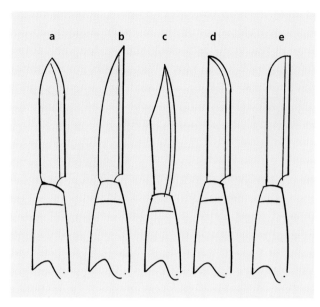

Fig 1.56 *The five basic blade shapes: (a) spear or pen; (b) slant tip; (c) sloyd or clip; (d) spey; and (e) sheepfoot*

Fig 1.57 *This orientation of knife blade is designed to be drawn towards the user*

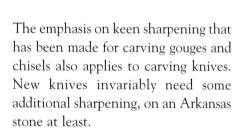

The emphasis on keen sharpening that has been made for carving gouges and chisels also applies to carving knives. New knives invariably need some additional sharpening, on an Arkansas stone at least.

SHARPENING

❶ Place the oiled benchstone end-on, and lay the blade flat on its surface with the edge pointing away from you.

❷ Lift the back of the blade slightly and stroke the edge backwards and forwards or in a circular motion on the stone, maintaining the same angle between blade and stone.

❸ Repeat equally on both sides. Use the method of looking for the white line along the edge to check the sharpness, as described for carving tools (see Volume 1, pages 149–52).

❹ Strop by dragging the blade *backwards* on the strop, at the same angle at which it was sharpened.

ADZES

The **adze** (Fig 1.58) is an ancient tool for shaping wood, and still has its attraction for some carvers of larger sculptures. It is often used, with an axe, instead of a mallet and gouge.

Fig 1.58 *This adze by Auriou has a substantial handle passing through the head; the anvil edge may be struck to ease an embedded adze out of the wood*

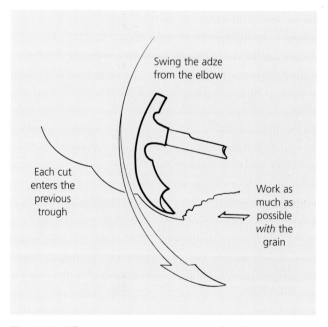

Fig 1.59 *The correct way to swing an adze. It is easy to bury the blade in the timber by trying to remove too much wood at once*

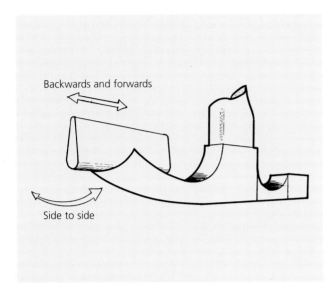

Fig 1.60 *Gouge-like adzes are sharpened only on the inside, with appropriate grades of large slipstone*

Fig 1.61 *A scorp (top) and a hook knife*

Adzes are available in flat or hollow cross sections, with the blade curved along its length to match the arcing swing from the shoulder or elbow (Fig 1.59). All adzes have just the internal bevel, and are best sharpened with large slipstones only (Fig 1.60). Double-ended adzes are quite dangerous if the non-working end is not covered with a proper guard.

Pick an adze with a large hole in the head through which to pass a substantial amount of the wooden handle. A good example would be those made by Auriou. There are great leverage forces at play when you carve and draw with it and the handle will snap at the head if the wood here is too narrow.

Adzes, in inexperienced hands, have a tendency to bury their edges in the wood and be used like crowbars to lever away a chip. A large gouge, propelled through its cut by a mallet, will cut more cleanly and accurately, so for most carvers it is a better option.

Scorps

A **scorp** is a strange-looking tool (a variant of the drawknife) which is drawn towards the user, carving large convex shapes. A similar tool – although not so tough – is the **hook knife** (Fig 1.61). Both are sharpened similarly, using a round slipstone on the inside and a flat stone on the outside as necessary (Figs 1.62 and 1.63).

Fig 1.62 *Sharpen the scorp with a round slipstone, working from the inside*

Fig 1.63 *A hook knife can be similarly sharpened with round and flat slipstones*

PUNCHES AND FROSTERS

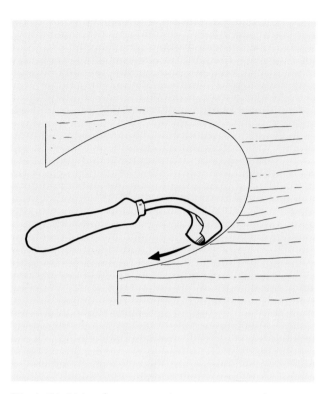

© Henry Taylor Tools Ltd

Fig 1.64 *Using the scorp requires a strong wrist, but it can be invaluable for working sculptural recesses, with the grain*

The advantage of these tools is that the edge cuts from the bottom of the hollow outwards, and in some circumstances will give a cleaner finish than a gouge worked in the opposite way. They can also get into deep, sculptural hollows where a carving gouge is impractical (Fig 1.64). They are hard on the wrist, and therefore most of the waste wood needs removing from such a hollow first. This can be done by drilling, with bent gouges, or using a burr on a flexible shaft.

These are the sorts of tools that are worth knowing about and keeping for specific needs or projects – in which case they can be indispensable.

Punches produce specifically shaped indentations, such as circles or crosses, when they are tapped on to the wood surface. They were very popular with the Victorians, who produced a large number of different punch patterns, some of which are still available today (Fig 1.65).

One shape which is particularly useful is the **eye punch**: an oval shape pointed at one end (Fig 1.66, right). This tool will sink and flatten the bottom of the 'eyes' that form in the junctions between certain sorts of acanthus leaves (Fig 1.67). Eye punches can be easily made by grinding or filing an appropriate size of nail. The eye must be carved properly in the wood first – using the punch on its own will only crush the fibres and leaf edges to bad effect.

Frosters or **frosting tools** (Fig 1.68) create a hatched effect made up of many dotted indentations.

Fig 1.66 *A close-up of the working ends of a variety of punches, including an oval eye punch, circular punches, two acanthus-eye punches (far right) and a floret*

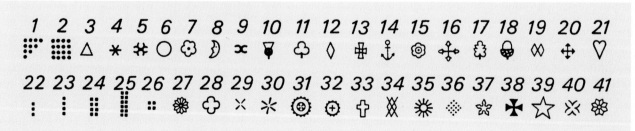

Fig 1.65 *A selection of decorative punches*

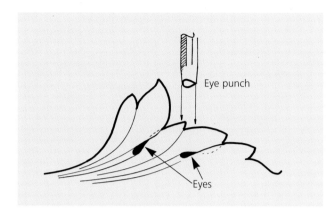

Fig 1.67 *Use an appropriate size of eye punch to flatten the bottom of an acanthus-leaf 'eye'*

Fig 1.68 *Different sizes of frosters are needed to work in different corners or shapes of the background*

They are used to finish a background and provide a contrast to some simple relief carving, or even to produce a decorative shadow effect. Frosters can be bought, or made by filing the flattened ends of large nails or bolts with small triangular files (Fig 1.69).

For the frosting to look its best, clean the surface or background properly with carving tools first. Frosters should not be used to hide rough work or a poor finish. Frosting is only a surface treatment – a contrast – and is not particularly meant to be noticed. It is therefore best to use the frosting tool with discretion and a lightness of touch (Fig 1.70). Overlap the edges of the indentations to provide a smooth transition across the frosting and work either to an even pattern or randomly, but not mixing the two.

Fig 1.69 *Frosting tools and many other punches can be home-made from nails or bolts*

Fig 1.70 *Tudor carving from Abbey Dore church, Herefordshire. If you look carefully you can see that different frosting tools were used, with various arrangements of points*

SCRATCH STOCKS AND SCRAPERS

Scratch stocks (Fig 1.71) will run lengths of small mouldings – particularly in furniture carving – which are then either carved or left unadorned. Although the idea and the construction of a scratch stock are simple – a blade is clamped between two L-shaped pieces of wood (Fig 1.71) – surprisingly accurate and detailed work can be carried out. Mouldings wider than about 1in (25mm) are not so easy to work this way, however, and more than one blade of different shapes may be needed to create a larger, more complicated profile in the wood.

The blade of a scratch stock can be made from an old hacksaw blade, shaped sharply square with a grinder and a file, and finished with slipstones. Do not blue the metal on the grinder. The shape is a negative or reverse of the moulding shape that is actually wanted. Check the profile on waste wood.

An exact amount of the scratch blade protrudes from the stock, which is kept butted against the edge of the wood to act as a guide or fence. Be sure to fix the blade tightly in the stock; if it works loose, the chances are you will not notice until too late, and the work will be spoiled. The metal shape is worked

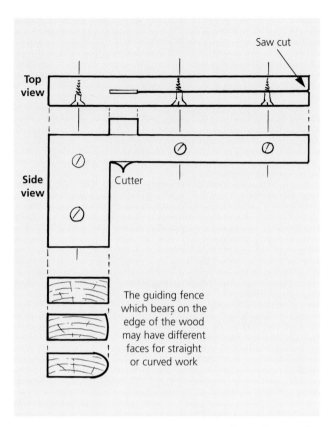

Fig 1.72 *A scratch stock for running small mouldings. The cutter can be shaped to a specific need*

backwards and forwards, stopping once the full depth of cut is reached. Start with light strokes, tilting the stock forwards. Do not try to take off too much wood at once, but proceed gradually and methodically. If the moulding is to be carved, avoid sanding – the grit will take off the edge of the carving tool.

Scrapers are pieces of hardened sheet steel used to flatten surfaces such as backgrounds, or to clean particular carved shapes. They are worked by hand, rather than in a jig like a scratch stock. Make them from old saw or hacksaw blades, shaping as for scratch-stock blades. The sharpening process is known as **ticketing**: once the edge has been honed smooth, a wire edge or burr is formed by rubbing an even harder piece of metal along the edge at a slight angle (Fig 1.73). It is this burr which forms the actual cutting edge.

Scrapers can be indispensable in some work, and surprisingly versatile. They can be bought in a variety of shapes, or easily reshaped to meet a particular need (Figs 1.74 and 1.75). They are used especially in

Fig 1.71 *Scratch stocks are quickly made and can produce a wide range of moulded edges; any number of interchangeable blades can be made for them*

furniture which is to be polished, prior to fine sanding (for example in cleaning up flutes in chair legs or bedposts), for the backgrounds of low-relief carving (such as is found in chair splats), or for cleaning up awkward grain.

MARKING-OUT EQUIPMENT

Carvers often need to make measurements – to ensure symmetry, for example – and occasionally need to work accurately to a pre-existing design. Callipers, dividers, compasses and rulers, as well as squares, marking gauges, carbon and tracing paper, and chalk, thick pencils or charcoal, all come in handy at different times.

Fig 1.73 *Sharpening a scraper involves burring over the edge (ticketing) – you can use the side of a chisel for this. This edge, if sharpened correctly, will remove a proper shaving and so must cut, rather than scrape*

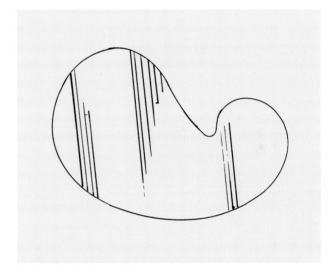

Fig 1.74 *A goose-necked scraper, available commercially*

Fig 1.75 *Different shapes of scrapers; they can be ground to specific shapes as required. The handled ones are home-made*

CHAPTER TWO

POWER TOOLS AND MACHINERY

AIMS

- To review the power tools and machines which are most likely to be useful to woodcarvers, both in carving itself and in the preparation of wood for carving

Carvers may use electrical tools in two ways: for working on a carving directly, and for preparing wood and general workshop purposes. I want to look briefly at the general-purpose tools first.

GENERAL WORKSHOP TOOLS

Electric tools – such as drills, power sanders and files; jigsaws, chainsaws and sabre saws; pillar drills and routers – can save a great deal of time by removing waste wood from carvings prior to working with gouges and chisels, or even power carvers.

Nowadays, large numbers of people possess power tools as standard kit; they need not have been bought specifically for carving. Exactly what use can be made of these tools depends on the nature of your work. As always, buy equipment on the basis of usefulness and cost-effectiveness, not just because other carvers have it.

There is not the space in this book to go into the detailed use of these tools, so only general pointers can be given. Although I do use different makes as examples, try to see as many as you can in action, in carvers' and other workshops, before buying; and *always read and observe the safety and operating instructions provided by the manufacturers.*

Every carver will have their own list of useful equipment but, depending on the pattern of work you want to undertake, my experience is that four pieces of equipment in particular are very useful – almost indispensable – for many carvers:

- bandsaws

- scrollsaws

- disc and belt sanders

- routers.

BANDSAWS

My bandsaw is the one piece of all my workshop equipment that I would hate to lose. Bandsaws, when used with due care and attention, are versatile, safe, precise, simple and friendly; a bandsaw will rough out carvings and save a lot of time and effort in a variety of ways.

Bandsaws range in size from small, bench-mounted models to large floor-mounted ones (Fig 2.1). They are principally designed to make curved cuts – the actual amount of curve possible depends on the width of the blade – but they should be able to cut reasonably straight lines as well. The blade is a continuous band passing over two or three wheels, with one section open for use and fitted with guides and safety guards. The blades eventually wear out or break – usually at the join – and need to be replaced.

When buying a bandsaw, the two important dimensions to consider are the **throat** (the distance from blade to machine body) and the depth of cut, both of which affect what you can achieve.

Blades will break as the flexing of the metal produces metal fatigue. This fatigue is greatest with:

- smaller wheels on the bandsaw

- three rather than two wheels

- faster speeds

- higher blade tension.

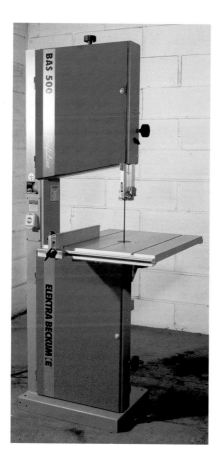

Fig 2.1
Bandsaws are very useful to the carver. A basic floor-standing bandsaw such as this will deal with a large range of work

USING THE BANDSAW

A typical carving use for the bandsaw is to cut out the two-dimensional outline of the object to be carved (Figs 2.2–2.4); this is one of the fastest and most

Fig 2.2 Using a template to draw an outline on the initial block of wood

Fig 2.3 The outline is then bandsawn, which saves a great deal of time over any other method

Fig 2.4 Back to the template to mark in the volutes. Provided the bandsaw was set up accurately, you can be sure the outline will fit on both sides exactly

accurate ways of removing waste material from a carving. Having cut out the side profile in this way, it is sometimes possible to cut the front or top profile as well, by turning the work round and temporarily re-attaching (with tape or glue) the part already removed.

When using the bandsaw:

- Always set the blade guides properly and accurately.

- Feed the wood into the saw lightly and let the machine do the work. Never direct the pressure of your hands towards the blade; keep them as far away from it as practicable, using a push-stick for small work.

- It is difficult – sometimes impossible – to reverse a bandsaw blade out of its cut, as it tends to be pulled forwards out of its guides by the fibres of the wood. Try to work out the best approach before starting to cut. Make **stop cuts** where necessary (cuts 2 and 3 in Fig 2.5), or work away the waste in smaller pieces, rather than risk getting the blade stuck in a position from which it cannot extract itself.

- If a blade does get stuck, stop and disconnect the machine. Raise the blade guides enough to allow you to place a batten of wood across the blade teeth above the work. Use this to hold the blade in its guides while drawing the workpiece forward.

- Curves are cut better if you think of the cut as originating from the back of the blade rather than just the teeth.

- The closer you can cut to your original design, the less wood that subsequently needs to be removed – but the less freedom there is to alter the design as you carve. Therefore you must be sure of your design if you are adopting the close-shave approach.

SAFETY

- Always follow the manufacturer's instructions and recommendations carefully: ensure that the correct width of blade is being used for the radius of curve you intend to cut, and with the appropriate tension.

- Always set the safety guards correctly, within ¼in (6mm) of the wood surface, and adjust them only with the machine stopped.

- Take care when coiling or uncoiling the blades – gloves are recommended.

- Double-check everything, including the locking of the table and any fence, before starting the machine.

- Be ruthless: remove blades as soon as they are blunt, and kink them to prevent re-use.

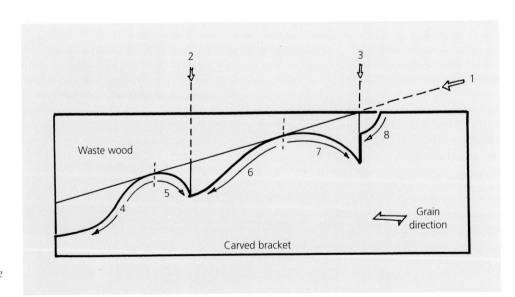

Fig 2.5 *Work out the order of bandsaw cuts before you start, so that the blade does not get trapped as it tries to reverse from a cut*

SCROLLSAWS

The scrollsaw (Fig 2.6) is a motorized version of the hand-held group of narrow saws, such as the fretsaw and the coping saw. In relief work these, and the power jigsaw, can be replaced in most circumstances by the scrollsaw. The handsaws are still extremely useful for carving in the round, but the precision and speed of the motorized version have made them obsolete for most other purposes.

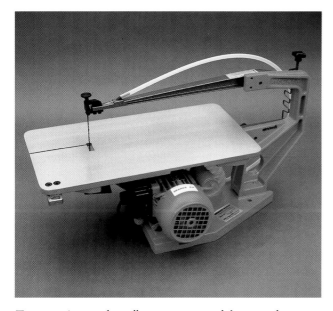

Fig 2.6 A typical scrollsaw or motorized fretsaw; this one is by Hegner

Scrollsaws will take a range of saw blades, from very fine (no. 00, with 11 teeth per inch) to coarse (no. 10, with 4tpi), for a range of materials from metal and plastic to wood. Quick-change adaptors allow for switching blades.

The blades cut by means of a long reciprocating arm, moving at around 1,400 strokes per minute (the speed of the motor). As on a bandsaw, the working distance the arm gives you is known as the *throat*, and the height of cut as the *depth*. Throat is normally about 16in (400mm), and you shouldn't buy a machine with less. Depth of cut can be up to 2in (50mm), although when you get to this depth you are probably better off with a bandsaw or some other way of removing wood. The work rests on a table for sawing, which itself may be tilted for angled cuts.

Scrollsaws cut on the down stroke, pushing the work on to the table. However, the return (up) stroke tends to lift the work from the table. This is not too much of a problem with thin wood, and any 'chattering' of the workpiece can be dampened as it is held down with the fingers (Fig 2.7). Hold-down arms, which double as finger guards, are usually available; I recommend using them whenever possible.

Fine blades will make intricate cuts: the work can be spun around on the blade. For internal cutting, small starting holes are needed through which to pass the blade.

Scrollsaws are mostly bought for scrollwork, an intricate style of fretwork which has a following in its own right. A woodcarver could use a scrollsaw whenever intricate cutting out is needed on thin wood. This would include fireplace urns, for example, and other **applied carving**, **pierced relief** (Fig 2.8), small parts and odd jobs for which the bandsaw is just too insensitive.

BUYING A SCROLLSAW

- You will need to assess your needs in terms of throat and depth. Always choose a larger size unless you are quite sure you will not need it.

- Motors are small, between 75 and 120W; running costs are very low.

Fig 2.7 A good-quality scrollsaw gives a truly vertical cut, ideal for small, accurate profiling. For delicate work, holding the wood down with the fingers is often quite adequate

Fig 2.8 This pierced relief carving was scrollsawn first. A great advantage of the scrollsaw is its ability to cut out interior shapes

- Although there are quite a few inexpensive machines on the market, you get what you pay for.

- Dust extraction is very important. Most machines have a blower/sucker unit to clear dust from the cutting area; of the two, a sucking arrangement, in connection with the workshop vacuum cleaner, is best, since blown dust just rises to be breathed in.

- The best machines are carefully engineered: there should be no side play on the reciprocating arms or movement in the table, for example.

- The heavier the machine, the less vibration you can expect.

- Two arm actions are possible: single or parallel pivoting. Single-pivot arms give a sloping cut, and are mostly found on cheap machines. The parallel pivot, found in well-engineered machines such as the Hegner, gives a perfect vertical cut.

USING THE SCROLLSAW

- Always set up and use the saw according to the manufacturer's instructions.

- Blades must be securely held, with the teeth pointing towards the table, and at the correct tension. Check the tension before you start the machine, and with each blade change.

- Vibration, arising from the reciprocating action, can be a problem; light machines may 'walk' across a bench top unless they are bolted or screwed down.

- Get a good adjustable light on to the work area. I find it easier to concentrate when sitting.

- Plan your work, boring all the holes together first, trying to minimize blade-changing or inserting time. It may be quicker to rough out on a bandsaw and leave the scrollsaw for intricate work.

- Don't force the work on to a blade to cut faster – blades are very thin and you will only break them. Let the blade do the work.

SAFETY

Scrollsaws are very safe machines: even if your finger does touch the blade, the skin is more likely to be vibrated by the reciprocating movement than cut (but don't try!). As a rule: never push towards the moving blade.

A peculiar danger is from a snapped blade, when the broken end stabs up and down in the air near your fingers. So, another rule: always keep fingers clear.

DISC AND BELT SANDERS

Commonly the belt and disc appear as part of a single unit, driven by the same motor, and designed to be mounted on a bench (Fig 2.9).

These simple machines can be fairly inexpensive; models are rated according to the degree of use to which they will be put, from continuous industrial to light hobby use. The difference is in build quality, the size and rating of the motor, the quality of the bearings, the accuracy of the adjustable table and other fences, and so on. When you buy one you need to consider how often you would use it, as well as the need for accuracy.

Various standard belts and discs are readily available both for wood and metal, in a range of grits similar to normal sandpaper.

Whatever sander you buy, make sure that there is a dust-extraction facility – something to which you

Fig 2.9 *A typical small disc and belt sander. Only the left side of the disc is available for use, so that the direction of rotation keeps the workpiece on the table*

can attach an industrial vacuum cleaner, for example (Fig 2.10).

SOME USES FOR DISC AND BELT SANDERS

- Flattening small surfaces accurately: for joints; for the bases of small carvings (say, when the hole left by a woodcarver's screw has been plugged); for cleaning up after a 'paper sandwich' glue-up (see pages 85–6).

Fig 2.10 *You may have to improvise a dust-extraction take-off, if the existing outlet does not match the vacuum cleaner you have available*

- Shaping: ends and protruding parts in particular. However, if you need to do a lot of this sort of shaping you would be better off with a power file, in which case the work is fixed and the tool moves.

- Flattening benchstones: this is possible even with an abrasive paper intended for wood. You must do this outside and with full dust protection, as this dust is usually silica-based and quite damaging.

- With a belt or disc suitable for metal, they can substitute for grinders when it comes to the preliminary shaping of carving tools and setting of bevels.

The disc and belt sander is one of those machines you can live without, but, when you have one, you will wonder how you managed.

USING DISC AND BELT SANDERS

- Set up and use the machine according to the maker's instructions.

- In particular, set up the table carefully, checking its alignment with a set square. Don't trust the calibrated guides which come with the machine – use these only when accuracy isn't a priority.

- *Let the machine do the work.* Pressing too hard can easily stop the belt on small machines and stress the motor. Never force the work.

- You can only use *half the disc* – the half that descends towards the table and so pushes the workpiece down against it. If you use the other half, the work will be lifted and may kick up.

SAFETY
Disc and belt sanders remove wood rapidly – or, rather, they transform wood into dust and particles, which they fling in the air. You must:

- fit a dust extractor (an industrial vacuum cleaner, say)

- protect your eyes and lungs appropriately.

35

These machines are best permanently fixed down to prevent 'walking' and the possibility of accidents; at the least, clamp them securely.

ROUTERS

What can a router do for a woodcarver? Here's a quick list from the top of my head:

Planing
Woodcarvers often need a wide area of wood – for a panel of lettering say, or a large relief carving. Usually this means joining narrower boards side by side, because wide boards are more likely to warp (see page 136). The resulting wide surface then needs to be levelled – but you may not have a planer, or the panel may be too wide for the planer you have. Your wood might also be a strange shape; or perhaps it is a lump, and it's only one face of it that you want flat.

Here the router comes into its own. With a simple jig, consisting of tracks along the side of the wood and the router on rails passing from side to side, the router will level any surface (Fig 2.11). The result may require a bit of finishing for your purposes, but you are practically there.

It is worth taking the time to make and set up the jig properly, because you can re-use the parts again and again, whenever you need to flatten a surface.

Fig 2.11 *Router planing is easy: use parallel side tracks on either side of the block you wish to dress, and a simple carriage to take the router. The router sweeps across the wood, and the carriage is advanced a little for each cut*

Relief carving
This is a principal use for the router: removing background waste around the subject of a relief carving, or rendering different levels of ground within the main carving. With a large cutter a lot of wood can be wasted away quickly. The router can only be used on flat surfaces.

'But', I have heard asked, 'isn't this cheating?' Not to my mind. When the routed surface is cleaned and finished by hand the result is exactly the same as if the background had been removed with mallet and gouge – but in a fraction of the time.

Plunge boring
Most routers have a spring-action 'plunge' ability, so you can push the router cutter, drill-like, down into the wood and easily pull it back out. The router base ensures the hole will be straight and accurately at right angles to the surface of the wood. With square-ended cutters the resulting hole has a square base.

Such routers also have a depth stop. With a narrow cutter you can neatly drop to predetermined depths within the elements of a detailed carving. This helps to clear out the waste as well as ensuring a uniform background to these tricky areas (Figs 2.12–2.13).

Making bench slots
This is not actually carving, but a slot in your bench top is often a better option than a hole for inserting a carver's screw or the screw fixing of some other holding device. It gives you more freedom of movement, particularly when carving on vertical surfaces, as described in my Elements of Woodcarving (GMC Publications, 2000), chapter 2. A router is ideal for making accurate slots – and for this purpose they don't even have to be straight.

Making mouldings
Carved mouldings for furniture or picture frames start with a blank, profiled strip of wood; this is then incised methodically with a pattern of cuts. Routers have long since replaced hand planes for this work. Indeed, most carvers find they now fit the carving to the available router cutter.

Fig 2.12 *This oak-leaf panel has been routed by a mixture of plunging and wasting, which saves a lot of time in the initial stages*

Fig 2.13 *This carving was initially routed like the previous one, then the background was given a hand-tooled finish. The work of the router is completely subsumed*

You can also use the router to rebate a frame for a relief carving. Indeed, many reliefs look like pictures, and need a frame; this can be carved as part of the original wood or made separately with a router, in the wood and pattern of your choice – which itself may be carved…

Jointing

A router can be used accurately enough to dress the edge of a planed board when jointing boards for panels or bench tops. Using a jig or fence, it can be used for cutting circular or oval panels, or repeat curves. You can run a groove for a loose tongue or spline between boards for extra strength. (If the boards are to be carved, remember to place this groove towards the back, away from the danger of being carved into from the front.) In addition, the router can be used to inset battens into the back of a panel to stop warping.

A router will easily cut mortises and tenons for woodcarving benches. A typical bench will have

four legs, and therefore eight of these joints, for the top rail alone. A router and jig will speed up the process a lot.

These are just some of the uses a woodcarver may find for a router. Buy a bigger one than you think you might need – you never know when spare capacity will be useful – and choose one with a plunging facility. Pay attention to the following points:

USING THE ROUTER

- Remove wood in small amounts; don't force the router. I always end up with a fine finishing pass.

- Secure the cutters into the router collet carefully; vibrations from the machine can cause the cutter to slowly work its way out, deepening the cut – sometimes disastrously.

- In particular, pay attention to the direction in which the cutter is revolving. A router 'rule' is to cut *into* the wood and *against* the direction the router is travelling. If you cut in the opposite manner, the cutter tends to run along the wood and pull the router with it, which is a less controlled operation.

SAFETY

- *Do use dust extraction as much as you can*; the router flings dust and chips everywhere: your view is obscured; dust gets all over the shop; and, of course, you breathe it in. I have an industrial vacuum cleaner in my workshop which is very easy to fit to the router, and which removes most of the dust and chips before they hit the air (Fig 2.14). For the rest I use a good face mask and protective goggles.

- Bear in mind too that routers are particularly, and excruciatingly, noisy. Ear protection is vital.

All in all, with dust mask, eye shield and ear protection, you may feel a bit of an astronaut, but there is no question that these are essential and eventually, like seat-belts, you will learn to accept and work with them.

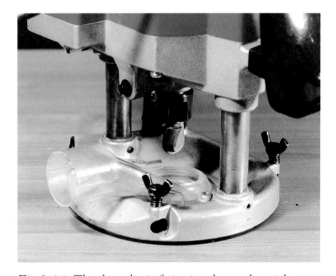

Fig 2.14 *The clear plastic fitting is a dust and particle extraction unit which can be connected to a vacuum cleaner. Make it a habit to use dust extraction facilities whenever you can*

PORTABLE POWER CARVING TOOLS

Some carvers take a purist attitude to their craft, shunning any electrical and mechanical aids as somehow 'cheating', or inferior in skill to traditional carving tools. Others adore the dust and drive of portable power tools, and might not even possess a conventional gouge. Some, such as myself, fall between the two.

I enjoy the intimacy and immediacy of carving with chisels and gouges. But I am happy to back them up with power tools that save me time, labour and money, and – crucially – don't detrimentally impose themselves on the result I'm after.

Woodcarvers use power tools in three ways:

- for removing waste wood prior to carving with conventional carving tools

- in conjunction with carving tools, swapping from one to the other as work progresses

- as shaping and finishing tools in their own right, with little or no recourse to traditional woodcarving tools. Sanders and power files in particular can finish surfaces smoothly by themselves.

When I discuss tools with carvers, I find it useful to differentiate – without a value judgement – between wood *carving* (using conventional woodcarving tools) and wood *shaping* (using fewer of these and more hand power tools, rasps and abrasives to produce a smooth surface). The tools, the approaches and the results are different. However, this distinction does disguise the common practice today, which sees carvers mixing the two.

For myself, I love the intimate personal engagement of conventional carving tools. I also love the purity of the forms and surfaces you get in the freer forms of wood sculpture in which power tools have a principal role. Both can be done well, or badly. The highest quality of design and workmanship is reached only by great skill and sensitivity, no matter what tools are being used.

It is important to understand that when we use any tool it is both a means to an end, and part of the very creative process in which we are engaged. *All* tools have advantages and limitations, whether they are hand tools or power-driven; all engage with the user in their own way, and all leave their particular marks on the outcome. We are free to choose the method and speed of working that best suits us, and the result we seek.

Broadly, the hand-held power tools that carvers may use fall into two categories:

- those less focused on carving, such as power drills, pillar drills, jigsaws, chainsaws, sabre saws and routers, which are to be found in many non-carving wood workshops

- those that are of more direct use to carvers, if not originally designed for them.

It is this latter category that I will be looking at here. Power tools of particular interest to woodcarvers fall into four broad classes:

- angle-grinder cutting discs

- high-speed flexible shafts

- hand-held high-speed motor units

- reciprocal carvers or power chisels.

For all hand power tools, keep the following advice in mind:

- *Always* read and observe the safety and operating instructions provided by the manufacturers.

- *Always* sharpen or adjust the blade with the machine isolated from its power supply.

- *Always* protect your eyes, your ears and your lungs. A feature of all hand power tools is the flinging out of dust and particles, with particle size varying from large (in the case of disc cutters) to extremely fine (high-speed abrasive burrs).

Remember that electric tools are designed to be fast, and events happen quickly – and sometimes suddenly. Besides the personal danger, it is very easy to remove more wood than you originally intended, with possibly disastrous consequences to your design.

These devices work in distinct ways and produce distinct results. Do understand that power carvers are only a substitute for traditional carving tools in limited areas – roughing out and texturing, for example. You need only to look at the breathtaking results of gouges throughout history to realize the inherent and unsurpassable advantages of the human hand and simple, sharp cutting edges over what has been done with power carvers so far. Which is not to say that power carvers don't have great advantages in the right instances, nor are capable of creating great beauty.

I do know for a fact that *some* carvers choose to work with power carvers not because these tools answer the needs of their vision better than hand tools, but because they find traditional carving tools, and their sharpening, difficult to master, and the results frustrating. To me this is understandable, but a shame: I know what joys they are missing. I always encourage carvers to see hand tools and machines as both different *and* complementary, not in competition with one another. In the final analysis, both are a means to creative ends.

I come to these machines as pre-eminently a user of hand tools, aiming to make some specific points about the advantages and disadvantages someone like myself might expect from them for woodcarving and shaping. I'll give an overview of each category of commonly used power carving tools, and mention some representative machines. It is important to try out these tools if you can – at least see them in action and discuss them with other users – before laying out your money. Some carvers hate the dust and noise, and prefer not to pay the price for the obvious advantages of speed and power.

ANGLE-GRINDER CUTTING DISCS

A power cutting disc will fit on to a small, hand-held **angle grinder**. The grinder itself you would usually buy separately; it only plays the role of a power unit. The disc rotates at high speed and its teeth bite out small bits of wood. Examples which are suitable for woodcarving include the Arbortech, and various designs made by King Arthur's Tools.

There are several possible designs. The cutting disc may be solid, with saw teeth or replaceable tungsten carbide teeth around the edge, as in the Arbortech; or the design may consist of a loose ring of chainsaw teeth around a steel centre, as in the King Arthur's tools.

Some small cutting discs can be fitted to high-speed flexible shafts. Arbortech also produce a very useful smaller version of their disc, as a 'Mini-Grinder', which I will also look at.

These discs remove wood in small bites. A third type is the heavy-duty abrasive disc, as made by Kutzall and King Arthur's Tools: slower than cutting discs, it works only with dry or seasoned wood which will not clog, and is used for smoothing over large surfaces. Abrasive 'flap discs' are also available, as well as sanding discs with which you can finish off surfaces.

Power cutting discs are essentially wasting devices, for cutting trenches and hollows and removing unwanted material rapidly. Both the edge and the free side of the wheel can be used, and they can replace the chainsaw, axe, adze, big gouge and mallet, sawing and splitting, and other means of removing waste wood.

There is space here to consider only a few of the most popular types:

THE ARBORTECH

The Australian Arbortech, which was one of the first in the field, is a patented circular blade that fits on a 4–4½in (100–115mm) angle grinder (Fig 2.15). Earlier versions were effectively saw blades, with the teeth pressed out of the steel disc itself and needing regular sharpening. The later versions (Industrial Pro) have replaceable tungsten carbide teeth (or 'tips'), and it is these that I recommend as excellent power discs (Fig 2.16). The teeth can be rotated in the disc to even out the wear and prolong the working life – which is considerable anyway – before sharpening with a diamond file or changing them.

The surface that results from the disc is surprisingly smooth; use the blade side-on for light dressing of surfaces as well as edge-on to produce grooves.

Fig 2.15 *The Arbortech blade fits to an angle grinder and wastes wood at an impressive rate. Safety guards are available and recommended*

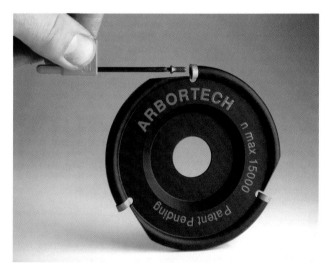

Fig 2.16 *Close-up of the Arbortech, showing the tungsten carbide tips. By loosening the central machine screw the tip can be rotated, thus prolonging its working life. They can be resharpened quite easily; instructions come with the blade*

KING ARTHUR'S TOOLS (KAT)

The American KAT cutting disc is a sophisticated circular chainsaw. Unlike a normal chainsaw, with 'skip teeth', every link of the KAT chain is a tooth. The chain itself runs between two stainless-steel discs that will spin to provide an anti-kickback clutch action for safety (Fig 2.17).

Several combinations of chain and disc are available: the Lancelot, 4in (100mm) in diameter with 14

Fig 2.17 *King Arthur's Tools' Lancelot cutting disc is a modified chainsaw cutter*

Fig 2.18 *In tandem, the Lancelot and Squire make a potent wasting tool*

or 22 teeth; and the smaller Squire with a diameter of 3⅜in (85mm) and 12 or 18 teeth. The really useful aspect of this is that Lancelots can be combined, either together or with the Squire, on the same grinder. Thus two Lancelots may be combined to give a large disc with 28 teeth for a really aggressive cut, or 44 teeth for a smoother cut. This wider double disc has great plunging and grooving capacity. Similarly, a Lancelot may be fitted in tandem with the smaller Squire for an offset arrangement of 26 or 40 teeth (Figs 2.18 and 2.19). This shape allows for more sideways scooping, to produce bowl-like forms.

In all there are seven options. In a well-chosen combination, no other disc can remove such a quantity of wood so quickly, so this is the disc of choice for large sculpture where the alternative might be a chainsaw itself.

Blades are sharpened like a normal chainsaw, with a ⁵⁄₃₂in (4mm) file. The chains can be replaced, so it might be more convenient to keep a spare one and swap them over while carving, saving the sharpening until later.

USING CUTTING DISCS

- Make sure you have an angle grinder rated for the scale of work you intend to do.

- Position the grinder guard carefully and according to the recommendations of the disc manufacturers; cutting discs should never be used without the guard.

Fig 2.19 *A close-up of the KAT teeth, which can be sharpened like a chainsaw*

- Additional guards are also to be had from the disc manufacturers. Most carvers find these get in the way, but do use them where you can.

- Cutting disc versus flesh is no competition: think ahead; relax and concentrate.

- Use both hands firmly on the angle grinder; always use the side handle. Don't, for example, hold the machine with one hand and reach into the vicinity of the rotating cutter with the other to pull away pieces of wood.

- The angle grinder will carry on rotating for a while after you have switched off. Wait until the blade stops rotating before putting it down.

The most important limitation to these power carvers is the diameter of the disc itself: roughly 4in (100mm). This is the shape with which you work, and you must bear it in mind at all times. No cutting disc can deal with any dish-like hollow of a *lesser* diameter, and certainly discs lack the sophistication of large gouges.

Until you are used to the shape, it is quite easy to remove the wood you wanted to keep. You must be careful not to unwittingly let the disc shape dictate the form of the carving. Having said that, in experienced hands quite delicate and subtle control is possible.

Cutting discs come into their own for relieving the labour of roughing out; they can speed up the earlier stages of a carving, sometimes even avoiding the use of a bandsaw. I find them so useful for this work that it is hard to imagine, now, a carving world without them.

A power carving disc works fast; in the concentration of noise and violence, and within the constraints imposed by the disc shape, it is easy to lose the vision of your carving.

- Work out your intentions carefully first, and proceed a step at a time. Check what is happening and then go on a bit further.

- I find it best to work with the disc a while, then slow down and use gouges and mallet while I re-gather my carving vision; then back to the disc (Fig 2.20).

- Light pressure should be used, with the blade doing the work. Adopt a light stroking action, stroking the blade towards you against its rotation and nibbling away, rather than making deep, heavy cuts.

Properly used, with all the necessary precautions, the cutting disc is a safe, rapid and effective way of removing wood; but, besides the limitation of shape, it does have one other major drawback. The grinders to which the discs are fitted have a no-load speed of around 11,000rpm, which means that wood chips and dust are flung everywhere around the workshop, and quite violently towards your wrists, body and face. Sometimes you can minimize this by using the

Fig 2.20 *The Buddha sculpture, shown complete in Figs 7.14 and 7.15, has here been roughed out by a combination of power disc and gouge*

grinder to cut a series of cross-grain grooves, then knocking off lumps of wood with a gouge and mallet (Fig 2.21).

In my opinion, the available angle-grinder guards are only partially adequate for protecting against flung waste. When I use my angle grinder and cutting disc for anything other than a small job, I wear:

Fig 2.21 *A close-up of the surface of the Buddha carving reveals a mixture of disc and gouge work*

- zip overalls (coveralls) with a collar and tight sleeve cuffs

- a face helmet with dust extractor

- gauntlets (leather gloves with wrist protection)

- steel-capped boots

- ear protectors.

This makes me feel a little more disconnected from reality than usual, to say the least, but I consider this the price I pay for the considerable advantages of using a cutting disc. To some people, though, the noise and speed are aesthetically and otherwise unacceptable. If you can, do try to use one under instruction (with another carver, say) before investing.

ARBORTECH MINI-GRINDER

The Mini-Grinder cutting disc is 2in (50mm) in diameter and slim. To use it, you must first fit a special kit to your angle grinder; this sites the disc forward on its own prow-like projection. Take great care to fit this kit according to the instructions which come with the Mini-Grinder.

The combination of extra projection and the precise high-speed blade gives a remarkable little tool. Wood is removed quickly but quite delicately. The disc, like the bigger Arbortech, can be used on its edge for grooving and deep hollows, or on its side for surfacing. It has the same limitations due to its shape, except, of course, that the diameter is smaller.

The Mini-Grinder disc is available either as a steel blade which has teeth pressed into it (which can be sharpened), or with tungsten carbide tips sharpenable with a diamond file.

HIGH-SPEED FLEXIBLE-SHAFT MACHINES

Dedicated flexible-shaft machines consist of a drive motor, hanging from a bracket (often on the wall), which rotates a flexible shaft at a high speed. The shaft itself ends in a handpiece that can be fitted with a large range of cutters, burrs, drills, sanding pads and other accessories. An example would be those made by the American firm Foredom.

Another set-up which is becoming more popular is taking a flexible shaft from a hand-held motor unit (discussed below); that is, a unit that may also be used without the shaft – perhaps even a power drill. For small work this is an economic option, as the shaft can be bought in a carrying case, with a range of bits to start you off. This might be a good way of finding out how you might use a dedicated flexible-shaft machine. An example would be the German Proxxon Micromot.

Although you cannot incise wood as cleanly as with conventional gouges and other carving tools, high-speed flexible shafts have rapidly become valuable supporting tools for carvers in many fields, and a mainstay in some.

The larger machines may be operated by a foot pedal or a bench-top speed control, allowing you to switch on and off and to vary the speed between 500 and 20,000rpm depending on the machine. With both hands free, the carver can hold the work in one while applying the cutters with the other. The size of the motor ranges from $\frac{1}{15}$ to $\frac{1}{4}$ horsepower, and you need to assess what use you will make of it: occasional or heavy. Handpieces vary within and between makers, but all will take the full range of available cutters and burrs. Once you have your unit, it is the cutters which dictate what you can do with it, and these add substantially to the overall cost.

SOME EXAMPLES

The Foredom machine is among the leading makes on the market, both for quality and for its range of handpieces and other accessories (Fig 2.22). Despite the speed, its operation is surprisingly quiet, and the motor is rated for continuous use. Regular checking and maintenance of the motor and flexible shaft is necessary, including regular lubrication and occasional bearing changes. As with servicing a car, the machine can only benefit and will last longer.

The Proxxon Micromot system is robust, well made and takes a full complement of smaller bits. The motor itself can be hung near the work or clamped in a special stand that sits on the bench. Speed is variable from 5,000 to 20,000rpm, adjusted on the machine so that, except for the absence of a foot pedal, it will operate to all intents and purposes

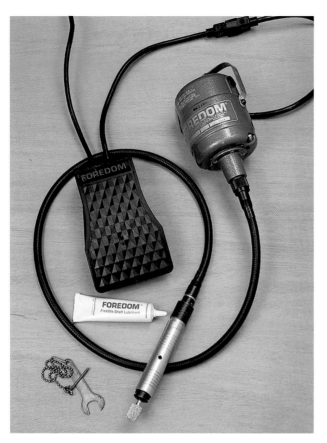

Fig 2.22 The Foredom high-speed flexible shaft, with its motor and foot pedal

Fig 2.23 The 'business end' of a high-speed flexible shaft. Tooling comes in a whole range of sizes and shapes: shown here are two sanding drums, chainsaw-type and tungsten carbide cutting discs (with their bearing guides) and various rotary burrs

as a dedicated flexible-shaft machine. The shaft and handpiece are proportionally smaller, so fine or delicate work is easy. The motor is usable for extended periods of time, but do remember that it is not in the same league as the large, dedicated machines; if you find you are working a machine of this kind hard, then it is time to move up.

BITS

There is now a huge and growing number of burrs, cutters, discs and so on to fit the handpieces (Fig 2.23). These items come under the term **bits**. Tungsten carbide or vanadium steel cutting discs, ruby- or diamond-grit coatings, and so on are innovative responses to the growing woodcarving market. *All bits have a manufacturer's recommended maximum speed, above which they should not be used.*

As bits for flexible shafts come in a very wide range of sizes, shapes and pin diameters, you need to gather manufacturers' catalogues. Start with a few

assorted bits that you like the look of, to get a feel of what these power-carving machines can do, and increase your stock as needs arise. Accessories are not cheap, and it is easy to start building up large numbers and find the overall outlay escalating.

Particularly good are the Tornado cutters, supplied by Rod Naylor. This is a miniature version of the power cutting discs used with angle grinders and, like these, is available in chainsaw or tungsten-tip versions. A bearing guide acts as a finger guard and depth stop. You will find yourself using cutters like these for rapid stock removal, and small burrs for further shaping and for cleaning up awkward corners and grain in normal carving. Shaping, texturing and very delicate work are all possible with appropriate bits.

USING HIGH-SPEED FLEXIBLE SHAFTS

This equipment may be used as a complement to carving tools or on its own. Apart from texturing, high-speed flexible-shaft machines cannot do anything that the right carving tool cannot do, although some of it they do quicker. Exactly what you can do depends on the variety of cutters you have available and on your skill in using them.

- As with all electric tools, allow the tool to do the work; that is what you have paid for.

- Use a stroking action like a paintbrush.

- The best control comes from the bit rotating *away* from you as the handpiece itself is stroked *towards* you, so you are working against the pull of the cutter. This is the same principle as using the router. If the cutter rotates in the same direction of the stroke, it tends to catch and run away.

SAFETY

High-speed flexible-shaft units are safe when used correctly – especially the dedicated machines, because of the delicate and precise control that a user can easily bring to the work with the foot pedal, freeing both hands.

- Cutters, burrs and sanding discs create a very fine dust, especially when used on hard wood; a face mask is essential. Chips of wood can fly off, and it is possible for a cutter or burr to break, so eye protection is also needed.

- In addition to eye and face protection, dust extraction is a very good idea if you are shaping any more than a small amount, or if you are sanding rather than cutting.

- Fit an ambient air cleaner in small, confined workshops: fine dust lingers in the air long after you have taken the dust mask off your face.

- There is a limit to how much you can flex the shaft. As you bend it, friction is created within, which eventually wears out the shaft.

- Always use a cutter or other accessory at or below its maximum rated speed. Used above this speed the cutter could fly apart, bend, or otherwise be damaged.

- Never use a bent or damaged cutter or burr, or one that vibrates or chatters; throw these away. Never force or pressure the accessories.

HAND-HELD HIGH-SPEED MOTOR UNITS

Essentially these consist of a motor unit that revolves the working bit at high speed (typically between 5,000 and 30,000rpm no-load speed) – rather like a flexible-shaft machine without the shaft. They are also called **micromotors** or **microtools**, and they are indeed small, taking comparatively small bits.

The Dremel Professional is probably the best-known example. Dremel has been a leading provider of high-speed motor units since 1934 and, with a range of over 150 cutters, sanders, burrs and other bits, Dremels are used in a wide range of crafts besides woodworking.

Recent models incorporate advanced electronics, giving variable speed and optimizing power. This allows them to start gently (without the 'kick' of some earlier models), and to run smoothly and at a constant power even though pressure on the bit varies. The manufacturer's manual suggests operating speeds, which can be adjusted on the motor unit, for various applications and attachments.

As with the flexible drives, it is the array of bits you have to hand which dictates what you can accomplish in the way of shaping and texturing. Besides woodcarving, you could, for example, grind an inside bevel on a gouge or groove the end of a frosting or matting punch. Comfortable to use and quiet, these are, at the least, a very useful support tool for the woodcarver.

USING HIGH-SPEED MOTOR UNITS

Most of what has been said about high-speed flexible shafts applies to these tools too, but the scale is smaller. Use them for lighter, more delicate shaping and texturing. If you work them beyond their limits – when you should be using a larger machine, perhaps with a cutting disc – then you will soon have motor damage.

SAFETY

As with flexible shafts, both eye and lung protection are essential. The main hazard is dust: very fine and insidious. If you are using these tools a lot during the day, an ambient dust extractor is essential for cleaning the atmosphere – remember you'll be taking your mask off sooner or later.

DIE GRINDERS

This category of tools also includes larger high-speed motor units, also termed **die grinders**, which are essentially the motors used for routers and milling machines. I have never been comfortable with the safety aspects of these tools when freely held, and recommend the other power-carving options described here, the designs of which have woodcarving more specifically in mind.

RECIPROCAL CARVERS OR POWER CHISELS

One of the advantages of using a mallet, besides the obvious ones of delivering force to a carving tool and saving wear and tear on hands and arms, is that it can deliver a discrete impulse. A unit of force propels the tool through the wood just so far – depending on the wood resistance and the amount of force – and no more. With small impulses, a carver can make quite accurate movements of the cutting edge.

Reciprocal carvers (also called **reciprocal** or **power chisels** or **motorized carvers**) work on a similar principle. The hand-held units deliver discrete impulses to a cutting blade, just like huge numbers of discrete mallet taps. A reciprocal carver can deliver 13,000 cuts in a minute, a blurred movement that pushes the gouge as if by hand, rather than by mallet.

This small vibrating movement results in a smooth cut that will eventually work its way through the toughest wood. However, because these machines still need to husband power, the carving tools supplied with them are not very big.

Reciprocal carvers may be:

- large, dedicated, flexible-shaft machines (such as the Bordet), designed for prolonged use on tough materials

- smaller, dedicated hand pieces (such as the Proxxon), designed more with the 'home workshop' in mind

- adaptations of power units, such as angle grinders, in which the rotary motion of the motor is converted to reciprocal (as in the Arbortech).

EXAMPLES
Bordet
The Bordet (Fig 2.24) is a top-range carving machine, designed for continuous hard work. A quiet motor,

Fig 2.24 *The Bordet carving machine*

designed to be hung up, drives a flexible shaft which delivers high-frequency vibrations to the carving tool via a cam mechanism in the handpiece. The cutting edge moves easily through even very hard materials – Bordet machines are regularly used by stonecarvers. The solid build of this powerful machine helps to minimize the amount of vibration. The chunky brass handpiece can be gripped somewhat like a normal carving tool, and the flexible shaft allows great freedom of movement (Fig 2.25).

The accompanying Bordet carving tools (Fig 2.26) have a simple rod-like shaft that is locked into the handpiece with an Allen key, so blade changing is very quick. The carving tools are very well made, somewhat thicker than regular tools and sharpened at a steeper cutting angle to make the edge tougher. The range of tools is perforce limited, but I have known carvers to grind the tang and shank of a favourite carving tool carefully and precisely to fit the handpiece.

A criticism would be the lack of a switch, either on the machine itself or foot-operated, which would be easily accessible to the user. You would be well advised to add an accessible switch yourself, rather than rely on the mains switch at the end of the power lead.

Fig 2.25 The Bordet power chisel can be held in much the same way as a normal gouge. The cuts it takes are light but smooth and easy, so, although it removes less at each stroke than a large gouge and mallet, you could carry on for much longer

The Bordet carving machine is a costly item – though no doubt it is not expensive for the engineering in it – and a carver would have to be serious about using it a lot to justify the outlay. However, for uninterrupted, hard use, there is no better machine.

Fig 2.26 A selection of tooling for the Bordet carver

Proxxon

Most carvers would find it hard to rationalize the cost of a continually rated machine, but there are several lighter-duty options: small, self-contained units taking thinner, smaller blades. These work best on soft to medium woods.

The Proxxon Carver MSG 220 (Fig 2.27) is a good machine of this sort: the body is a comfortable size to hold – a very important consideration – and, although heavy, the weight gives authority to the cutting action. The motor delivers 13,000 cuts a minute, and the sense of vibration is low and the cut very smooth. At 65 watts, this is a machine designed for occasional, light use rather than heavy-duty work; stressing the motor too hard will only shorten its life. Larger machines are more powerful (180W, say), but the same advice applies.

Fig 2.27 The Proxxon MSG 220, a lightweight reciprocal carver

Although this machine, like the others, comes with a selection of blades, the Proxxon will also take those Flexcut blades (see Volume 1, pages 97–9) which are designed and sold for this sort of machine. The flexing of the blade works very well indeed with the scooping action.

Arbortech

An economic alternative to buying a self-contained reciprocal carving machine is to convert your angle grinder: this is Arbortech's quite successful approach. By adding an extension kit, a 4in (100mm) hand-held angle grinder is converted into a power chisel

(Fig 2.28). This method takes advantage of the not inconsiderable power of the grinder motor, although such grinders are heavier in the main than the self-contained units. The chisel extends from the end of the grinder, and so you find yourself wielding a large, hefty device – but not one you can't get used to.

The chisels and gouges are big and tough, reminiscent of the Bordet ones (but not interchangeable with them); and shapes and sizes are similarly limited. It is not possible to adapt your own because a locking slot is needed in their shaft. This slot wears, and the chisel must be replaced when it reaches a specified thinness at this point.

Not all grinders suit the extension kit, so you need to check beforehand. The kit must be carefully fitted according to instructions, and maintained by oiling regularly.

USING RECIPROCAL CARVERS

Reciprocal carvers do not suit everyone's style of carving by any means, and you should definitely try one before buying.

The main action of these machines is a scooping or running cut, so your woodcarving design must arise out of this approach. Detailed incising must be added with regular woodworking tools. There is no comparison to what can be done with conventional carving tools, in terms of subtlety and intricacy. Reciprocal carvers are simple machines with simple blade options: simple designs work best.

My feeling is that reciprocal carvers find their greatest value where dexterity or strength is lacking, either from age, lack of physical fitness or the toughness of the material.

Control of the cutting edge is quite precise, because of the discrete packages of force which are delivered to the carving tool. This same 'softly-softly' nudging will push the cutting edge through hard timber. Though not as fast as cutting discs, reciprocal carvers will rough out work with little effort while maintaining the 'feel' of a carving tool to a far greater extent. Lack of dust is one great advantage.

Bear in mind that you have to sharpen the carving tools with a steeper bevel than usual (around 20–25°). Let the machine (the cam drive) do the work, and don't push it too hard.

SAFETY FACTORS

- Reciprocating carvers are very safe: to activate the tool – to make it vibrate and thus cut – the edge must be pushed against the wood. Only then does the cam engage. Nevertheless, it is possible to substitute flesh for wood, so normal, sensible carving rules ('hands behind the cutting edge', for example) still apply.

- All reciprocal carvers are noisy. Noise inevitably arises from the cam rapidly striking the shaft of the tool. It may not be excessively loud, but has a harsh, buzzing quality. I find I need ear protectors to work comfortably.

- This is not hand carving; I strongly recommend eye protection.

- Some people are affected in some degree by Raynaud's syndrome: a waxy whiteness of the fingers as blood vessels constrict. A prime instigator of this condition is vibration. Since vibration, even if only lightly felt by most, is an essential part of reciprocal carvers, there is a danger here for the susceptible.

Fig 2.28 *The Arbortech Power Chisel, available fully assembled or as an extension kit to fit your own angle grinder*

CHAPTER THREE

MODIFYING TOOLS

AIMS

- To describe some simple ways of changing the existing shapes of woodcarving tools to make them suitable for particular carving situations

- To indicate the possibilities for making entirely new tools

- To look at some methods and equipment

- To promote confidence with woodcarving tools

It must be said at the outset that this chapter is not a treatise on tool making. Based on my own understanding, experience and efforts, it is not without its limitations. However, my attempts to modify tools, or to make new ones when I have had the need, are worth sharing. The information and understanding that follows is gathered from simple processes that have worked well for me. Read through all the information before attempting these techniques.

WHY MODIFY TOOLS?

With the huge numbers of woodcarving tools on the market, you might think that carvers must be hard customers to satisfy if they cannot find what they need. But the truth is that the shapes and sizes available (in the Sheffield List, for example) were, and are, standardized through decisions relating to commercial production. Reasonably enough, manufacturers need to sell tools to stay in business – and

the more obscure a carving tool, the less financial contribution it will make. The shapes and sizes available today will be those that sell best, being the most useful to most carvers.

Carving, however, can involve very complicated three-dimensional shapes, and the carver may find that access to difficult corners or recesses will tax his or her carving tools to the limit. In these circumstances carvers, tending to be adaptable, will work with what they have and make one tool do the work of several others, even if this means using it in an unorthodox way. And, within the range of tools produced by different firms, there will usually be something which will do the necessary work.

Failing these options, there is the possibility of changing the design of the carving. One approach is to incorporate **flats**, or areas where an extra piece of wood is added to increase the depth of carving at some point. The deeper layers of carving are finished first, then the next layer of wood is added and carved (see Fig 3.1). In this way a great depth of carving can be achieved using ordinary woodcarving tools – when

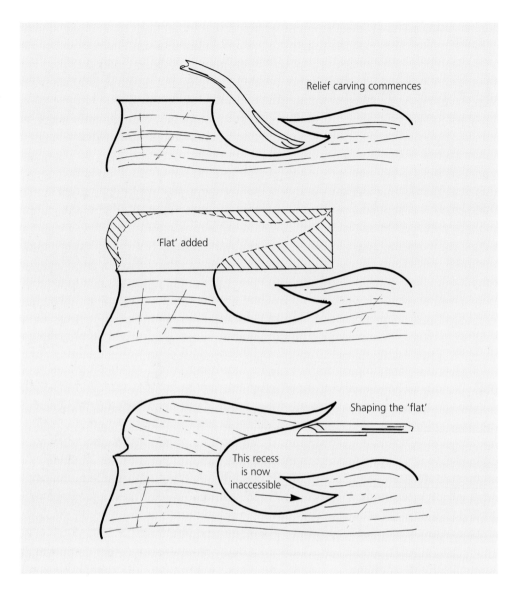

Relief carving commences

'Flat' added

Shaping the 'flat'

This recess is now inaccessible

Fig 3.1 By planning ahead and leaving surfaces to which wood may later be added, deep carving effects can be achieved by using 'flats'

Fig 3.2 This large frontbent gouge was made from a boatbuilder's caulking chisel (similar to the bolster in the foreground) using a blacksmith's forge. Smaller shaping work is possible with a much leaner set-up

the deepest layers would otherwise have been impossible to carve. This is a long-established carving practice, used, for instance, by medieval carvers, and by Grinling Gibbons.

Sometimes, however, neither versatility nor redesigning solves a particular problem of access and, unless a new carving tool can be made, that part of the carving may be inaccessible. Rather than creating an entirely new tool, it is more usual to modify one already in use, perhaps a spare one (Figs 3.2 and 3.3). You may have been using a bent gouge which is not quite bent enough, or needs to be bent in a more appropriate direction (Fig 3.4); or perhaps a skew is not quite skewed enough. This level of modification is well within the capabilities of most carvers.

Fig 3.3 *Old and disused tools like these can be remade or changed into something much more useful*

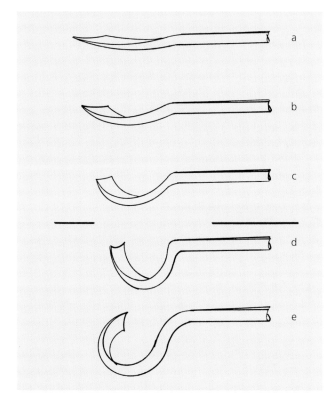

Fig 3.4 *How much bend you get in a bent tool varies between manufacturers (a–c); for a particular job, you may need something which is not made commercially (d–e)*

Repairing and reclaiming broken or worn-out carving tools is an offshoot of the ability to modify their shape. Exactly the same processes apply to these tools, including retempering a blade that has been overheated or poorly tempered, and reshaping a tool that has one of the faults mentioned in Volume 1, Chapter 4.

Gibbons is also thought to have made special tools to cope with certain kinds of carved work; this allows the possibility of designing carvings outside the compass of normal carving tools. If, in the execution of the work, the availability of tools is not a problem, then there is one less barrier to imaginative design.

Some carvers who enjoy smithing make carving tools from scratch – which means finding the appropriate high-carbon steel, forging it to shape and then rendering the edge hard and strong enough to cut. Huge quantities of high-carbon steel are to be found in scrap yards (for example, in the form of leaf and coil springs), where rust is only superficial. The high carbon content of the steel reveals itself in the bright showers of sparks that come from contact with a fast grinding wheel (Fig 3.5). Such metal can be made into perfectly serviceable woodcarving tools.

But, although the process is simpler than most people think, it involves more of a commitment to the idea – more expenditure and time to set up – than most woodcarvers wish to make, and cannot be dealt with here. Some manufacturers, such as Henry Taylor, will make a tool to a carver's specification if it falls outside the range of tools they normally produce.

THE POSSIBILITIES

Having said that this chapter is not a treatise on tool making, but that carvers, being practical by nature, should have no problems with the techniques and suggestions being offered here: what can a

Fig 3.5 *Plentiful sparks from a piece of steel indicate that it is made of high-carbon steel and is suitable for making into a woodcarving tool*

carver reasonably expect to achieve in the way of modifying tools?

Perhaps the most useful area is creating a new bend – forwards, backwards or to the sides – or indeed straightening a blade. This is relatively straightforward if you are reshaping an existing tool of the right width and sweep (Fig 3.6).

Hardening and tempering (or retempering) carving tools is also relatively straightforward, although it involves some means of generating the necessary heat. Both procedures entail heat-treating the metal so as to render it hard enough, but also resilient enough, to carve with. Bending a tool usually involves upsetting or destroying its temper, after which the tool needs retempering, so this process supplements the previous one.

Lengthening, broadening or forming a new sweep are more skilled procedures and are more akin to the smithing work needed for new tools (Fig 3.7). Sweeps

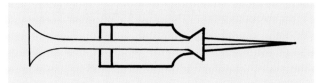

Fig 3.7 *An old tool which is short and wide has enough metal to be forged into a longer, narrower one*

are forged around suitable formers (Figs 3.8 and 3.9). Given time, care and some experimentation, these skills can be acquired to give further scope to the simple modifications that follow.

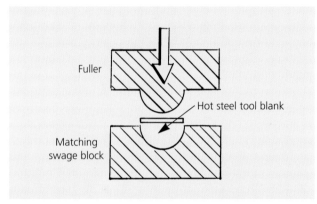

Fig 3.8 *Tools are shaped commercially by hammering a convex fuller into a matching concave swage block*

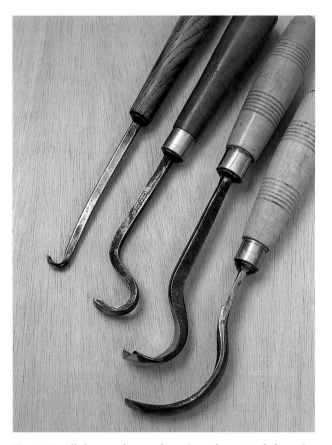

Fig 3.6 *All these tools were bent from the original shape for a particular purpose, using the basic techniques discussed in this chapter; in each case the original sweep is retained*

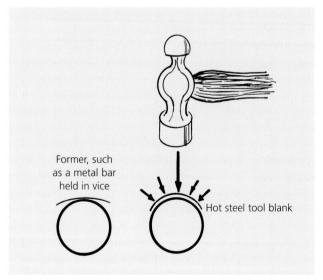

Fig 3.9 *It is not too difficult to change the sweep of a blade using a suitable former. Any roughness in the former will be transferred to the hot metal, so make sure the former surface is smooth*

BASIC PROCEDURES

The shapes of carving tools can be modified while they are cold, while they are heated, or through a combination of both, depending on what changes are needed.

COLD PROCEDURES

Other than a small amount of bending to the soft parts of a tool – such as the tang – working with a cold tool involves removing metal. This is a limited, but valuable, process; grinding the bevel, and even sharpening, are instances of it. Another example is resetting the angle of a skew chisel to make it more acute (Fig 3.10). As removing metal always results in something smaller, a larger tool, or a larger amount of metal, is necessary to start with.

Grinding wheels and sharpening stones do take time to remove metal from a blade if the steel has already been hardened; there is also the danger of blueing when a high-speed wheel is used. But if the tool has been **annealed** – that is, the hardness taken out – grinding and so on becomes a lot quicker. It makes no odds if the steel turns blue, and files can be used for sensitive shaping – but in order to carve with the tool, it must first be rehardened.

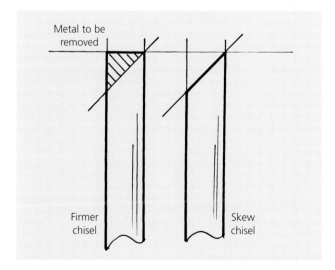

Fig 3.10 *Changing the angle of a skew chisel, or making a new one from an old firmer, is an example of a simple cold procedure*

HOT PROCEDURES

Removing cold steel is a limited procedure, but when combined with heat, new possibilities are opened up. As the metal temperature rises, it becomes ductile, plastic and eventually liquid. At the ductile temperatures it can be bent (Figs 3.11 and 3.12) and forged. **Forging** involves shaping the steel by hammering it: it can be made wider or longer, or the sweep can be changed. This procedure is more appropriate to a discussion of entirely new tools, and from the point of this chapter will be touched on only briefly.

Fig 3.11 *Even rasps and files can be reshaped successfully, though their tempering makes them harder, more brittle, than carving tools*

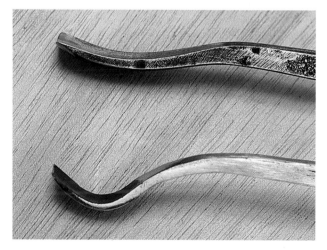

Fig 3.12 *Increasing the amount of bend in a bent tool is simply a matter of manipulating the metal while it is hot enough. A little more skill is needed to refine the shape, yet more to harden and finally temper it*

Probably the simplest source of heat for most carvers is a propane torch, which is available with different sizes of nozzles or jets to produce corresponding flames. Such torches, working from a cylinder of gas, will generate the necessary heat for most tools. Wood stoves and fireplaces may also be usable. More information on heat sources is given on pages 58–9.

After heating and shaping, further refinements can be made by grinding with the metal cold, before using heat treatment to restore the necessary hardness and temper.

HARDENING, TEMPERING AND ANNEALING

The steel that is used in woodcarving tools is known as a 'high-carbon' steel; this has a certain amount of carbon in it (usually around 0.5–1.5%, but definitions vary), as well as other trace elements. Put simply, the iron atoms in the steel form a latticework; this crystal lattice expands as the steel is heated above a certain temperature, and the carbon atoms enter. If the steel is cooled quickly (**quenched**) the lattices contract, trapping the carbon atoms within their framework. Tension is thereby created, which appears as hardness. This process of heating to a high temperature and then quenching is known as **hardening**. The degree of hardness depends on how rapidly the tool is cooled – how much carbon is trapped in the lattices.

When the steel is gradually heated – with the intention of hardening it – the metal will begin to show a dark red colour, the first visible glow of heat. The steel changes colour as it gets hotter: to a blood red, then to a dark cherry red, a medium cherry red and then a light cherry colour (Table 3.1). It is at this medium-to-light cherry-red colour, sometimes called 'bright cherry' (about 1,375°C or 2,500°F), that the tool is quenched. Toolmakers in the past would have learned to judge the temperature solely by the colour of the metal.

These heat colours are best seen in a semi-dark room. If you have never seen them before, experiment on an old chisel or screwdriver. Try to observe

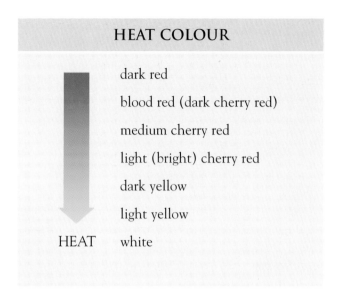

HEAT COLOUR

dark red

blood red (dark cherry red)

medium cherry red

light (bright) cherry red

dark yellow

light yellow

HEAT   white

Table 3.1 *Heat colour changes when hardening steel*

these colours always in the same quality of light, so that your assessment is consistent. Heat the steel evenly with the torch, moving the flame around as necessary.

Beyond the light cherry colour, the steel becomes gradually more yellow, light yellow, and then white. When a white colour is reached, sparks will start to fly from the metal – this is carbon leaving the steel or being burnt out. Heating the tool to white-hot will probably ruin it.

From the first visible heat glow the metal starts to become malleable, becoming more so as the temperature rises. If the steel is heated to a cherry-red colour and then allowed to cool slowly (without quenching), all the carbon atoms leave the lattices of iron and the result is the softest, most flexible condition the steel can be in. The metal is said to be **annealed**. Annealed steel can be filed and worked much more easily than when it is in its hardened state.

A degree of annealed, softer metal is desirable behind the cutting edge – in the shank – of a woodcarving blade, to give the tool resilience to mallet impact and general use without the metal cracking. The tense hardness that arises from heating and quenching makes the steel brittle, and carving with a tool in this state would probably lead to a fracturing of the metal. Reheating to a much lower, but still precise, temperature causes some of the carbon atoms to escape the lattices of iron, so relieving the tension.

This second process is known as **tempering**, and seeks a balance between hardness and brittleness.

When steel is heated, but long before the malleable temperatures are reached, oxides are formed with the air on the surface of the metal. These oxides vary in colour according to the temperature of the metal. A distinct range of colours appears, which can be used as a guide to the temperature of the blade at any particular point. Again, in the past these colours would have been the only measure available to the toolmaker, who would have been sensitive to their gradations and what they signified. Different colours indicate a specific degree of softening of the steel from its original hardness, making it suitable for particular purposes.

To temper a blade, it must be hardened first. After hardening, you need to polish the surface in order to see easily the colours of the oxidation spectrum as the temperature of the metal is raised (Fig 3.13).

To get an idea of what these **tempering colours** look like, polish a bar of high-carbon steel or the surface of an old chisel with emery paper (Fig 3.14). The colours reveal themselves best in daylight. Gently and slowly apply heat to an area of the metal. The first colour to appear is a faint straw colour, starting the sequence given in Table 3.2.

The range between the first and last colours is only about 70°C (125°F), so care and stealth are needed in the heating. It is not always easy to see or separate out the colours, as each colour merges with the next like

Fig 3.14 Polishing the surface of the tool before heating means that the tempering colours can easily be seen; they will remain visible unless removed by subsequent polishing

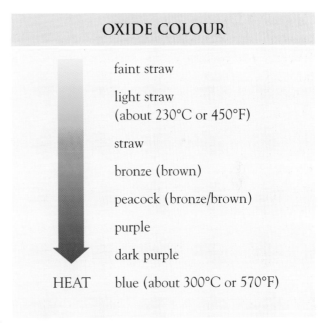

OXIDE COLOUR

	faint straw
	light straw (about 230°C or 450°F)
	straw
	bronze (brown)
	peacock (bronze/brown)
	purple
	dark purple
HEAT	blue (about 300°C or 570°F)

Table 3.2 Oxide colour changes when tempering steel

a rainbow. With a little practice the colours become familiar and can be made to appear as bands distinct enough to serve as indicators of hardness. The colours themselves are entirely superficial and rub off easily with fine emery paper.

The colour at which a woodcarving tool should be set or fixed by a second quenching is that of light straw.

Fig 3.13 A typical oxidation spectrum produced by heating a polished steel surface. Normally the lighter colours are 'floated' into position from a hotter, annealed part of the blade, the blue representing the highest temperature. From left to right, the colours follow the sequence listed in Table 3.2

A mid-straw colour would be acceptable, perhaps even a slightly dark straw colour, particularly for sculpture tools taking a lot of hard work. However, heating to further along the colour range results in a softer metal which is no longer able to hold its edge. The blue colour is seen when an edge is 'blued' on a fast grinding wheel. At this temperature hardness has been removed sufficiently from the edge to make it too soft to use for woodcarving.

If, having quenched to fix a temper colour, you find you have gone beyond what you intended, the tool can be rehardened and another attempt at tempering made – this will do the tool no harm.

If you heat the centre section of a polished metal bar, the spectrum of colours appears to either side of the heated (blue) part as heat is conducted both ways (Fig 3.15). Stop heating, and the bands of colour will continue to travel along the metal for some time,

with the straw colours moving in front. The blue area can be used as a reservoir of heat, and, with deft use of the propane torch, the required colours can be 'floated' along the metal of the blade and into their required positions (Fig 3.16). Try doing this. You can cool the metal between attempts and polish off the oxidation colours.

When the exact colour is reached in the tempering process, the blade is quenched by rapidly dipping into water. This fixes the degree of hardness represented by the colour. Experiment with quenching at particular colours.

It is not necessary to render a large amount of the blade light straw colour. In specialized woodcarving tools, only a good working amount behind the cutting edge is needed. However, different parts of the blade do need different degrees of hardness. Softer, more resilient and stronger metal is necessary behind the

Fig 3.15 *The oxidation colours on the polished metal surface spread in both directions away from the source of heat and vary according to the temperature*

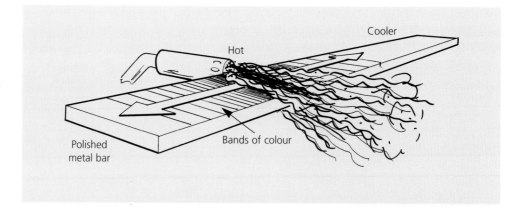

Cooler

Hot

Polished metal bar

Bands of colour

Fig 3.16 *Using the metal itself to hold a reservoir of heat, which can be subtly floated along by deft application of its source, is an important tempering technique*

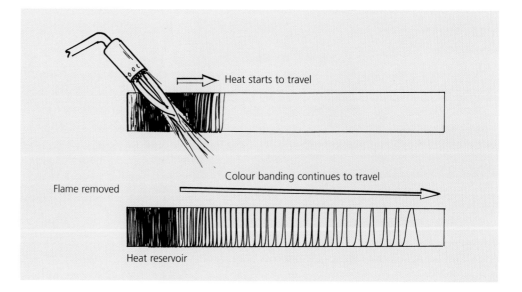

Heat starts to travel

Flame removed

Colour banding continues to travel

Heat reservoir

56

harder, but more brittle, cutting edge (Fig 3.17). For example, the edge of a shortbent tool should be tempered to a light straw colour, but the bend is rendered gradually darker, becoming blue at the shank.

Points were made earlier, in the discussion on bench grinders, about the relationship between mass and temperature (see Volume 1, page 157); that information is relevant here. As heat is deliberately applied to a blade to temper it:

- the thinnest parts of the carving blade, being of least mass, will rise in temperature the quickest;

- the heat will travel slowest in the thicker parts, moving more quickly as the blade becomes thinner.

So the colour changes to light straw can appear very quickly as the heat approaches the thin cutting edge and corners (Fig 3.18). A close eye must be kept on the movement and appearance of the colour banding – reacting quickly and dipping the tool into the water prevents further change to the colours.

Although this method of tempering by eye may seem a little casual, it has a long tradition. Long before computer-regulated furnaces, toolmakers using such methods were producing the fine qualities of

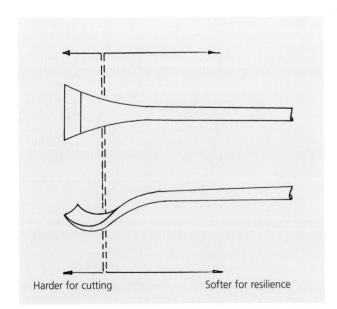

Fig 3.17 *Different tempers are needed in the different parts of a blade; in general, the metal needs to be harder towards the cutting edge*

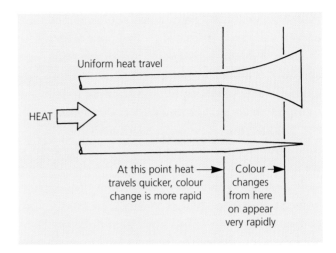

Fig 3.18 *The speed at which the oxidation colour changes depends on how fast the temperature rises; this in turn is determined by the thickness of the metal*

tempering seen in many old tools. My experience is that by learning to trust your eye – and with a little practice – not only can hardening and tempering be successful, but you may actually be able to improve on the temper of the original tool.

Experience is, of course, necessary, but correctly tempering a tool is far easier than usually thought. But, at the end of the day, the proof is in the cutting of the wood. If the resulting tool seems a little soft, or is still not quite the right shape, there is no harm in repeating the process or experimenting further.

QUENCHING

In practice, when the metal has been heated to a cherry-red colour in the hardening process, you must maintain this colour evenly for a little while, soaking the metal in the heat to maximize the movement of carbon. The tool is then quenched – dipped into a cooling liquid and moved up, down and around, to dissipate the heat rapidly and fix the crystal lattices.

The main liquids used for such cooling are:

- oil (old car oil is adequate)

- water (fresh).

Both should start at room temperature.

Water is used for large tools – plunge the tool in vertically, edge first. There is quite a shock to the metal when it is cooled rapidly in this way, and with smaller or more delicate tools there is a danger of the blade warping or cracking. For these tools oil is safer. Oil boils at about three times the temperature of water, and therefore cools the steel more slowly and with less shock. The resulting blade is slightly softer than if it were quenched in water, but this is not a problem in practice. Some toolmakers plunge really fine tools into tallow; others use brine (saturated salt solution) as a midway between water and oil, so increasing their options.

It is important to be aware that when a large, cherry-red, hot piece of metal is plunged into a small amount of oil there is a danger of the oil igniting. The blade should be dipped *completely*; if part of the red-hot blade is left above the oil, it may ignite the fumes. So, for safety when quenching in oil:

- Keep the oil in a lidded metal can.

- Use at least 1 litre (1.8 pints) of oil.

- Keep a cover or safety blanket to hand.

- Dip the blade completely under the oil.

- Work in a well-ventilated area – unpleasant fumes will result from the quenching, the amount depending on the size of the blade being quenched.

- Wear eye protection at least, or better still a face shield.

Water, when used to quench red-hot metal, should be kept in a metal container close to where you are working. Obviously there is no danger of its igniting, but the heated water may well 'spit' when the tool plunges in.

Hardening in oil gives rise to a harmless black patina on the metal; even water will leave the blade dirty and discoloured. The patina needs cleaning off in order to show the tempering colours of the subsequent stage better. 'Wet and dry' abrasive paper, made from emery or Carborundum, is available in various grits and will polish the surface.

The final quenching of the much lower temperatures used for tempering should be done in clean water. Plunge the blade straight in and swirl it around. On emerging, the polished surface is normally clean, and the beautiful tempering colours clearly visible for inspection.

EQUIPMENT

The three main procedures at our disposal for modifying tools are:

- removing metal

- bending and shaping

- hardening and tempering.

Most of the necessary tools for these procedures are to be found in the average workshop, and any further equipment need not be expensive.

HEAT SOURCE

The blacksmith's forge contains special coal, which is said to create a carbon atmosphere around the hot metal and improve the quality of the steel. In practice I have found a good propane torch – such as plumbers use – quite adequate (Fig 3.19). The direction and amount of heat are accurate, and it does not seem to

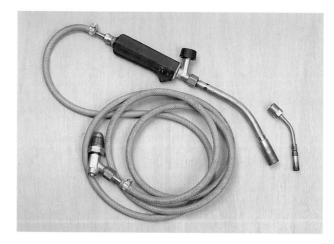

Fig 3.19 *Sievert propane torch with different sizes of interchangeable nozzles*

affect the steel adversely. A large nozzle will give a good overall heat for larger tools and hardening; switch to a smaller one for more delicate tempering.

Fix the torch securely in position, in a vice or clamp. Alternatively, you can hold the torch in one hand while the tool is held, with tongs or Mole grips, in the other. As a naked flame is being used, work away from the wood area of the workshop; always work carefully and safely, and preferably outside if possible.

Start heating the metal slowly so as not to shock the blade. Water or oil coolants should be in metal containers and placed to hand before heat treatment is started.

VICE

A small metalworking vice – designed to be roughly handled – is useful in a carving workshop, for example for gripping blades to fit or remove handles. A portable vice which clamps to the bench top will probably be quite satisfactory (Fig 3.20).

If you need to work on your woodcarving bench, try and keep the surface clean – metalwork tends to be a grubby business. Black slate-like roof tiles make a good protective surface.

Bear in mind that a metalworking vice or clamp may act as a heat drain, absorbing the heat away from the blade (Fig 3.21). As a consequence, the blade may conduct heat unexpectedly, need more heating up, and cool down quicker.

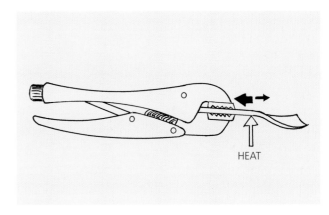

Fig 3.21 *The means whereby a tool is held may itself act as a heat drain; the effect of applying the heat may then be unpredictable*

ANVIL

A solid, and reliably flat, surface is sometimes needed to true up part of a blade using a hammer. Small anvils are available, but there are also anvil-like surfaces on metalworking vices. Suitable lumps of metal can be found in scrap yards.

GENERAL TOOLS

How you are going to grip the hot carving tool, safely and securely, needs to be thought out before you start heating the metal. Tongs, locking grips (Mole grips) or different sizes of pliers are all possible devices (Figs 3.22 and 3.23). A vice, for instance, is no good for holding a blade that must be quickly dipped.

Fig 3.20 *A fixed metalworking vice, a small portable vice and a bench-top anvil*

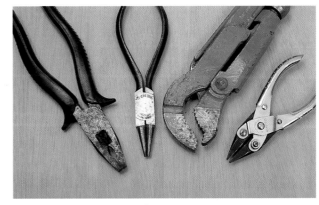

Fig 3.22 *Four types of (non-locking) pliers or grips. Choose the one which grips the particular tool you are working on most securely and suitably*

Fig 3.23 *Mole (locking) grips lock securely on to the tool on which you are working*

Hammers, pliers (for bending) and a hacksaw are tools which will be needed according to the work. There is plenty of scope for improvising but, again, try and work out what you might need before starting. It is quite frustrating to have to stop in the middle because you do not have the right tool.

Metal files of different sizes, shapes and roughness can remove metal more accurately than the grinding wheel. Use them when the metal is annealed.

Pliers with sharp jaws may mark the hot, soft metal during the bending. These marks can usually be filed off when the metal is cold. Pliers that are round in section, smooth-jawed or without sharp corners, mark soft metal far less. It is quite useful to have different sorts available.

Slipstones and 'wet and dry' abrasive paper will finely shape and polish the metal surface. Ordinary woodworking sandpaper will abrade annealed metal too.

BENCH GRINDER

Details of grinders are given in Volume 1, Chapter 10.

SAFETY

Safety, as ever, lies in being in control, being aware of the dangers and not being distracted. Modifying tools in the ways we are discussing need give no problems, especially if the following basic points are observed.

- The woodcarver's environment tends to be dry and to contain inflammable wood chips, finishing agents, etc. – work well away from these.

- Never leave a naked flame unattended. Keep water nearby, or better still a fire extinguisher or fire blanket.

- Make sure a source of heat is safe before using it. For example, if the torch is to be clamped or held in a vice, work out the arrangement before lighting it, rather than wandering around with a naked flame, looking for a home. *Do not clamp the hot torch to a wooden surface.*

- Have good ventilation – fumes arise from the use of torches and other heat sources, as well as from quenching blades in oil.

- Remove the wooden handle completely before heating up a blade. Even if it does not burn the handle, an expanding tang may loosen the hole.

- Sharp tools left clamped in vices with their tangs and edges exposed are very dangerous.

- Eye protection, if not a whole face shield, should be worn.

OVERVIEW OF THE HOT SHAPING PROCESS

In general terms, the procedure for modifying a woodcarving tool, using heat, is as follows:

First heating: annealing

- Heat the tool to cherry red.

- Cool slowly to anneal.

Second heating: shaping

- Heat beyond the red colour to bend, shape, hammer, etc.

- Cool slowly to room temperature for cold working.

- Grind and file accurately to shape. Finish surface well.

Third heating: hardening

- In semi-darkness, heat to bright cherry red, holding the colour for a little while.

- Quench in water or oil.

- Clean and polish the metal.

Fourth heating: tempering

- In daylight, heat to between light and dark straw in the region of the cutting edge; darker for the supporting, more resilient parts.

- Quench in water.

- Check blade colours. Hardening and tempering can be repeated if necessary.

BENDING

Work out the amount and position of the bend – forwards, backwards or to the side – before you start. While the metal is still cold, decide on your plan for gripping and bending it. For example, part of the blade may be held in a metalworking vice, using a pair of pliers for bending in one hand and the torch in the other. Or you may fix the torch safely and use both hands to work the blade, in which case position the torch to point safely away from where you are working.

Heat the part of the blade to be bent to at least red-hot. It is always best to anneal the metal first to safeguard against cracking. Do not try to bend the metal when it is less than a dull red colour. To do so can result in the metal fracturing.

Bending the hot part over a corner of metal (or round metal bar) by hammering is another option, especially suitable for larger tools (Fig 3.24). Be careful not to damage the sweep.

If the bend is not quite what you wanted the first time, the metal can be reheated and reworked.

FORGING

Forging refers particularly to hammering the metal to shape: shortening or lengthening the form; creating the internal curve (or sweep) by hammering the

Fig 3.24 *Detail of the crank in the home-made shortbent gouge shown in Fig 3.2*

cutting edge over suitable metal formers; or bending and forming tangs and shoulders. All this is possible with enough practice.

At a simpler level, forging will augment bending. For example, you can straighten, lengthen or flatten part of a blade using the anvil (Fig 3.25). For this sort of work both hands are needed, with the heat source safely to one side. Again, reheating may be necessary.

After bending (or other shaping), allow the metal to cool slowly; do not quench it. Refine the shape with files, emery paper glued to wood strips, slipstones and so on. Smoothing the surface at this stage makes it easier to polish after hardening.

Fig 3.25 *In the absence of swage blocks, a simple fishtail shape can be forged by hammering the hot end on an anvil. The shape can then be further refined over a round bar, filed and shaped*

SOME EXAMPLES OF TOOL MODIFICATIONS

The following examples of tool modifying follow from the information given so far in this chapter, and illustrate just some of the possibilities. If you wish to attempt these projects, read through all the instructions first.

COLD SHAPING

SKEW CHISEL

To emphasize the working point of a skew chisel, grind metal from the back of the long corner (Figs 3.26 and 3.27). The point becomes very useful for delicate work and getting into tight corners – a specialized tool, not the everyday working skew. Because it is weakened, take care not to rock the tool from side to side for fear of breaking it; store with a plastic cork on the tip.

As the point itself is susceptible to overheating, a light touch on the grinding wheel is necessary, with frequent cooling. Stop the grinding a little before the cutting edge, and finish the ground surface with slipstones.

Fig 3.26 *A cold procedure: grinding the back edge of a skew chisel to emphasize the point and so gain access to tight corners*

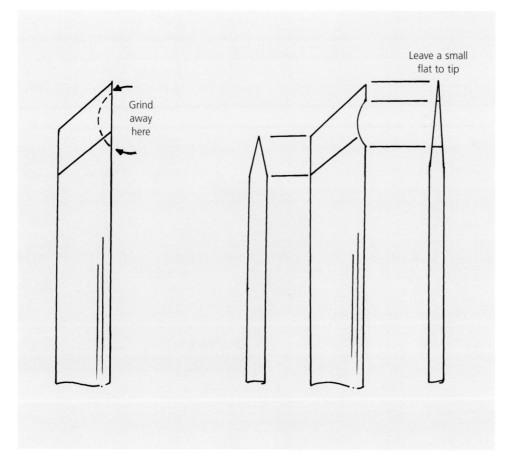

Grind away here

Leave a small flat to tip

Fig 3.27 *Simple cold shaping to produce a useful skew point*

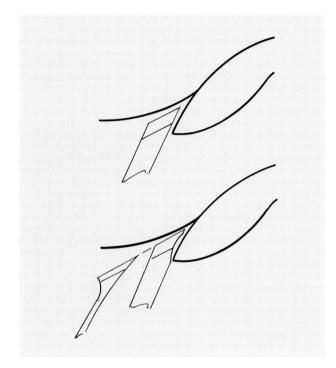

SKEWED FISHTAIL CHISEL

A skewed fishtail chisel is another tool that helps the carver to get into awkward recesses (Figs 3.28 and 3.29). It is also useful for cutting the flat ends of serifs in lettering, and for finishing lightly convex surfaces. The shape itself goes back a long way and can be seen in woodcuts of medieval carvers at work. A socketed version from China, dated around 1850, is to be found in the Science Museum in London (Fig 3.30).

Fig 3.28 *Sometimes the sides of the skew prevent it making a clean cut in a tight recess; in these cases a tool with an even more pronounced point may gain access. Note how even the reground skew cannot reach quite as far as the skewed fishtail*

Fig 3.29 *The skewed fishtail chisel: another tool useful for getting into tight corners*

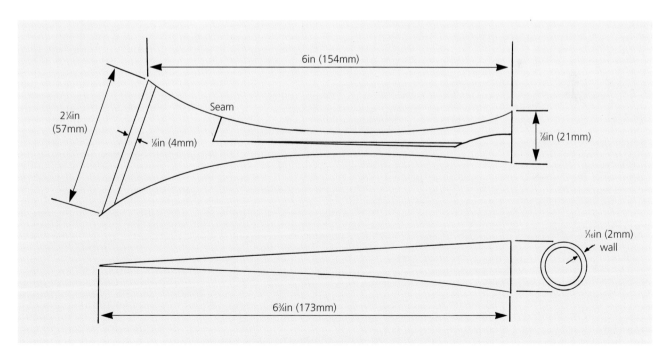

Fig 3.30 *A socketed skew chisel, of a type common in China around 1850, from the Science Museum, London (inventory no. 1873–53). The basic 'plate' was turned and seamed to form the socket, and surplus metal dressed forward to form the blade itself*

There are three different ways of making this shape:

- Bend a normal fishtail chisel sideways; the shank then has to be hammered straight and the edge lined up again (Fig 3.31).

- A simpler way is to take an oversize fishtail or other chisel, anneal it and grind away the surplus metal (Fig 3.32). As when sharpening a normal skew chisel (see Volume 1, pages 193–4), set the skew angle first – try about 30° to begin with – then the bevels. Sharpen as normal and retain the corners.

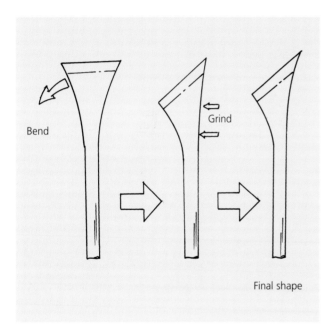

Fig 3.31 *One way of making a skewed fishtail chisel using both hot and cold procedures*

- The shape can also be made, more satisfyingly, by actual forging. Heat an unwanted short, fat chisel and draw out the shape on a small anvil (Fig 3.33). The tang and shoulder remain from the original chisel, and the hammering improves the grain of the metal.

HOT SHAPING

KNUCKLE GOUGE

A knuckle gouge is an extra-tight shortbent (or spoonbit) gouge. It can cut within awkward recesses denied to normal shortbent tools (Fig 3.34). Knuckle V-tools and backbent gouges can be created in a similar way. Start with a shortbent gouge that has the width and sweep that you want, but inadequate longitudinal curve.

Method

1. Heat the blade to cherry red; allow to anneal by slowly cooling in the air.

2. Reheat to blood red the part which is to be bent (Fig 3.35), and bend using round-section pliers (Fig 3.36). If you grip the blade too tightly across the width you may flatten the sweep, so work lightly. Reheat as necessary to get the bend just right.

3. When the shape is correct, allow the metal to cool slowly and clean up the blade with fine files, slipstones, emery paper, etc.

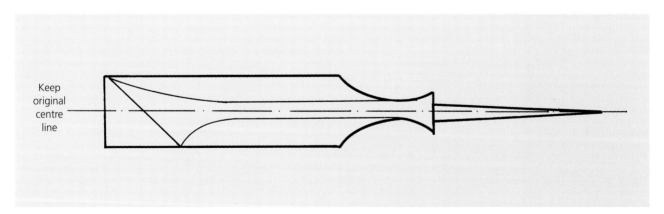

Fig 3.32 *An alternative method: once annealed, surplus metal can be ground away quickly, and it does not matter if the metal becomes blued*

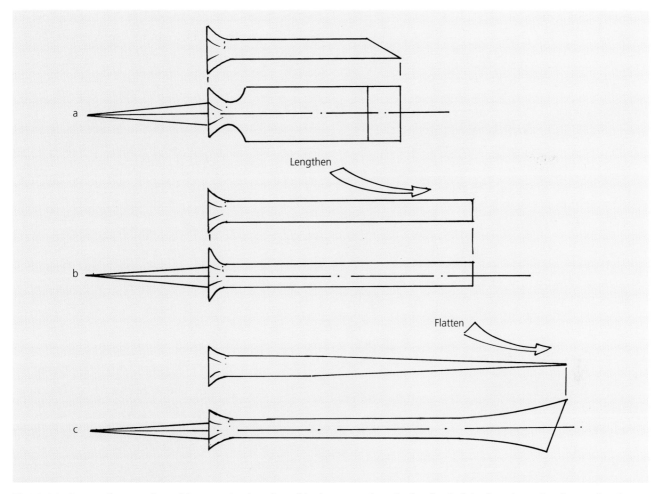

Lengthen

Flatten

Fig 3.33 *In true forging, the red-hot metal is lengthened by beating it from both sides (a–b), then the end is flattened and formed to the required shape (c). Further forging could turn it into a fishtail gouge. Keep the centre line as a guide. Some cold finishing may be needed before hardening*

Fig 3.34 *A knuckle gouge like this may enter a recess and remove wood by cutting with the grain for a clean finish, where other gouges would be cutting against it*

Fig 3.35 *Heat to an adequate temperature the part of the blade which is to be bent*

Fig 3.36 *Use round-nosed pliers to form the bend*

❹ Reheat the bend to a bright cherry colour, soaking it in the heat for a little while, then quench in oil by plunging the blade and moving it around.

❺ Clean off the oily residue and repolish the metal. At this stage the gouge is hardened but too brittle to use.

❻ Temper the gouge using a fine torch nozzle or flame in one hand, and tongs in the other to hold the gouge. Lightly start the heat along the shank, turning the polished metal blue. Apply the torch deftly to extend the colour spectrum so that the purple–bronze–straw colours start to separate and creep along the steel away from the blue (hottest) colour. Try to float the colours along the blade so that as the light straw reaches the cutting edge, more bronze colour appears in the first crank of the bend, turning to purple-blue at the shank.

❼ At this point quench rapidly in water.

Dry the blade, and the colours should be plainly visible, showing the range of hardening. These oxidation colours may be left on or polished off. The tool can now be sharpened ready for use.

BACKBENT V-TOOL

If a shortbent original is not available, a different type of operation from the one described above will produce various bent V-tools from a spare straight one of the right width. A long backbent V-tool – not available commercially – is described here (Fig 3.37).

Method

❶ After annealing (by heating the whole blade blood red to the shoulder and slowly cooling), clean the inside cannel of the V-tool well.

❷ Reheat the centre part of the blade blood red from the shoulder to around 1in (25mm) from the cutting edge – say about three quarters of the blade length. When this metal has become light cherry red, *verging on yellow*, hammer the sides of the V-tool together on an anvil, without spreading them, and leaving the part towards the cutting edge untouched. The hammering will heat-weld the two sides of the tool together, effectively making them a single piece of metal – the shank of the new tool (Figs 3.38 and 3.39).

Fig 3.37 *A backbent V-tool made for a particular purpose*

Fig 3.38 *An example of the hot welding technique, where the sides of the V-tool are fused into one*

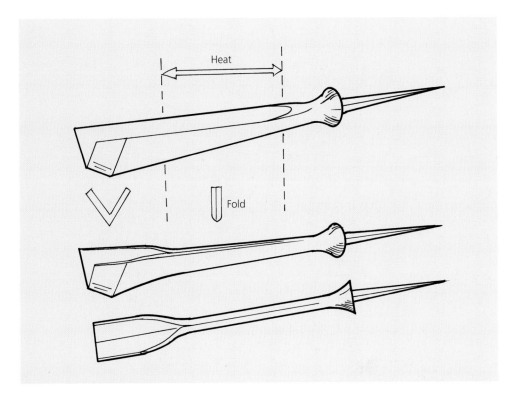

③ Keeping the blade hotter than dark red, tidy the shape on the anvil and then bend it, using pliers, to the shape you want.

④ Refine the shape when cold, using files, grinder, etc.

Once the shape is right, continue as for the knuckle gouge – hardening, tempering and sharpening in a similar fashion. You could go straight to bending without welding, but this is an interesting technique.

SMALL V-TOOL

A worn-out spoonbit or shortbent gouge can be reborn as a very useful parting tool for delicate and accurate work (Fig 3.40).

Method

① Anneal as before.

② Grind or cut off any remaining spoon profile, but keep the bend in the shank to work on.

③ Reheat and establish a 30° crank over the first 1in (25mm) of the shank towards the cutting end. Cool slowly.

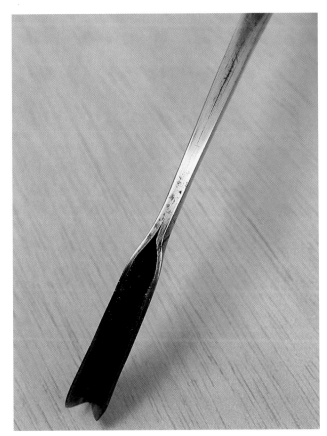

Fig 3.39 *The weld in this tool is a fusion of the two sides into one shank of metal*

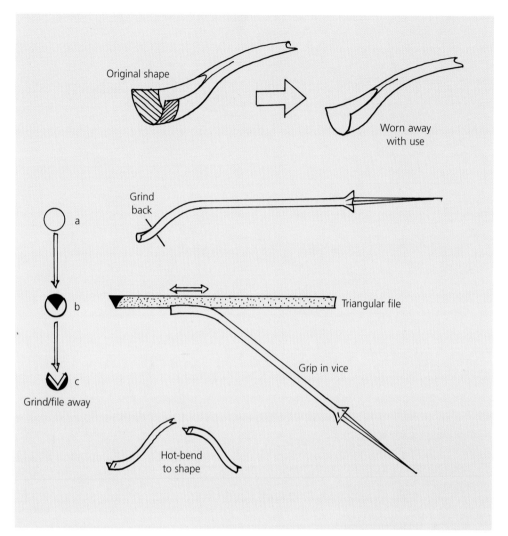

Original shape

Worn away
with use

Grind
back

a

Triangular file

b

Grip in vice

c

Grind/file away

Hot-bend
to shape

Fig 3.40 *An old shortbent gouge turned into a useful fine V-tool. Anneal and clean off the end (a); shape the inside (b), then the outside (c); and then hot-bend to shape. A final cold finish to refine the shape, then harden and temper*

❹ Grip the shank in a metalworking vice and file a V-groove using a fine triangular file – such as a needle file – in the bent part of the blade. Finish with slipstones. Work the outside of the V-groove with flat files, making the walls a uniform thickness.

❺ Reheat and bend the blade into the shape you want: straight, spoonbit or backbent. Check over the cannel and finally refine the shape.

❻ The end can now be hardened and tempered to a light straw colour, with a bronze colour at the junction of angle and shank.

Sharpen the tool and see how it cuts the wood.

SUMMARY

People are often surprised at how easy it is to modify carving tools, by bending, hardening, tempering, etc. There is something alchemical about using fire to create a new tool – a process far removed from woodcarving. These are useful skills to have or know about, and you never know when they may be needed. The day they are, may be a day of great satisfaction. There is a great pleasure to be had in making or modifying such a tool yourself, and using it to overcome a particular carving problem.

CHAPTER FOUR

HOLDING DEVICES

AIMS

- To consider the important aspects of holding carved work securely

- To discuss a repertoire of techniques and possibilities

- To encourage improvisation

- To increase confidence

The means of holding a carving is given only a passing mention in many woodcarving books. There are probably two reasons for this. The first is that as the methods are fairly simple and straightforward it may be supposed that little can be said about the matter. And secondly, since work is so varied – flat, round, abstractly shaped; from large sculpture to small, delicate netsuke; horizontally or vertically placed – it is important for the beginner to be a good improviser, which is something not so easily taught.

With experience, carvers build up a pool of techniques to hold the piece they are working on – even going so far as to design their carving with the means of holding it in mind, so important is this aspect of carving. For example, waste wood, used to clamp the work to the bench or to grip it in a vice, can be left until the last moment before being removed (Fig 4.1); or separate pieces can be carved and then assembled before finishing (Fig 4.2). Carvers tend to have their own favoured methods, just as they have favourite carving gouges.

For the beginner, holding the carving so as to get safely to the part you want can be quite a conundrum

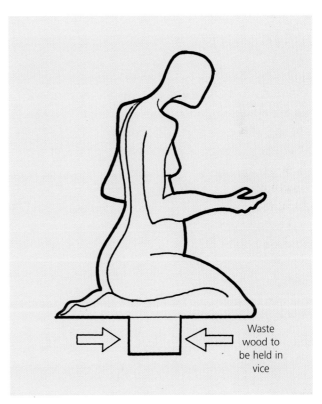

Waste wood to be held in vice

Fig 4.1 *Holding work by a waste element, to be removed later, is often a convenient approach*

THE WORKBENCH

Let me start by saying three important things:

❶ It will take you some time, as a beginner, to settle down and establish what range of work you will be carving, what exactly you need to hold your carvings and, thus, the size, height and shape of bench that will be most useful. This is normal. Just begin with *something* (I discuss the traditional options later), and move on as your experience grows.

❷ Unless you carve the same things all the time, you will *always* be adapting; always looking for the best, most helpful, way of holding your work. I confess to having several, and *still* search for the perfect workbench, or work-holder – but it doesn't exist. With experience, though, and a range of options, you will develop an ability to improvise and adapt.

❸ Although I use the term 'workbench', think 'work station'. Like an operating table in a hospital or an artist's easel, this is where it all happens.

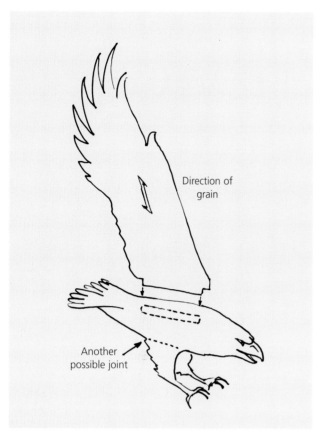

Fig 4.2 *Part-carving separate components before assembly may be easier than trying to work on the whole piece from the start*

– and may remain so until a repertoire of methods has been built up. As with so much that needs to be learned, this repertoire will grow as a result of problems being solved and possibilities explored. It is only fair to say, however, that even experienced carvers are sometimes at a loss for a while when trying to work out how to hold something exactly as they want.

The correct holding of a piece in order to carve it cannot be over-emphasized. This chapter will look at the reasons why this is so important, as well as the range of possibilities that is available.

First, however, we need to look at the workbench – the centrepiece of carving activity. It may be true that in Bali carvers sit on the floor and hold the carving between their feet, or that Japanese carvers sit cross-legged and use a simple plank – but in the West most work is gripped by one means or another to a carving bench. The bench, for us, is the indispensable starting point to holding work properly.

Workbenches vary enormously between carvers, not only because the size and weight of work that is undertaken varies so much, or because of workspace constraints, but also because the size, shape and preferences of carvers themselves vary. Some carvers like to work outside on a summer's evening. Others have to make do with a kitchen or a spare corner of the house. Others again may have infirmities that make standing in the usual way difficult.

Though there is no such thing as a 'standard carving bench', there may be an ideal one for a particular individual: a bench which works well, supporting and helping the carver achieve his or her ends. Most carvers make their own benches, or at least have them made to suit their own specific needs. These benches become like old friends in whose company many hours will be spent. This is perhaps the only occasion when an old friend can be designed by yourself.

Despite their individuality, all carving benches have certain attributes which make them useful. The following general features need to be borne in mind while thinking and planning out a bench to suit your own requirements.

HEIGHT

It is usual for carvers to stand at their work, and this should be done wherever possible as it gives the greatest freedom of movement around the piece that is being carved. A workbench for a carver is higher than that for a carpenter or joiner, to allow a good standing posture to be maintained – too low a bench is bad news for the back. Lower benches suit carpenters because they position themselves over the work to plane it and so on.

Fig 4.3 *An adjustable carving platform, mounted on a small, movable bench, provides a variety of work-holding options*

Some books recommend a particular height for a carving bench, but in fact the appropriate height varies with the heights of different carvers. A tall person will obviously need to work on a higher bench than would suit a shorter person.

The rule is that the work, and your ability to stand (or sit) comfortably to it, dictates the height of the bench. This may well mean that you end up with several at different heights, perhaps with removable work surfaces or with 'duckboards' to stand on, and so on. Swivelling, adjustable work-holders will allow you to get at taller carvings by tilting them, but this changes the perspective; I eliminate this problem with a small carving platform that can be raised or lowered (Fig 4.3), as described in my *Elements of Woodcarving* (pages 21–3).

Although the design of the 'work station' or bench arises from the needs of the work, as a beginner you may well not know what kind of carving you will eventually take on. In this case the best guide to the height is the traditional one: stand comfortably upright, raise your forearm horizontally and measure the height from floor to elbow. The bench height is this measurement, less the width of one of your hands (Fig 4.4).

You may need an accomplice to do the measuring, but the result should give a good, useful working height for the bench surface. Problems may still arise with particularly tall or large carvings, but for average work this height will be appropriate.

Carvers who need to sit will have to experiment to get a comfortable height and position – one that allows them to work for a long time without strain or discomfort. And this is really the point: carving can go on for many hours and, without the correct ergonomics, tiredness, backache and so on can spoil an otherwise enjoyable experience. Try, for example, raising the back legs of the chair about 1in (25mm), which tilts the seat a little towards the bench.

If a carpentry bench is the only one available, then you can either raise the height or make a false top. False tops are discussed on page 74. To increase the height, insert glued-up blocks of wood or plywood under the feet. Make the blocks wider than the feet of the bench, with strips of wood around the edge to keep the blocks in position (Fig 4.5). This is a good

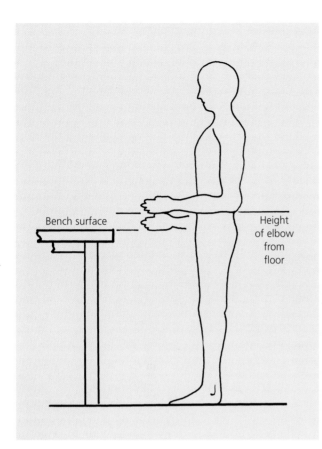

Fig 4.4 A well-tried guide to finding a bench height appropriate for carving

Bench surface

Height of elbow from floor

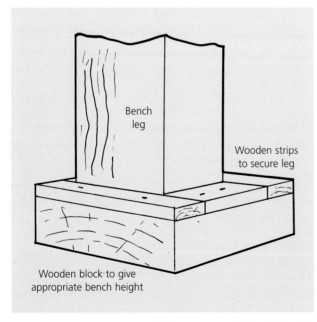

Bench leg

Wooden strips to secure leg

Wooden block to give appropriate bench height

Fig 4.5 Blocks, of varying thicknesses, stored by the bench, give a ready means of altering the height of your working surface when necessary

method for a carving class using the woodworking room of a school. The blocks can be placed under the benches quickly with a team effort, and easily stored away afterwards.

STRENGTH AND WEIGHTING

For the average carver, a good workbench will last a lifetime, even though it may be subject to considerable battering – but it does need to be strongly constructed. In practice this means a working surface of at least 2in (50mm) thick, and legs at least 3 x 3in (75 x 75mm). The best joints are mortise and tenon, to which cross-bracing may be added (Fig 4.6). It is preferable to make the legs and framework from hardwood, such as beech, glued and pinned – although softwood is acceptable.

Pine or another softwood is best for the top, as it has good gripping and deadening qualities, absorbs impact and minimizes 'bounce'. It is also easily nailed or screwed into. Hardwood can be a bit bouncy for the top, but is still preferred by some. Of the manufactured materials, MDF (medium-density fibreboard) has a slippery surface, and plywood can be dusty.

The idea is that the bench should be solid (in the sense of immovable), but with a certain amount of resilience. Various devices can hold the work steady, but beneath them the bench must be firm. The size and strength of a carving bench depends not only on the height of the carver and the size of work, but also on the amount of violence that is intended. Good advice for beginners is to build the bench stronger than you think you need. A bench can never be too strong – but it can be too weak.

Even when strong in itself, a bench may still tend to 'walk' around the room under the impact of heavy carving, especially vigorous mallet work. Two options to counter this are:

- Screw or bolt the bench to the floor or wall, using angle irons or brackets.

- Weight the lowest part of the bench, which may mean building in rails to the base. Compacted concrete blocks, such as are used for paving slabs, make excellent weights in manageable sizes; a box of sand (which can be dampened) also works well.

Fig 4.6 *Some construction details for a carver's bench*

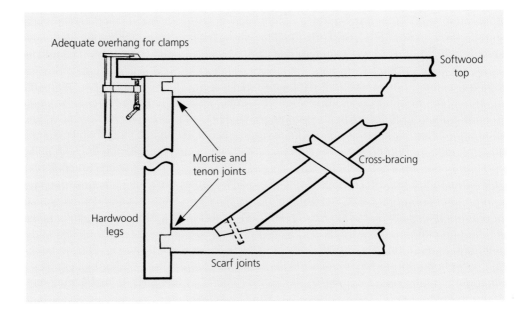

Adequate overhang for clamps

Softwood top

Mortise and tenon joints

Cross-bracing

Hardwood legs

Scarf joints

PROPORTIONS

In addition to the height, the surface area of the bench is important. It used to be common practice for professional carvers to use a bench made from planks 3–4in (75–100mm) thick, running the whole length of the workshop. Too big is better than too small.

The surface of the bench should be flat, and have enough room for:

- the workpiece

- laying out carving tools, other tools and bits and pieces – some of which can be out of the way towards the back when not being used

- changing the orientation of the carving or the position of the tools, and generally shunting things around.

This also has to be seen in the context of available space in the workroom.

As a guide for those starting with no idea of what sort of bench they will need, a working surface of 3 x 2ft (1m x 60cm) is a useful working area. If you expect to undertake work in a whole range of shapes and sizes, then increase these dimensions. Benches of 6ft x 2ft 6in (2m x 75cm) are not uncommon, but do not make your bench deeper than you can comfortably reach.

There are many different sorts of carving bench – some of which appear later in this section – suitable for different types of work. You may, for example, like to change the proportions to give yourself a tall bench with more of the appearance of a sculptor's modelling stand. Such a bench would be suitable for small figure work, raising the piece nearer to eye level.

FITTINGS

A bench not only holds the carving off the floor at a comfortable working height, it also has features which help to hold the carving, thus making the work of the carver easier.

The working surface of the bench should overhang the under-framework by at least 2½–3in (65–75mm), as this allows versatile clamps to be used. An ordinary woodworker's vice might be fitted (Fig 4.7); there may be bench stops and pegs; and there may be holes for holdfasts, carvers' screws, bolts, etc. You can make most changes to the bench as the need arises.

Drawers, cupboards and shelves are useful additions for the tools and equipment which relate to the bench (Fig 4.8). Make sure drawers and doors will not be obstructed by clamps and so on – it is quite irritating to have to undo a carefully arranged clamp in order to get at a drawer or cupboard. Position them lower down, or to one side at least.

Fig 4.7 An ordinary woodworking vice has its uses for the carver; note the strong diagonal bracing beneath to ensure rigidity

The strongest part of the bench is over the legs, so this is the best place for heavy thumping. Keep the ends of the bench clear, as these are good parts for working around.

Fig 4.8 Shelves and drawers make use of the prime storage space beneath the bench

A tool rack at the back of the bench is useful; so is a lip at the back to stop small items rolling off. A step, perhaps forming part of a low shelf, can also make a very good footrest.

You should see the carving bench as the focus of the working area – almost an operating table. Large amounts of time may be spent at the bench, so make yours as comfortable, efficient and friendly as possible. It is not unusual for beginners to start with such a nice bench that they are afraid of marking it. By all means care for your bench, but remember that a bench is primarily a work station, contributing to the carving – a means to an end.

ALTERNATIVES

The bench described so far is probably the most common sort of working arrangement that carvers use. What follows are some variations and different ideas for benches and work stations that might suggest possibilities, or suit the needs of different carvers. You will find a few more suggestions in my *Elements of Woodcarving* (GMC Publications, 2000).

TABLES

If you are carving in your spare time, a table in the kitchen or bedroom may be all that is available. This arrangement can work well for small pieces, provided it is strong and stable enough, but there is usually a problem with the height, as most tables are designed for sitting at.

A working surface can be clamped to the table top to give extra height, and this surface can be marked with impunity (Fig 4.9). Line the underside with cork tiles to give a good grip and protect the table top. Unless the table can be fixed to the floor or wall for added stability, it may still only be suitable for light work.

PORTABLE WORK CENTRES

A portable work centre is a collapsible system that doubles as a bench and a saw-horse. It is designed for mobile carpentry, and there are several varieties on the market. The best known is probably the Black & Decker Workmate, but there are several other types available. They tend to be small, low and lightweight.

Fig 4.9 *Detachable work surface for use on a table top. The dimensions should suit the table's height, etc.; the top can be made of plywood*

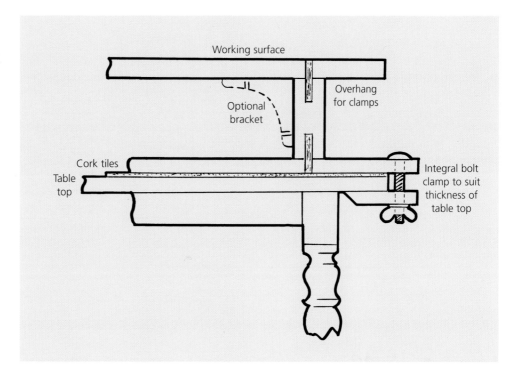

Nevertheless, if this is all that is available, try weighting the base and clamping on a table-top bench as described above to increase the height. It may be necessary to sit while carving, to prevent backache.

SCULPTURE TROUGHS

For very awkward shapes, a trough such as shown in Fig 4.10 may be useful. The trough should be lined with an offcut of old hessian-backed carpet – reversed so the hessian is outside. The V-groove will easily jam

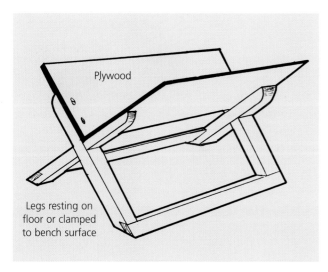

Fig 4.10 *Sculpture troughs may be floor- or bench-standing*

and grip many odd shapes. Various sizes of sandbag packed around a carving will hold a large sculpture in a similar way. There is a tendency for the sand dust to leak out, but otherwise this can be a simple way of holding a difficult shape, especially if you want the work horizontal for carving.

COLLAPSIBLE BENCHES

Perhaps even before the kitchen table, amateur carvers were banished to the garage to make their noise and wood chips. If this puts the carver in competition with the car over space – and the car is winning – fit a collapsible bench. The car in turn can be consigned to the outdoors for the duration. The back edge of the working surface is hinged to the wall and, when not in use, the top drops away vertically (Fig 4.11). Strength can come from diagonal cross-bracing to the wall and floor corner, and from using robust hinges.

Such a bench can make a substantial work surface, while collapsing to quite a narrow intrusion on the garage space. Racks and shelves can also be fixed to the walls to store tools and equipment – if the garage is dry. Check the wall fastenings regularly, and arrange the cross-bracing to minimize 'bounce' in the work surface.

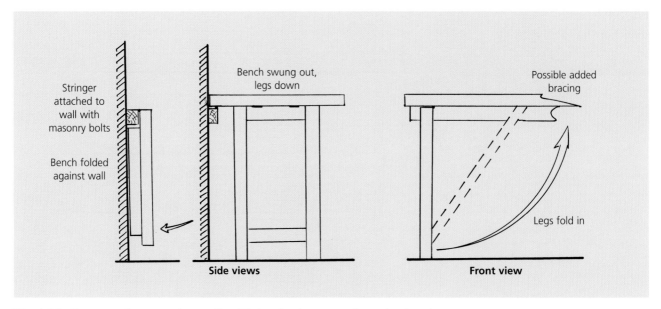

Fig 4.11 *One way of constructing a collapsible bench where space has to be shared*

TILTING SURFACES

Reliefs above a certain size are best carved in a vertical position, or slightly sloping back, for a variety of reasons: the perspective is correct – especially if the wood can be turned and adjusted easily – wood shavings fall away by themselves, and less room is required in the workshop. Disadvantages are the need to place tools to one side, and the fact that you can't exert the pressure that comes from being 'over' the work. Nevertheless, the advantages are strong and it is worth trying.

In my *Elements of Woodcarving* (pages 20–1) I describe my 'Deckchair' stand, which is very easy to make and will give you a taster for carving with the work vertical. Essentially it is a simple, portable and adjustable frame that clamps to the bench, with a central slot through which a carving is mounted using a carver's screw. Be sure to construct such tilting surfaces strongly and use substantial hinges.

Besides specially made stands like this, a panel or something that will naturally be wall-mounted might simply be clamped or screwed to a piece of wood, in turn gripped upright in a vice. Check that the workpiece is securely held before you start exerting pressure!

Gino Masero's design for a portable bench doubles as a horizontal and vertical working surface (Figs 4.12 and 4.13). The arcing metal brackets can be cut by most engineering firms. A revised version is shown in my *Elements of Woodcarving* (pages 16–19), and has proved to be one of my most useful benches.

METAL BENCHES

Although wood is the traditional material for carving benches, excellent subframes can be welded up quite cheaply from lengths of metal found in scrap yards. The actual working surface must always be wood, but the subframe can be either all metal, using say 2 x 2in (50 x 50mm) square-section welded tube; or a wood and metal mix, for instance angle iron bolted between wooden legs, acting as stringers and bracing.

MANUFACTURED BENCHES

Manufacturers have responded to the increasing interest in woodcarving with widening ranges of tools and equipment, noticeably holding devices such as adjustable clamps and carvers' screws. At least one manufacturer, Veritas, is taking on carvers' benches too, which are designed to fit with other well-thought-out products such as the Veritas work-holder, hold-down, bench dogs, clamps and carver's screw.

The Veritas carver's bench is the only one I know of at present that is designed specifically for wood-carvers (Fig 4.14). It has a cast-iron stand, weighs some 68kg (150lb), and can be bolted down or further weighted as necessary. The thick hardwood top has

Fig 4.12 *This idea for a tilting surface with arc-shaped supports can be adapted for many purposes. The important consideration is the placing of the pivot point*

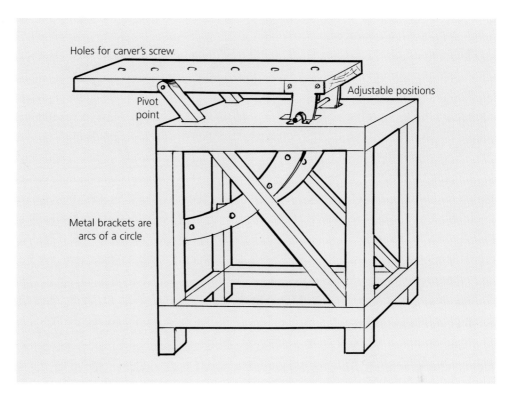

Holes for carver's screw

Pivot point

Adjustable positions

Metal brackets are arcs of a circle

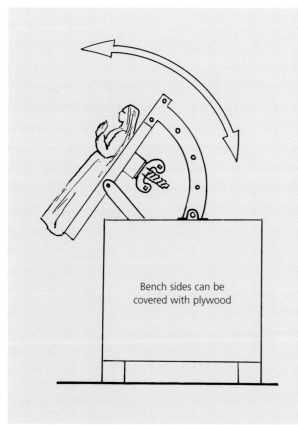

Bench sides can be covered with plywood

Fig 4.13 *A sketch drawing of a multi-purpose portable bench using metal arc stays*

Fig 4.14 *The adjustable woodcarver's bench by Veritas. Work is held by a combination of 'Pup' screw clamps (available separately) and metal bench dogs, which can be positioned in any of the drilled holes as required*

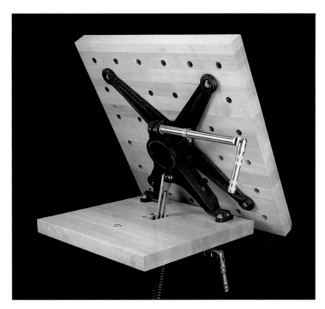

Fig 4.15 *The tilting mechanism of the Veritas bench. The top lever allows the bench top to swivel completely round; the bottom lever allows the bench top to tilt upright*

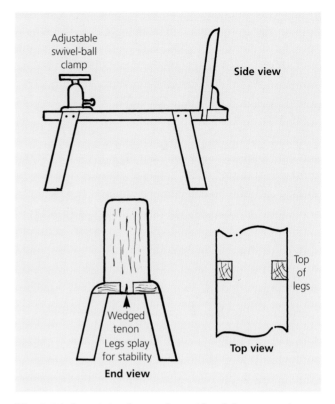

Fig 4.16 *In a sitting horse, the weight of the carver gives stability. Splay the legs so that the horse will not tip, especially when you lean backwards to view your work*

plenty of overhang, and can be swivelled through 360° or tilted upright by an ingenious spring-loaded mechanism (Fig 4.15). The work surface is drilled to accept various stops, **dogs**, and so on.

The height is not adjustable; at 35in (89cm), it is a compromise. It is probably too low for most carvers to work a relief flat down, but with the Veritas work-holder in place a round carving would be lifted to a comfortable working height. The manufacturers recommend sitting when the top is tilted for relief carving, an option I favour only when there is no alternative. Nevertheless, if the bench is seen as a 'work station', to be adapted to the work in hand, it is easy to bolt on false tops or other accessories to increase its scope and capacity. There is no such thing as 'the perfect carver's bench', but this one tries hard.

SITTING HORSES

Standing is the best position to carve in, but for some people there may be a choice between sitting to carve, or not carving at all. A carving **horse** is an option here. The carver sits astride something similar to a saw-horse, part of which is designed to take a vice or clamp (Fig 4.16). The weight of the carver keeps everything stable, while padding and a backrest add to comfort. Make sure the timber and joints

are strong enough – use a hardwood and wedged through-tenons, with the legs splayed. For small carvings, there should be little problem with such an arrangement.

TALL STANDS

As with modelling stands, tall carving benches raise smaller pieces of work nearer to the eye (Fig 4.17). The working surface itself is usually small. A stand can be a useful addition to a larger bench in the work-shop – perhaps even clamping to its surface.

PEGBOARDS

For carving panels, house signs and so on, a board like the one shown in Fig 4.18 can be clamped to the main bench. The 1in (25mm) holes are set at 2–3in (50–75mm) intervals, rather like the Veritas bench shown earlier. Dowels are dropped into a few appropriate holes and the work itself caught with wedges. Easily knocked apart and repositioned, it allows a carved panel to be shuffled around as required.

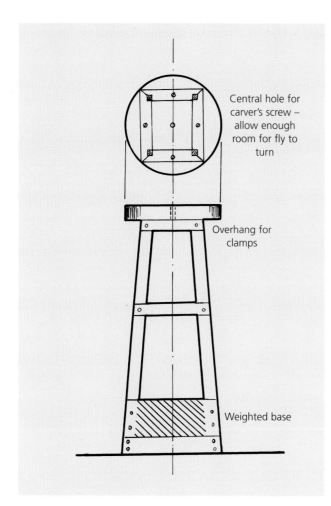

Central hole for carver's screw – allow enough room for fly to turn

Overhang for clamps

Weighted base

Fig 4.17 A tall bench for smaller carvings. Tools must be laid on a separate surface to one side, but the extra height can make working a lot easier

MEDIEVAL CARVING FRAMES

Nowadays figures tend to be carved vertically, but in the past they seem to have been carved horizontally, held in a frame between ends. Fixed with large carvers' screws, the work could be rotated to get at all parts conveniently. This is still the practice in some places, for example southern Germany.

A suitable floor- or bench-standing framework, which is both adjustable and collapsible, is shown in Fig 4.19. Taken from a medieval etching, the principle of the design is simple and quite elegant. Etchings of the time show very large pieces of work held in this way, and it is an idea worth remembering – possibly as an adjustable way of carving turned work. Waste wood in the carving is allowed at each end where it meets the frame to take the screws.

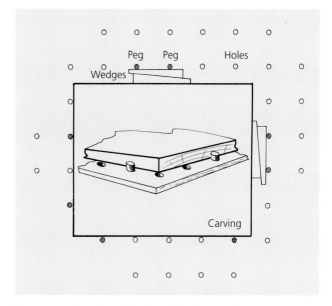

Peg Peg Holes

Wedges

Carving

Fig 4.18 A pegboard with wedges for small panels avoids the need for clamps, which might get in the way

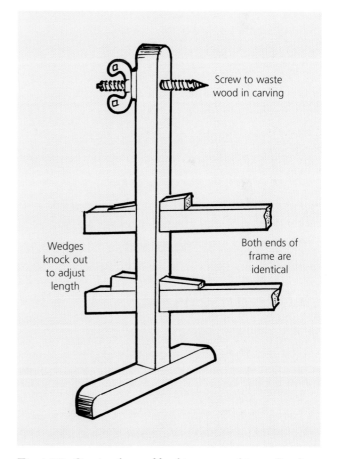

Screw to waste wood in carving

Wedges knock out to adjust length

Both ends of frame are identical

Fig 4.19 Carving frames like this were used in medieval times to hold quite large and heavy carvings; the work can be rotated to allow access from all sides

Without this, small plugs may be needed when the screws are removed.

CONSTRUCTION NOTES

The sort of bench needed by a carver varies with the size and type of work, the size and type of the carver, and the size of the workshop.

It is always best to make the bench to personal requirements, or at least have one made to your specifications. The possibilities described above are by no means exhaustive, but constructing any carving bench will need to begin with consideration of the following points:

- The height must be appropriate to the user.

- The working surface must be flat and of adequate size for the intended work.

- For strength, it is best to use mortise and tenon joints, possibly with cross-bracing; 3in (75mm) square hardwood legs; and a 2in (50mm) thick softwood top.

- For stability, consider weighting the base and perhaps anchoring it to the floor.

- The edges should project at least 2½–3in (65–75mm) at the front and sides to allow for secure clamping.

- Drawers, shelves, etc. need to be located out of the way of clamps. Keep the ends of the bench free for working around, and fit a tool rack to the rear.

BENCH DISCIPLINE

The idea of 'discipline' has arisen in various parts of this book. Disciplines are working practices and habits that contribute to a more satisfying experience of carving; they help the carving proceed towards the best possible result. Such practices also protect tools from damage, and yourself from accidents. With the proviso that those people who love chaos may care to skip the following list, here are some particularly good habits that are centred on the carving bench and are worth cultivating:

Keep the working area uncluttered as far as possible

This means bringing forward tools in immediate use and keeping others out of the way, if not actually putting them away. Consciously *arrange* things, rather than just letting them happen.

Have regular clearing-up sessions

Clear up the bench between different stages of the carving, or at natural breaks such as the end of the day. Keep a bench brush and pan handy to remove wood chips and shavings (Fig 4.20).

Line up carving tools

Arrange the carving tools neatly with their blades towards you – they are more easily distinguished and are far less likely to have their edges damaged. Putting gouges to one end, or bent tools to the other, also speeds their selection.

Always pick up and put down carving tools carefully

Beware of metal objects, such as clamp heads, against which edges may knock.

Attach work securely

Make sure the work is properly and securely held to the workbench, leaving both hands free to use

Fig 4.20 *Keep a couple of useful brushes by the bench: a stiff one for cleaning carvings (actually an ex-horse brush); and a soft one for the bench (ex-wallpaper brush, with or without handle)*

the carving tools. When moving or adjusting the work, avoid crashing it into – or putting it on top of – the carving tools.

Never try to catch a falling gouge or chisel

With the best will in the world, a tool may fall or get knocked from the bench. If you have a concrete floor, an old hessian-backed carpet, upside down and in front of the bench, may well save the edge – as well as being easier on the feet.

Use the different parts of the bench appropriately

The strongest parts of the bench are over the legs towards the corners, so use these parts for heavy thumping. Keep the corners clear, as these are the areas that allow the greatest freedom of movement.

INDIVIDUAL HOLDING DEVICES

FUNDAMENTALS

The carving bench is the centre of the workshop – where the carving actually happens. How the work is held to the carving bench is equally important. There are several criteria that an appropriate holding device must fulfil; let us consider these in order of importance.

EFFICIENCY
Holding a woodcarving in the right way at any given time increases working efficiency. This is true to the extent that if a piece of work is going slowly or laboriously, holding the carving in a different way (or even just changing its position) may well get the flow going again.

CONTROL
You need to be able to get to any part of your work at will, even if this means adjusting the way the carving is held. The more adjustable a holding device, the greater facility you have, the more control you have,

and the more confidence that the piece can be carved successfully.

INDEPENDENCE
The means of holding the work should not damage it. This may be an obvious point, but we are not just talking about forgetting to pad a metal clamp – the holding device should not dictate or interfere with the design either. In effect, the device should remain independent of the carving: enabling it to happen and working with the process, but imposing as few dictates on the design as possible.

CONVENIENCE
The means of holding a carving should not obstruct the act of carving itself. This can become unavoidable – clamps, for example, can become awkwardly positioned and a hazard to tool edges. At this point some adjustment may be necessary, or a different holding device may have to be used. The wood also needs to be placed so that you can work comfortably and without strain.

SAFETY
A carving must be held securely so that the carver need never worry about it coming loose, or springing out, from the holding device, even under the jolts and pressures of cutting.

The work should remain perfectly still – it is the tools that move. If the workpiece moves suddenly, or unpredictably, and control is lost, not only can the carving and the carving tools get damaged, but the carver may be hurt as well. Whatever the method of holding the work, check for safety before starting to carve, as well as at regular intervals while working.

Any holding device will have advantages and disadvantages, making it suitable for some situations and not for others. This is why a repertoire of methods and devices is necessary. Within the development of a particular carving, several different approaches may be needed.

As with all carving tools and equipment, it is best to acquire things as they are needed – or as you come to know what direction your carving is taking.

A good vice and a few G-clamps will be enough to start with if no specific needs are obvious.

The following options are all well-established methods for holding carving work. Although I have classified them as devices for holding panels and others for holding three-dimensional forms, their uses will often overlap.

HOLDING PANELS

Very large panels present their own problems and may need a special structure to hold them, but smaller work done on the bench can normally be contained by the following devices.

CLAMPS

The principal clamp used by the carver is the **G-clamp** (also **G-cramp** or **C-clamp**). The term is used here to describe both the well-known clamp that looks like a letter G, as well as the quick-action version which slides on a bar, looking rather like a small sash clamp (Fig 4.21). **Sash clamps** themselves are principally used for gluing up work, especially panels, but it is possible to use them for holding the carved panels themselves.

The words *clamp* and *cramp* are synonymous in this context, deriving from the Old High German *krampf*, meaning 'bent' – a clamp or cramp being a metal bar bent at both ends. From the same root comes the sense of *cramp* as a violent contraction of the muscles, and the word *crimp*.

G-clamps come in sizes that increase by 2in (50mm) increments: 6in (150mm), 8in (200mm), 10in (250mm) and so on. This measurement is the

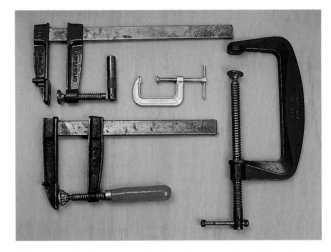

Fig 4.21 *Quick-action* (left) *and conventional* (right) *screw G-clamps. The one at top left with the swivel handle is particularly good*

maximum open span; remember to allow for the bench-top thickness. The most useful sizes of clamp to start with are probably the 8in (200mm) and 10in (250mm).

Clamps work from the front edge of the bench; usually the pad or foot is uppermost and the tightening bar, or *fly*, beneath. A piece of waste wood is placed between the metal pad and the work to stop bruising or other damage. Make up a few special packing pieces from cork-lined plywood, and keep them by the bench and always ready to hand.

The part of the clamp above the bench can get in the way of working and be a danger to cutting edges. One way round this is to use clamps in conjunction with 'bridges' of scrap wood to exert pressure on the panel (Fig 4.22). A variant of this technique is shown in Fig 4.23a.

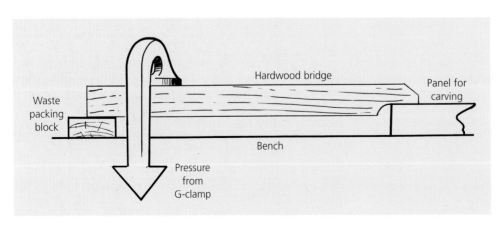

Fig 4.22 *The metal body of a G-clamp can be kept out of the way by a using a bridge of hardwood*

Waste packing block

Hardwood bridge

Panel for carving

Bench

Pressure from G-clamp

Fig 4.23 *Coach bolts with wooden bridges, and screw clamps are cheap ways of holding panels*

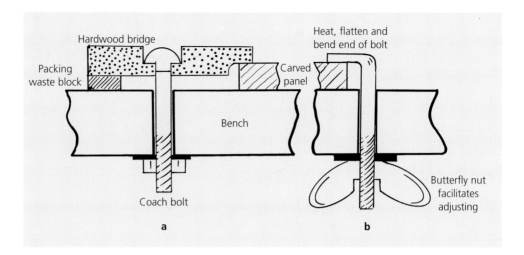

Fig 4.24 *Cutting slots into the waste part of a carving enables it to be gripped by G-clamps to the corner of a bench, over the leg*

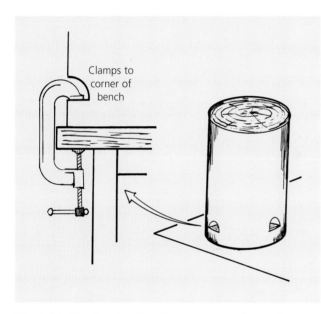

A screw clamp, a variation on the carver's screw (see pages 88–90), can be made from a bolt, the head of which is removed and the end flattened and bent (Fig 4.23b). Ideally, wings can be welded to the nut to make a fly which can be tightened by hand.

G-clamps will hold work in the round as well. In this case, waste wood is left on the bottom of the carving, in which recesses are cut to take the clamp pad (Fig 4.24). Slope the recesses downwards into the wood to get a good purchase. The work is held towards the end of the bench so that it can be clamped from two sides.

HOLDFASTS

The original **holdfast** was an L-shaped dog of metal thumped through a hole in the bench, which gripped the work by dint of friction (Fig 4.25a). Later models, still available in two sizes, have a screw thread which exerts considerable leverage (Fig 4.25b). They grip

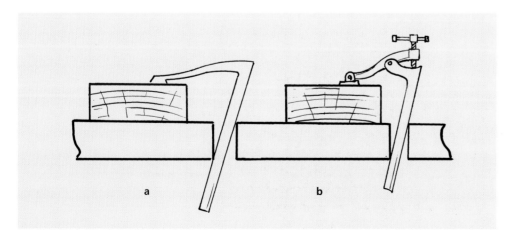

Fig 4.25 *The original holdfast (a), probably deriving from a bench dog (see Fig 4.28), was jammed into position and relied on friction inside the bench hole. More recent versions (b) can be adjusted and released more easily because of the screw*

very well and are as effective as a G-clamp, but work from the back of the bench to hold the panel. These two forms of bench clamp complement each other.

A holdfast needs an appropriately sized hole in the bench surface and can only reach a fixed radius from this hole (Fig 4.26). It is best not to bore large numbers of holes in the bench top in the hope of using holdfasts, but to start with a hole at each end of the bench and one in the middle, boring other holes only as they are needed.

Some holdfasts come with metal collars which fit into the bench top to reinforce the holes. As these collars themselves can cause damage to the carving tools, sink them below the surface a little and keep them covered with a thin plywood or perspex disc when not in use (Fig 4.27).

Like G-clamps, holdfasts need some padding beneath their foot, and can project awkwardly where you want to work. A bridge of wood used with the holdfast can also help here.

DOGS, SNIBS AND FENCES

These ways of holding a carving use the working surface of the bench directly, and will mark it.

Dogs are metal staples, hammered across the bench top and the workpiece (Fig 4.28). They are not particularly versatile, as the work is fixed immovably – although this might be entirely appropriate. If the wood does not need to be moved during the carving, then screwing or nailing it down through a waste part is also a very simple and quick approach.

Fig 4.26 *The bench holdfast reaches through a radius from its hole*

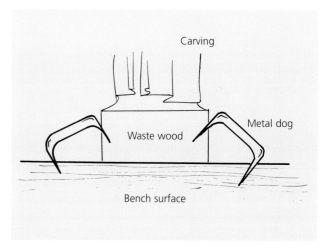

Fig 4.28 *Dogs are very old methods of holding work and, while limited, demonstrate that the means of holding a carving can be simple and cheap*

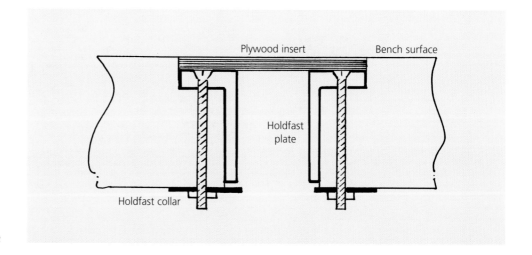

Fig 4.27 *Details of the holdfast hole in the bench, with collar and cover plate*

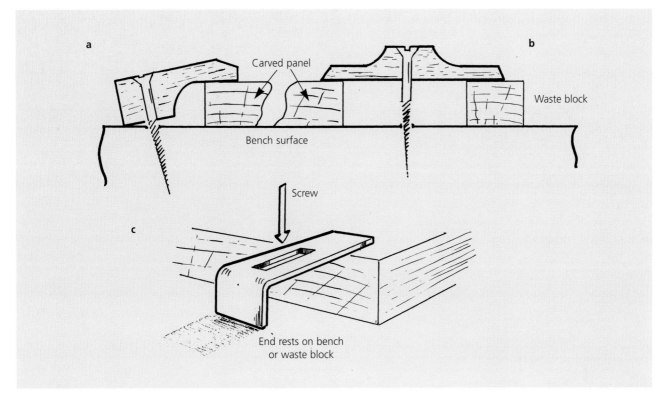

Fig 4.29 Two wooden snibs (a and b) and a metal version (c)

Snibs, sometimes also called dogs or **buttons**, are wooden pieces screwed to the bench top and projecting over the edge of the panel to hold it (Fig 4.29). They need to be unscrewed to adjust the work, but represent a quick, makeshift way of holding a carving. Even a washer with a screw through it can be useful at times.

Fences are strips of wood, nailed or screwed to the bench, that simply wall in a panel. The strips of wood, being lower than the panel, do not obstruct the work and are not a hazard to tool edges. In the basic arrangement the panel cannot be moved; however, if you add wedges between fence and workpiece this allows the work to be quickly removed from the bench (Fig 4.30).

PAPER AND GLUE

This is an old method for holding thin panels – ones that are too thin, or have not enough room, for conventional cramping. A typical example might

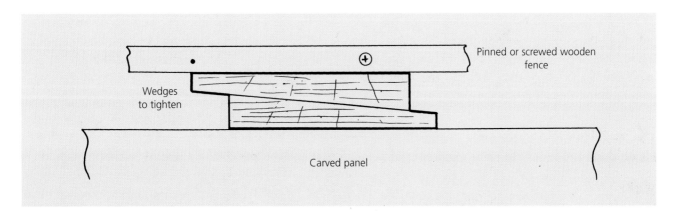

Fig 4.30 Fences, although they mark the bench surface, are a simple and effective option for panel carvings

be **paterae** or swags which are fretted out first and then applied to a fireplace surround. Bear in mind the possibility of designing strengthening ties or other waste pieces to be cut away at the last moment.

The idea is to glue the more fragile piece of wood to be carved to a larger piece that can be clamped or fixed to the bench. A piece of newspaper or brown wrapping paper is sandwiched in the join. A spatula, decorator's filling knife or other thin knife will easily divide the paper and separate the joint afterwards, but the joint is strong enough to hold the piece as it is being carved (Fig 4.31). Woodturners use this method to hold work taking considerable stress.

Fig 4.31 *A spatula releases a finished patera by slitting the newspaper to which it is glued*

Brush the lower piece of wood with white PVA (polyvinyl acetate) glue that has been thinned a little with water. Lay on the paper, making sure that it is soaked in the glue. Brush glue onto the back of the carving wood and clamp the whole together. Make sure the glue is dry before starting work.

After slitting the join, any paper left on the reverse of the carving can be scraped off, soaked off, sanded off (by rubbing the carving on sandpaper stuck to a flat board) or just left to disappear when the piece is glued into its final position.

HOLDING WORK IN THE ROUND

VICES

The common woodworking vice (Fig 4.32) is a useful, if limited, addition to the carving bench. Vices with

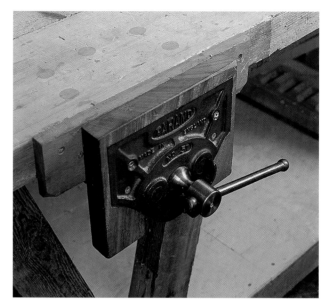

Fig 4.32 *A standard woodworking vice fitted with wooden jaw linings*

quick-release action are the most useful. The term *vice*, referring to jaws that open and close by means of a screw, first appears in the sixteenth century. The word itself comes from the Latin *vitis*, meaning 'a vine', or more exactly the stem with winding tendrils.

Exactly where the vice is fitted to the bench is a personal decision, but it is usual to have it more towards one side than the centre. Fig 4.33 shows a way of fitting such a vice to the bench so that no metal parts are exposed.

There is a fixed and a moving part to the vice; you will find a pin that, when removed, disengages the two. The fixed part is then easier to fit to the bench, housing its face flush with the bench edge, but a little below the surface wood. The underside of the vice will need packing to set the vice in its final bolted position. Make sure the face is at a dead right angle to the bench top. The underframe of the bench will need cutting to take the moving section of the vice – remove only the minimum amount of wood. Sink any fixing (coach) bolts below the bench surface and fill to hide the metal. Pad the jaws to prevent them bruising whatever they are holding.

When using the vice, a spigot or waste shoulder may be left on the workpiece; or the carving can be bolted (or screwed) to another block of wood which is then held in the jaws of the vice. Other holding

Fig 4.33 Cross section
through a carpenter's vice,
showing how all the
metalwork that might
damage the tools or the
carvings is hidden or
padded

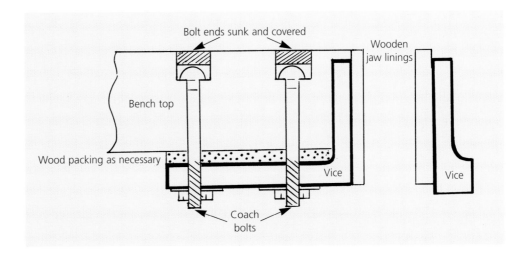

devices can also be gripped by the vice – for example, a block of wood to which a swivel-ball system is fixed. Because the vice is stationary, the possibilities for repositioning or adjusting work are limited.

Engineers' vices are an alternative, although, sitting on the bench surface as they do, the jaws are higher than those of the woodworking vice. It is therefore easy to knock tool edges against their metal bodies. Engineers' vices that swivel are the most useful; these can be quite small, and fitted to the bench for a particular job. Again, the jaws need padding.

WOODCARVERS' CHOPS

Chops is the name given to a particular type of wooden vice, like a pair of jaws, that sits on the bench surface (Fig 4.34). The vice is fixed by means of a bolt passing through the bench top to a butterfly nut underneath (Fig 4.35). When this bolt is loosened, the chops can be rotated to reposition the work, or it can be completely removed. The best chops are made of ash with leather- and cork-lined jaws and brass runners. Because the apparatus is made of wood, carving tools are safe from damage.

Fitting carvers' chops involves boring only one hole, but several may be arranged for different working positions on the bench. The jaws open towards the back, and the whole device can be moved horizontally. These movements, together with the rotation of the vice, can push tools and equipment around the bench top if care is not taken. The vice also sits rather high on the bench, like an engineer's vice.

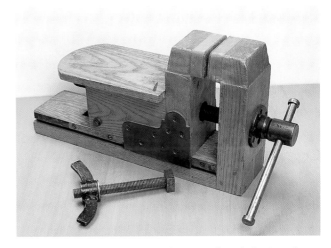

Fig 4.34 *Carvers' chops, with its attaching bolt. It is the back jaw which opens, sliding with the brass plate in a groove in the base. The jaws need relining now and then with cork and/or leather*

Fig 4.35 *The holding bolt passes through a square hole in the base of the chops, then along an internal rebate. The vice can be slid forwards and backwards as well as rotated*

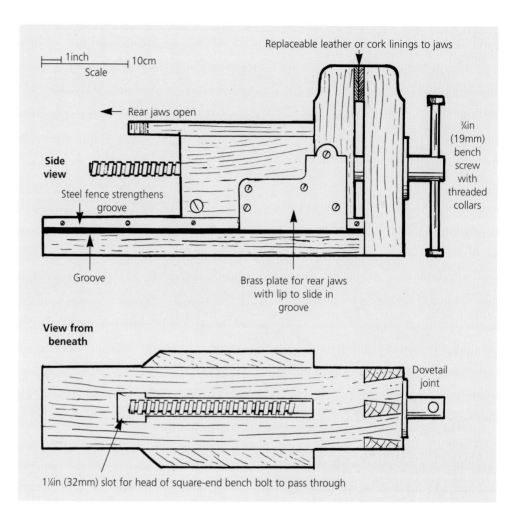

Fig 4.36 *Some basic construction details of the woodcarvers' chops*

Carvers' chops are certainly very useful means of holding some work on some occasions. For someone who has not used them before, it is probably best to see a set in action – perhaps even trying them out – in the first place, as they do not suit everyone.

Quality woodcarvers' chops with an overall length of 18in (450mm) are available from Alec Tiranti Ltd, who have been making or supplying them for generations. Any other size will have to be custom-made, and a scale working plan is shown in Figs 4.36 and 4.37. The dovetail joints and metal side cheeks give strength. Use ash for the woodwork, and a square-threaded screw.

WOODCARVERS' SCREWS

These are a very elegant way of holding some types of work (Fig 4.38). The tapered part of the screw is wound into a pre-drilled hole in the base or back of the carving, and tightened using the square hole in

the fly as a spanner (Fig 4.39). The rest of the screw is then passed through a hole in the bench; when the fly is tightened underneath, the work is gripped. Loosen the fly, and the work can be rotated.

As the main thread of the woodcarver's screw is normally a strong, square type, a lot of pressure can be exerted by tightening the fly (Figs 4.40 and 4.41). There is a tendency for the screw to loosen in the carving, so it will need retightening periodically. Be careful not to overtighten it.

If the screw is inserted into a carving with the grain running vertically, the screw will tend to cut the fibres rather than wrapping round them as it would if the grain was running across the thread. Screwing anything into end grain is the weakest fixing; and into cross grain the strongest fixing. To help support the screw when it is inserted into the base end grain of a carving, a hole may first be bored a little way into the work, equal to the diameter of the

Fig 4.37 *Front and back views of the carvers' chops*

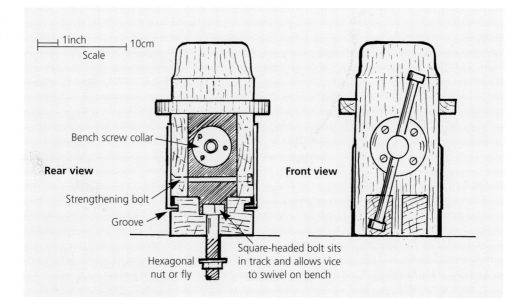

Bench screw collar

Rear view

Strengthening bolt

Groove

Hexagonal nut or fly

Front view

Square-headed bolt sits in track and allows vice to swivel on bench

Fig 4.38 *A collection of carvers' screws. Top: small and large Stubai screws; Marples screw; washers (not supplied with these models). Centre: custom-made long carver's screw. Below: Veritas screw; large and small Axminster screws; large square washer*

Fig 4.39 *A square hole in the fly engages a spigot on the end of the screw in order to tighten it into the workpiece*

Fig 4.40 *The working ends of carvers' screws differ in taper and thread according to what the manufacturer thinks will give the best grip*

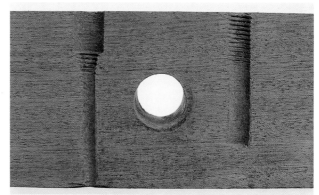

Fig 4.41 *The Veritas screw (right) fits the workpiece with a taper of about 5°; the older Marples model about 35°. The difference in the amount of grip they can get on the wood is obvious*

parallel thread. A drop of wood glue to the end point of the screw helps to bind the wood fibres together and give a surer grip. Sometimes two screws are used, although then the workpiece cannot be rotated.

Instead of holding the carving to a horizontal bench, the woodcarver's screw can be used to fix the work to a thick plank, angled or vertically placed, and perhaps held in the bench vice (Figs 4.42 and 4.43). This arrangement is especially suitable for pieces intended for wall mounting.

One drawback carver's screws have – as do expanding bolts, coach screws and similar holding devices – is the resulting hole in the back or base of the carving. This may or may not be acceptable. It is sometimes possible to design around the hole – for example by allowing waste wood in the preliminary stages – or to conceal it by using a mounting base or a neat plug.

Carver's screws come in various sizes, some of the larger ones being made in continental Europe.

SWIVEL-BALL SYSTEMS

Most of the holding devices mentioned so far have limitations to their movement and the adjustability

Fig 4.43 A screw post, or board, held in a vice allows work to be held vertically

of the work they hold – at best, two-dimensional repositioning is possible. Fixing the carving to a ball which can rotate, swivel and be locked, moves the holding ability into three dimensions. There are several such clamps on the market, some crudely mechanical – but still very effective – and some based on hydraulic systems with amazing locking ability.

These swivel-ball holding devices are becoming increasingly popular, and this is not surprising because they represent in many ways the carver's dream come true: the work can be rotated in any direction and locked horizontally or at an angle. They are worth serious consideration and investigation.

The Spencer Franklin Hydraclamp, which has been well established and proven over many years, is a hydraulic system in which a plate is attached to a spigot extending from the ball. The plate has many slots and holes, allowing a range of adaptations (Fig 4.44). The carving can be fixed directly to the plate using bolts or screws; or an attachment for a woodworking vice can be improvised; or the spigot can be

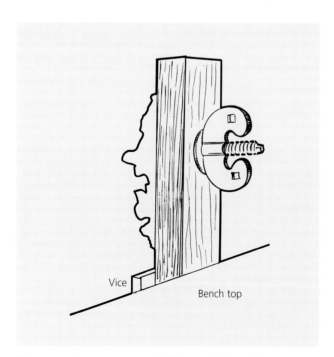

Fig 4.42 A carver's screw holding work through a vertical post; the screw will also work well in conjunction with the tilting surfaces mentioned earlier

Fig 4.44 *Two different sizes of the Spencer Franklin Hydraclamp. The top plate has slots to take bolts into the base of the carving. It is also possible to fit a vice on top*

Fig 4.45 *The Veritas Carver's Vice, with its mounting bolt. This one is fitted with the larger of the two available mounting plates*

modified to meet a carver's individual needs. Although a little ingenuity may be required, the carving, once fitted, can be positioned so that any part can be got at easily. The work can be locked and moved safely. The clamp itself may be bolted directly to the carving bench, mounted to a block of wood clamped to the bench top, or held in a vice.

The Hydraclamp 1400, for example, will support 100lb (45kg), held at 45° and 12in (300mm) away from the centre of the ball, and there are larger and smaller versions available. In fact this tremendous holding ability creates a particular problem: the strength and weight of the bench may not be up to taking the weight of the carving, under what can become conditions of considerable leverage, and may 'walk'. A free-standing, floor-mounted metal stanchion or stand is one answer.

The Veritas Carver's Vice is a well-made example of a genre of small bench-top holding devices (Fig 4.45). Work is screwed from below to the faceplate and, when the faceplate is rotated or tilted, a wide range of carving positions is made possible.

The Stretton Carver's Clamp is designed to be held in a carpenter's vice (Fig 4.46). The faceplate is mounted on a ball which swivels and tilts as the spanner (which remains loosely in place) undoes the clamping nut.

The Koch clamping system has a vice to hold the work, rather than a faceplate; it locks mechanically and is adjustable, but not quite to the same extent (Fig 4.47). Bench-mounted, the angled metal bracket

from bench to ball makes it feel lighter and springier than the other types. The carving will vibrate and bounce when struck even lightly with a mallet.

As all these metal swivel-ball systems fit to the bench top, they do pose a danger to the tool edges. Using a bench vice to hold them keeps their metal bodies out of the way, lowers the working height and makes them easily removable.

Fig 4.46 *The Stretton Carver's Clamp, with its integral spanner for adjustment*

Fig 4.47 *The Koch clamping system, with extension bars to take small relief panels*

HOLDING TURNED WORK

The application of carving disciplines to woodturning has a long history – you only have to look at such furniture as four-poster beds for an example. This sort of work would have been undertaken by two separate tradesmen: a turner and a carver. Today, however, many turners will have a go at carving their own work and vice versa.

Essentially, no turning is of a more complicated shape than can be found in carving; and most of the problems with holding turned work are the same as those for carved work.

Spindle turnings are often best left on the lathe – locking the mandrel, or using an indexing plate, to adjust the position of the work. Arrange a board, with a fence around it, under the turning and on the bed of the lathe. This will act as a bench, and the carving tools can be placed on it normally. With delicate spindles, extend a wooden supporting trough from the toolrest or saddle – such spindles can be quite flexible, if not fragile. The work may need reversing to get at the other side, or to work with the grain.

Faceplate work may, again, be best left on whatever device was used to hold it for turning – though not necessarily on the lathe – and many of the holding methods described above can be used.

A bowl may be gripped between two bars of wood, bolted across, for lettering purposes (Fig 4.48). If the edge is not strong, grip it in a similar way but using a packing block to the centre. This arrangement can then be clamped to the bench surface or held in a swivel-ball clamp. Many other ways of holding turned work for carving are described in my *Carving on Turning*.

Carving should be done before any sanding, to prevent the grit damaging the keen edges of the carving tools.

SUMMARY

This chapter cannot hope to cover all the ingenious ways that carvers find to hold their work. And that really is the crux of the matter: ingenuity, adaptability and foresight are often needed, unless only a limited range of predictable work is undertaken.

Although holding a particular piece of work efficiently, conveniently, safely and securely may be a problem, there will always be some way to achieve it – found from within a repertoire of techniques. Part of the challenge and joy of carving comes from successfully finding a creative response to these sorts of problems.

Fig 4.48 *A simple way of holding a bowl in order to carve lettering on the rim*

CHAPTER FIVE

THE WORKPLACE

AIMS

- To advise on what makes a suitable and pleasant working environment for carving

- To encourage, in newcomers, the right balance between tools and carving

- To look at safety in the workplace

The type of workplace needed by a carver varies with the nature of the carving work. Small and intricate netsuke, for example, can be carved with a tray on the carver's lap, sitting in an armchair. Huge log sculptures, at the other extreme, may need a block and tackle to handle them. In these cases the workplace is adapted to the carving work.

On the other hand, many carvers have to fit the carving to the workplace. They work on kitchen tables, on benches attached to garage walls and in garden sheds. Some are lucky, but most do not have purpose-built workshops and the available space dictates the size of work that can be undertaken (Fig 5.1).

If the size of the workplace is one factor influencing the type of carving work, whether the workplace is large or small, purpose-built or improvised, there are other physical requirements that matter. Some non-physical factors also need to be considered.

A carver needs to feel comfortable and at ease, even 'at home', in the workplace. This applies as much to those whose carve only an hour or two a week as to those who spend more of their waking hours inside a workshop than they do outside it.

A workplace must feel safe, secure, comfortable and attractive to the user, supporting the mental states that will express themselves in their work. It is really worth the trouble to make your own workplace as

Fig 5.1 *Despite the size of this book, it does not take much to make a woodcarver happy*

supportive as possible (Fig 5.2), rather than try to work in a makeshift environment that is continually unsatisfying or annoying .

I would like to include a plea for spiders and the like, who love to dwell among wood and behind benches. They are completely harmless (unless you live in Sydney or somewhere similar) and are only being what they are. Carving can be an isolated occupation and these creatures are always there to talk to – you only need to worry when they answer back! So, please treat them kindly and allow them to share your space.

Fig 5.2 This corner of a well-organized workshop shows a small carving bench with an adjustable stand on top, and wall-mounted storage for clamps and other tools. Even quite a small space can be pleasant to work in, provided it is carefully planned

FEATURES OF A WORKPLACE

The following thoughts concern some of the physical qualities which help to make the workplace function well and support the carving process. One other useful facility to the workplace is running water.

POSITION OF THE BENCH

See the workbench, whatever its shape or size, as the hub of all your carving activity. It is here, after all, that the actual carving takes place. Give your bench prime consideration and fit, arrange or orientate everything else around it – and not just around the tea-making facilities.

FLOORING

The floor must be solid enough for the bench to stand firmly on it. A bench will 'walk' on a springy wooden floor, especially when a degree of force is used. Concrete floors, on the other hand, are hard and cold on the feet, and can damage any tools that happen to fall from the bench.

A wooden floor laid over a concrete one is an ideal compromise: firm but friendly. Alternatively duckboards, or a section of chipboard, or a reversed piece of hessian-backed carpet laid on the concrete in front of the bench will make standing to your work a lot more comfortable.

LIGHTING

The bench cannot properly be arranged without careful consideration of the lighting. Carving or sculpture is essentially about light and shadow. The quality of the workplace lighting affects the carving and the final result enormously. Complete all-round lighting will produce no shadows, and it becomes difficult to see what is happening to the carving.

Ideally the workplace lighting should reproduce that in which the finished carving will reside. To produce a working pattern of light and shadow, a variety of adjustable sources is needed. Many workplaces have single fixed windows to which the carving must be continually orientated; this can be entirely satisfactory. Daylight is considered by most to be by far the best light to work in, and workplaces that have no windows at all and depend entirely on artificial light are at a disadvantage.

There are some options to increase the quality and flexibility of the lighting. The best illumination is like that used for photographing objects: a main source of light (from above or to the side) and secondary lights 'filling in' from right angles to the first. But the important thing is to *control* what is going on.

NATURAL LIGHTING

Being able to adjust the amount of sunlight with venetian or roller blinds is a good start. The most useful light for carving comes in the lower half of a tall window, so blocking off the top half is an advantage. This is not the same as an overhead skylight or transparent panel in the middle of the room, which gives a good light for three-dimensional work.

Northern light in Britain is the most constant and mild, whereas southern windows give the maximum but most variable quality of light. Of the two, northern light is preferable.

Painting the walls and ceilings of the workplace bright white will increase the amount of ambient light (Fig 5.3); as will the large acrylo-plastic mirrors which are available – throwing light back from dingy corners of a room.

ARTIFICIAL LIGHTING

Normal light bulbs give a yellow tinge which affects the colours of the wood, but need not be a problem if you are considering only the relative light and shadow of a form. Fluorescent tubes are harder on the eyes, give harsher shadows, and in general are a bit insensitive. Daylight tubes and bulbs are better.

Adjustable angle lamps in various places greatly help in controlling the light direction (Fig 5.4). They can be turned on or off, swung here or there, closer to or further away from the work, thus allowing changes to be made quickly.

TOOL AND EQUIPMENT STORAGE

Some carvers like to work in chaos with tools scattered everywhere. But if you are not like this, then it's a case of the old adage 'a place for everything and everything in its place', as far as is practicable.

Fig 5.3 White-painted walls make the most of the light coming through this window

Fig 5.4 An adjustable lamp on a strong tubular frame allows light to be targeted on this sharpening area

Use shelves, cupboards, hooks and so on (Figs 5.5 and 5.6).

It is helpful to divide tools and equipment into two categories:

- those which are stored for a long length of time

- those which are used often and only put away in the short term.

Keep the most frequently used tools nearer the work area – that is, in, on or by the bench. Relegate the others to less useful areas of the workplace.

Do pay attention to the security of the workshop; replacing tools is both expensive and inconvenient.

HEATING

It is said that carvers, in the main, are a long-lived lot. This may be because they have a habit of working in cold workshops and – in Darwinian manner – the weaker members of the species are

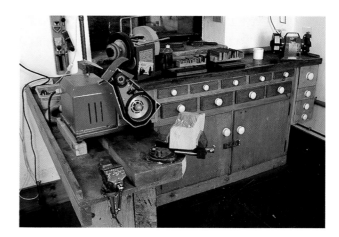

Fig 5.6 Additional storage can be built into the workbench or sharpening bench itself

weeded out early on. This habit may be due to stoicism or meanness. However, having a warm enough workplace does make a lot of difference to the well-being of the carver.

Temperature often goes with humidity: too hot an environment makes work hard and sluggish; too cold, and the hands feel lumpy and insensitive. Too dry an atmosphere can lead to wood splitting; too moist, and rust and mould thrive. A balance needs to be found within these variations.

First of all you need to look at the workshop itself:

- Check over the insulation: perhaps consider double-glazing the windows and soft-boarding (or fibre-boarding) the walls. Look for draughts.

- A wooden floor is much warmer than a concrete one. If you place a wooden floor over concrete, insulate the space between.

- Heating a workshop that is divided into smaller areas of use is more manageable.

Much less heat is needed to heat a workshop where these points have been applied.

Wood-burning stoves have always been popular, if a little hazardous. Do check any insurance policy you have, as many insurers will not allow any naked flame – such as in these stoves, or in bottled-gas fires – in the workplace.

Remember that paraffin (kerosene) and bottled-gas fires give off both fumes and water vapour – in

Fig 5.5 Open racks, situated near the workbench, are ideal for tools in frequent use.

fact, when one gallon of paraffin is burnt it produces one gallon of water vapour. Both types of fire need good ventilation; if they can be used in an indirect form of heating – ducting the fumes externally – so much the better.

Electric heating is probably the cheapest form to install, if not the cheapest to run. Both installation and running costs need to be considered when working out overheads. Electric convector heaters with thermostats, and infra-red heaters, work well, as do night-storage heaters on cheap electricity.

WOOD STORAGE

It is worth thinking about where and how wood is to be stored when setting up a workplace initially. Will it be kept in the workshop or separately? How soon will the wood be needed? How much space is available? Are racks necessary? Can the wood be got at easily? Is there woodworm in the place? Where is the source of heating to be, and where will you be wanting to move or work?

Keep wood dry and aired, and stored in such a way that you can see exactly what you have.

CLEANING

Although some carvers thrive on chaos, it does have its drawbacks for most of us: tools get lost, damaged or broken; dirt gets onto carvings, etc. Carving is a disciplined craft and generally keeping the workshop tidy and clean is good practice.

Having found places for tools, it is a matter of putting them away when not in use. The best habit is one of 'policing the area' – for example, if you are crossing the workshop anyway, take something with you that can be put away. This saves on intensive clearing-up sessions.

An 'industrial' vacuum cleaner is a definite asset in a workshop for clearing up. A bench brush and soft floor brush are useful, but tend to raise the dust. Wood chips and shavings from carving are fairly large and easily cleared up; dust, on the other hand, floats around in the air for a long time. Routing or power-sanding in a small workshop can soon cover every surface in fine dust.

It is a good idea to keep carvings covered between working sessions.

BEGINNER'S SYNDROME

This book is mainly about the tools and equipment used for carving; notes about woodcarving itself are only made as they apply in context. There is, however, a real danger for newcomers to carving, one that may be reinforced by the nature of this book, and which needs to be considered.

Someone coming new to carving will buy their carving tools, sharpen them, build up a bench, set up a workplace, hunt around for wood, read many books... all of which can be very exciting, interesting, and enjoyable – and make them feel as if they are getting somewhere. But none of this is *actually carving*.

These activities are very important and contribute to the carving process, but there are many would-be carvers who actually never get round to carving, or carve very little, because they spend all their time and effort on the tools, equipment and other paraphernalia. If only they had this clamp, or those tools, a better place to work, a nicer bench or whatever – then they could get on with it. But it never seems to happen, or rarely. A student carves in a class for a couple of hours a week and is always planning to carve at home, but years later they have never managed to get the conditions right. This state of affairs is common enough to need discussing.

One of the main reasons for this 'beginner's syndrome' is that carving itself is very demanding and challenging, especially when you are beginning. There is a lot to learn and initial efforts can be disappointing. There is also the well-known 'blank canvas' problem, which can faze even experienced carvers. Tools and equipment are much less threatening and a ready diversion. They represent a definite, and understandable, siren-call to the unwary beginner. The solution involves a sort of strapping of yourself to the bench – in a friendly way.

The first thing is to notice the prevarication. If you recognize the condition I have described, in whole or part, you have to ask yourself whether you really want to carve. If you do, then the following approach may get things moving:

- Having acknowledged and accepted where you are, strongly try to visualize yourself carving.

- Decide what sort of carving is within your grasp and what you are really capable of. It does not matter whether this is just a few decorative strokes to the surface of a chopping board. Assess what is the 'bottom line' of your vision, what you could actually achieve as a project. Beginners often set their sights too high.

- Decide that for the moment you have enough tools; that you will just finish this one simple project and not concern yourself with others right now. Decide to enjoy the carving, no matter how 'good' or 'bad' the end result. 'Practice makes perfect' and you are starting to practice.

- Allocate an amount of time within which to start the carving – write this down – and a period of time to finish it.

- Start the carving. If you do not manage to start and finish within the time frames, then you must try to understand the reasons.

- Enjoy the carving and the result; carving at any level is no mean achievement. Assess your carving – not by comparing it with other carvers, but by deciding what you might have done to make it better, a happier result for yourself. Consider keeping a journal for these thoughts and others related to your carving.

- Try and make bench time a regular pattern or habit.

- Decide on a second project. See how much carving you can do before buying any new tools, working out your needs from actually carving before buying them.

The attitude to establish in your heart and mind is that you are a carver – no matter at what level (Figs 5.7–5.9). Which means that you carve – by definition – not collect tools.

Fig 5.7 St Michael, *southern Germany, about 1490. The great confidence the unknown carver has in his ability to use his tools has given rise to this mixture of easy posture and tense lines. Even such a master must have started somewhere, as a beginner*

SAFETY IN THE WORKPLACE

Good advice about safety in the workplace is to stand at the entrance with a notepad and challenge yourself to think of all the ways you could be hurt in the space in front of you, once you start using it, the tools and the equipment.

The following specific notes should be read together with the other safety notes in this book.

Fig 5.8 *Detail of Fig 5.7. Tool cuts are visible all over: in the precision of the mouth and the eyes as well as the hair and armour. Certainly there must be natural talent, but carving is also the result of hard work and constantly seeking to improve. We, too, must put steel to wood if we want to make headway in the craft*

Fig 5.9 *Detail of Fig 5.7. It is easy to overlook the effort that is required, the deep and deft use of tools that have liberated this hand, so loose and relaxed, from a solid block of wood. Rather than be intimidated by such work, we can be inspired and challenged to do better*

- Make sure that where you walk is free from the danger of sharp edges and corners, things to bump into and wires to trip over. See that you can easily and safely work around your bench.

- All electric wires should be installed, earthed and protected properly, and replaced as soon as they show signs of wear.

- Bag up and remove dust and debris regularly – especially rags that are used for finishing – all of these are fire hazards.

- Install a smoke alarm and extinguisher.

FIRST-AID BOX

There are notes on safety practices in the introductory pages of this book, as well as interspersed where appropriate throughout the text. Despite care, accidents are always possible – mostly unpredictable and sudden. A fully equipped first-aid box should be present in every workplace.

Carving is a solitary occupation, and therefore carvers may well be on their own when an accident happens. The first-aid box should be readily accessible.

The most common accident is a clean cut to the hand or finger from the razor-sharp carving tools. These nicks are more annoying for getting blood on the carving – sweat and tears are enough – than for the personal injury. But remember that you may have to deal with this, or a larger cut, dexterously, using only one hand. Do be aware of this, and make sure that you can get at, and open, things easily – as well as knowing how to use them.

Carvers should always be up to date on their tetanus jabs.

Some useful items to include in the first-aid box are:

- plaster strips, sterilized strips and individual plasters

- lint and cotton wool

- crêpe and cotton bandages in assorted sizes

- scissors

- antiseptic

- needle for removing splinters

- eye-bath and wash.

Always replace items in the first-aid box as soon as they are used and keep it stocked. When you want an item, you want it straight away.

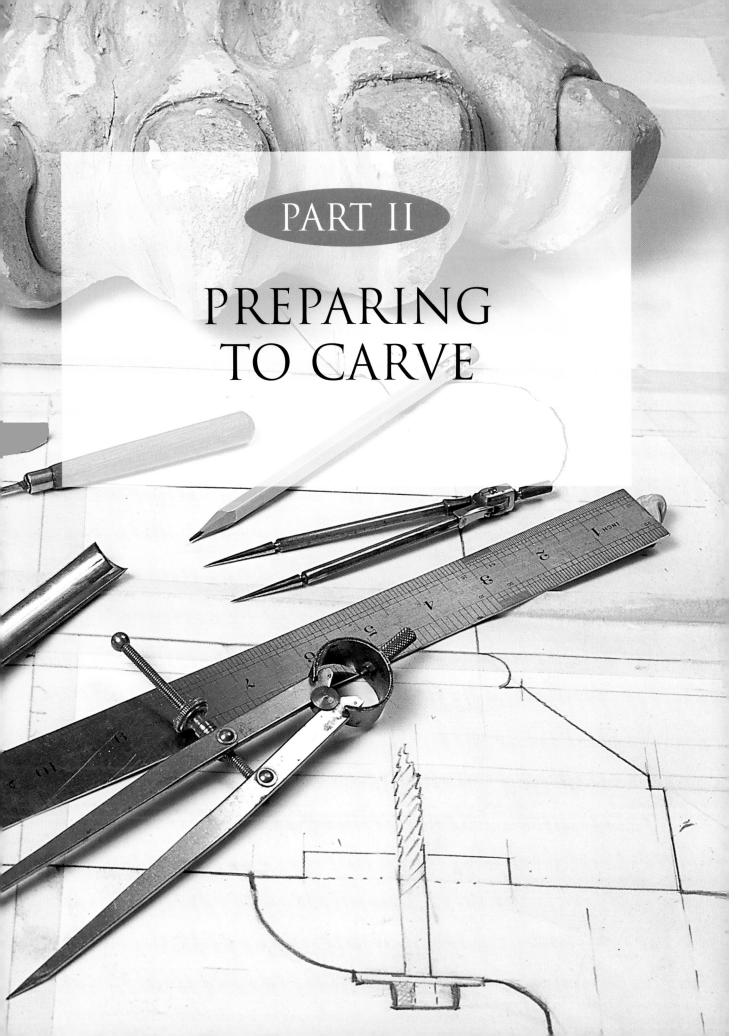

PART II

PREPARING
TO CARVE

AIMS OF PART II

- To describe what carvers need to know about the nature of wood, and to advise on the selection, seasoning and care of wood

- To discuss why surface finishes are needed, and to describe some simple, reliable and effective finishes which can be used on a wide range of carvings

- To give advice on planning and designing your work.

- To instil the confidence you need to make a start on this absorbing and rewarding craft

What carvers need to know about the nature of wood

A woodcarving is the result of three things: the tools, the materials and the design. It is like a three-legged stool: each part is vital to the whole. Thus knowing your material, wood, is essential. You cannot know too much, but you can know too little. And carvers need to understand wood in a different way from, say, a carpenter or furniture maker. Chapter 6 looks at your chosen material closely so as to provide the basis for that understanding which comes only from experience.

Surface finishes, and why they are needed

It amazes me how many carvers seem to have the attitude that 'finishing' is something you 'do' to carvings, almost as an afterthought. The finish of a carving really needs to be taken into account right from the start: in the initial vision and in the designing process.

Most carvings need only a minimal finish, to protect the wood and reveal its beauty. Others need so much that the wood itself is invisible and could be replaced by another substance. In Chapter 7 I look at what 'finishing' can do for your carving, and describe some well-tried methods with which it is hard to go wrong.

Planning and designing your work

Where does a carving start? Not when edge cuts wood. Woodcarving starts in the mind's eye, with an idea, a vision. Between this and the finished carving is a process that will start with a certain amount of pinning down and clarifying of the idea, even if you later change your mind as you go along. It is here that drawing and modelling really help. As many carvings fail because of a lack of planning as through defects in the carving itself. You also need to be sure where wood can safely be removed – it is hard to carve wood back on. So Chapter 8 looks at these supporting skills, with which your carving will have more chance of success.

Having the confidence to make a start

Many beginners, as well as experienced carvers, hesitate over starting a carving. It's a lot of work, relies on visualizing a form within a block of wood, and demands patience and effort. To begin with, you can only bring to the work what you have. The more you carve, the more competent you become, and the more confident. But the crunch is, you must carve to be a carver and to gain the necessary experience that begets confidence. I have written this book to give you information and knowledge to help you start what, to me, has always seemed an endless journey.

There are only two rules to learning to carve: start, and don't stop. Oh yes, and don't be too serious: relax and have fun!

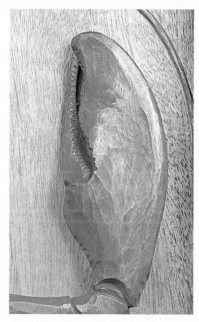

A detail of the lobster carving shown complete in Fig 7.18

CHAPTER SIX

UNDERSTANDING WOOD

AIMS

- To show how the growth of a tree produces and affects the wood within it

- To describe those properties of wood which carvers need to understand and work with

- To help choose the material to suit a specific project or design

- To give some general advice on the selection, seasoning, storage, gluing-up and care of wood

- To clarify some of the terms used in talking about trees and wood

- To help beginners feel more at ease with the material they are working in, so adding to their general confidence

Let us begin by considering each of these aims in a little more detail.

How the growth of a tree produces and affects the wood within it

Unlike the material of stonecarvers, which is relatively fixed and unchanging, the material woodcarvers work with has changed and unfolded as it grew – and continues to change as it is worked. The massive 400-year-old oak tree started as a single acorn, lost in the dark soil one autumn day (Figs 6.1 and 6.2).

As the leaves of a tree are lifted higher and higher to catch the sunlight, rising further away from the roots, so the connecting food and water channels grow longer and longer. These hollow channels are the fibres which are bound together in bundles and masses, tighter or looser, thinner or thicker – depending on the species. It is this fibrous material that is carved. A woodcarver may be cutting into what was once the very heart of a great tree.

Once planted, and the seed having sent its roots deep into the soil, the tree can never leave that spot. It constantly absorbs the changing environment:

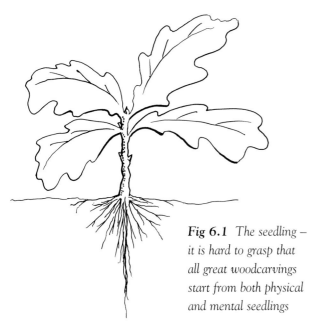

Fig 6.1 The seedling – it is hard to grasp that all great woodcarvings start from both physical and mental seedlings

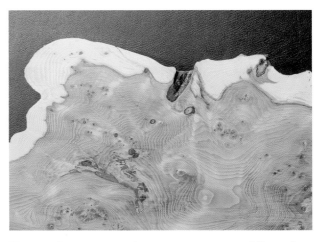

Fig 6.3 Some trees, such as yew, grow quite wildly, and this is reflected in the fibrous structure within

Fig 6.2 From seed to tree, tree to timber, to carving. This oak carving on a door at Berkeley Castle, Gloucestershire, shows a fine understanding of grain in the layout of the design

the rainfall; the sunlight; the wind, frost and lightning; the warmth of summer and the cold of winter that makes for a temperate climate. Trees of the same species on the south side of a valley will grow quicker than those on the north. And even the north side of a tree is different from the south side. Each tree grows according to its individual experience.

Woodcarvers not only work with a fibrous material – a tree – but with different species of trees; with unique examples of a particular species; and with singular parts of any one tree – with knots and burls, wavy grain and unusually thick sections (Fig 6.3). The starting material of a carver is often of a size and composition that workers in any other wood craft would not use.

Wood *can* be treated as a passive material on which a design will be imposed whether it likes it or not. But this would be to miss one of the rich veins of joy available to a woodcarver – the wood itself. Each piece of wood is unique, and carvers need to be alert to get the most out of the material in front of them. This should not be done in a dewy-eyed, romantic way, but with the realism born of true intimacy.

The properties of wood with which carvers in particular need to understand and work with

Tilman Riemenschneider (Fig 6.4) used great lumps of limewood; the carvers of cathedral misericords used oak; Henry Moore used the boles of elm trees; and in the Victoria and Albert Museum, in London, there is

Fig 6.4 Presumed self-portrait of the master, Tilman Riemenschneider (1460–1531), whose woodcarvings are almost exclusively in the limewood (linden) of the region of southern Germany in which he worked

exquisitely detailed work in boxwood. Why is it that these carvers chose these particular timbers – and not others – for their designs?

Undoubtedly availability and cost were, and always have been, factors. In the days when transporting anything was a fairly major undertaking, artisans tended to live nearer the source of their materials and woodcarvers would naturally work in the woods available locally.

Often overlooked in appreciating the history of sculpture is the circumscribing effect that the attributes and limits of any material have on the sculptor who works it. The designs that can be expressed through one particular species of wood can be very difficult, if not physically impossible, to express in another. Looking at carvings in the past, the designs

that particular schools and styles of carvers used always seem, at their best, to fit perfectly with the type of wood used. The designs do not appear to have come before the material or vice versa; it is as if they arose naturally together. Sometimes the link is strikingly obvious. Limewood, for example, is noted for its tractability, elasticity and ease of working. It can be said that if limewood, with its unique characteristics, had not been available locally, the whole phenomenon of the limewood carvers of Renaissance Germany could not have taken place (Fig 6.5).

Fig 6.5 Part of the Altar of the Holy Blood, St Jacob's Church, Rothenburg, Germany, by Riemenschneider. The clarity and intense detail of all the carving in the altar are possible only because of the material qualities of limewood

Suiting the material to a specific project or design

An understanding of wood grows with experience. Carvers who have been working in the medium for some time will have at least an adequate understanding, if not a very good understanding, of their material – they will know what they can expect from it.

This chapter is aimed mainly at beginners who perhaps have never worked with wood before; consequently they may have little knowledge or experience of the material. There is a lot of knowledge, relating to wood, that is shared between the different woodworking crafts. But what do woodcarvers – as opposed to, say, carpenters – need to know about wood?

It is not possible to know too much about the material you are working with – but it is possible to know too little. And the consequences of knowing too little are quite likely to be some adverse effect such as the wood splitting, reacting badly to a stain, or lacking strength in a part where the design calls for it (Fig 6.6).

Fig 6.6 *A Victorian ceiling boss in pine. Each element is supported by its neighbour to create the web of support that safely allows both the piercing and the thinning of the stems – an essential consideration when using wood which has little inherent strength*

Some general advice on the selection, seasoning, storage, gluing-up and care of wood

Husbanding wood is a concern of all woodcarvers – without the wood, what are they? Husbanding can involve the relatively minor exercise of choosing a piece of wood from a timber yard specializing in the needs of carvers, or it may involve a large-scale operation such as buying and converting whole trees.

Whatever need a carver has, the final carving will rarely look anything like the original tree, and only a small amount of the original tree will have been used by all those woodworkers interested in it. The rest will have been burned on site, removed in the timber yard, succumbed to the weather or other defects, or will have been swept up from the workshop floor and thrown away.

Time, effort and financial outlay are needed to obtain the wood, so thought must be given to the material in order to make the most of it – from the tree to the finished piece.

From the point of view of the planet, nobody in the West can now claim to be unaware that resources can no longer be taken for granted. Carvers are working with woods from all over the world and from all levels of forest and woodland management. In the long term, carvers have a responsibility to trees over and above their being vehicles for short-term creative achievements. Indeed, it should not just be a matter of 'responsibility' for trees, but a love of them.

Clarifying some of the terms used in talking about trees and wood

Being able to name what concerns us is tantamount to acquiring a language with which to understand and share our experiences. For those who have arrived at woodcarving with little or no experience of wood, this chapter will help them find their way around by clarifying terms that are commonly used.

Feeling more at ease with the material being worked and so adding to general confidence

It is not just the terms themselves that need to be understood by the beginner, but the substance these terms describe, and this involves time, exploration and experience.

A carver works *with* wood, not against it. Newcomers to carving not only have to gain the skills of sharpening, using their carving tools and working out the designs they want to carve, but must also learn how to bring all this information to bear on the material itself. This particular combination of challenges is what makes woodcarving and wood sculpture such a stimulating occupation.

The wood itself may suggest an idea and actually form the design in your mind. Or you can find a piece of wood to fit the idea. Either way, as a feeling for working wood grows – how to cut it and shape it well – the carver becomes more free. Carving becomes more of a lovers' dance – even if at times dancing with an old piece of oak feels more of a tussle – where both dancers must contribute to the final display. There is no need to think in terms of fighting or subduing the material. You have to seduce and cajole, read and listen, direct with affection and be prepared to be directed. The material must become a means of expression, not something that keeps getting in the way.

HOW TREES GROW

Trees dwell in two worlds: growing their trunks, branches and leaves into the sunlit air, and their roots into the dark earth. The ancient Chinese believed that trees held heaven and earth together and that without trees, heaven and earth would separate.

The root system can be deep and extensive, or surprisingly shallow – as in the trees from tropical rainforests. Roots seek out water and food elements such as sodium, potassium and iron, which ascend the tree to the leaves as a watery sap (Fig 6.7). Sunlight and carbon dioxide act to transform the inorganic salts into chemicals which go into the life processes of the tree, including its growth (Fig 6.8). The sap, now much heavier, passes to buds and branches, and back down the trunk to the roots. If you burn a piece of wood, the ash represents all the solid material which has been taken from the soil by the tree; the smoke will be some of these chemicals, as well as carbon dioxide absorbed by the leaves; the heat from

Fig 6.7 *Water, with dissolved nutrients, is drawn right up the tree by the considerable force exerted by evaporation from the leaves, far above*

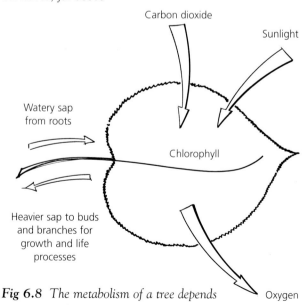

Fig 6.8 *The metabolism of a tree depends on trapping the energy of sunlight*

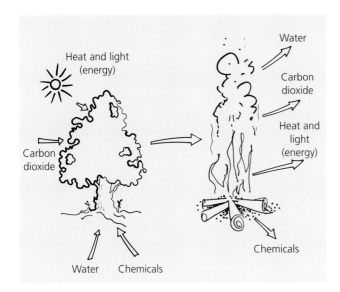

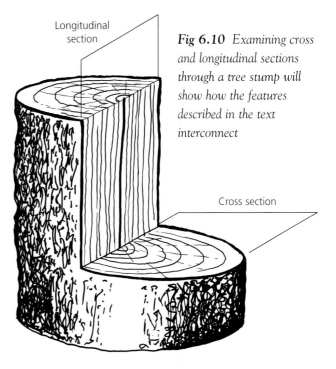

Fig 6.10 *Examining cross and longitudinal sections through a tree stump will show how the features described in the text interconnect*

Fig 6.9 *The law of conservation of energy: what you get out is what went in*

the burning is trapped sunlight – the fire in the grate is, ultimately, heat from the sun (Fig 6.9).

Trees are products of their immediate environment: the amount of sunlight, its direction, the availability of water, the chemicals in the soil, and seasonal changes. All these factors will affect its growth.

We are all familiar with logs or felled tree stumps. In such a cross-section of a tree, the places where the growth and life processes take place can be seen (Fig 6.10). Starting on the outside, the **bark** (Fig 6.11) protects against the weather, insects and animals. It is almost completely impervious to water, but pervious to air.

Just inside the bark is the **bast**, a spongy layer in which most of the sap travels as it returns from the leaves. If a tree is bark-ringed (Fig 6.12), this layer is destroyed and nourishment is denied to the roots of the tree, which subsequently die, terminating the tree itself.

Inside the bast, but before the wood proper, is a microscopic layer of cells extending throughout the whole tree; it is sometimes just visible to the naked eye. This is the **cambium**, a protoplasmic layer of cells which creates the bast and bark to the outside, and the wood itself on the inside. Wood has a fibrous structure with hollow channels (like veins) and sheets of fibres which conduct food and water and act as a mechanical support. It is these fibres which

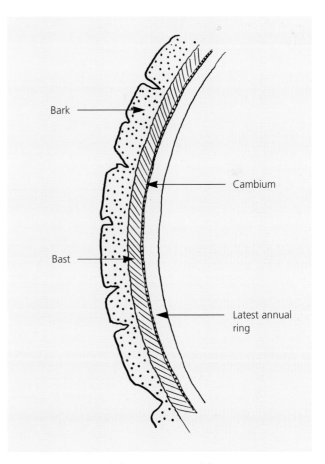

Fig 6.11 *A magnified cross section of the outer part of the trunk*

with the inner springwood and outer summerwood, together, forming an **annual ring** (Figs 6.13 and 6.14). Table 6.1 summarizes the properties of springwood and summerwood.

The annual rings represent the story or history of the tree. They can be wider or tighter depending on how well the tree grew in a particular year (for instance, growing faster with more sunlight), or they can vary in width across the trunk depending on whether the tree grew bent or straight (Fig 6.15). Annual rings only appear circular in a cross section; cut them any

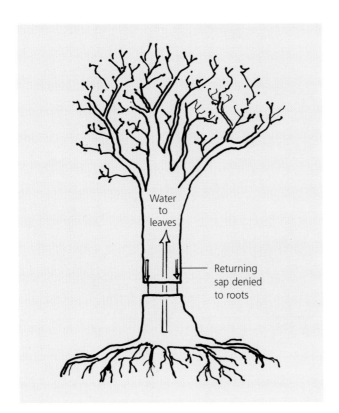

Fig 6.12 *The effect of 'ringing' a tree*

form the **grain** with which woodcarvers work. The cambium is the growing part of the tree, the most alive and active part – rather like a skin draped over a skeleton of wood.

A tree grows both in girth and height as the cambium adds layers of fibrous tissue everywhere, including the veins of leaves. This fibrous tissue is correctly known as **wood**. An amount of usable wood is technically called **timber**. In practice, however, these two terms are loosely used to mean the same thing, i.e. the material that is being worked.

In temperate zones, spring is the occasion for a great eruption of activity. Warmth evaporates water from the leaves, and more is drawn in from the roots. The cambium quickly responds, laying down a layer of **springwood** or **earlywood** – wood that is light in both weight and colour, and carries large amounts of water and mineral salts upwards. As the season moves on, the activity of the cambium slows down, producing a darker, heavier, and stronger layer of fibres – **summerwood** or **latewood**. Summerwood is more supportive than conductive. In winter the cambium is virtually dormant. This pattern is repeated every year,

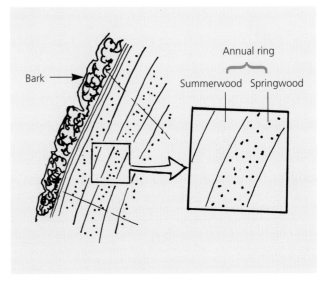

Fig 6.13 *The exact form of the annual rings depends both on the species and the individual history of the tree*

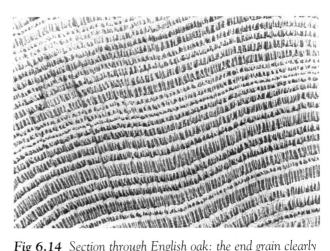

Fig 6.14 *Section through English oak: the end grain clearly shows the light springwood and dark summerwood that make up the annual rings; medullary rays are also visible*

SPRINGWOOD	SUMMERWOOD
Grows first in the year	Grows later in the year
Forms the inner part of the annual ring	Forms the outer part of the annual ring
Conductive	Skeletal
More porous	Less porous
Lighter colour	Darker colour
Lighter weight	Heavier weight

Table 6.1 General differences between springwood and summerwood of a tree

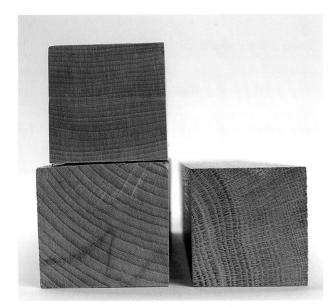

Fig 6.15 Cross sections of beech (left) and oak. Wider annual rings in the same species indicate faster growth and softer timber

The base of a tree is thicker because it has been growing for a longer time than the higher parts. As it grows, low branches that were part of the original sapling – having fallen or broken off – will be incorporated into the body of the trunk, becoming **knots**. Wood laid down later tends to be clear or free of knots, although later branch growth will affect the pattern of the grain. 'Knotty heart' in a tree is caused by the sapling having a large number of small branches early on.

The cross section shows a few more features worth noting (Fig 6.16). The very centre of the tree is the **pith** or **medulla** of the original seedling. This is mechanically always a weak point, and often the source of rot in the middle of a tree.

From the centre – though not necessarily reaching it – radiate the **medullary rays** (Fig 6.17). These are sheets of tissue that store and conduct food and water across (in and out of) the tree. It is the medullary rays that produce the 'silver ray' figuring in English oak (Fig 6.18). Again, they are a weak point; when a tree starts splitting, it is almost always along the lines of these rays.

As the tree grows, the central parts take on more of a skeletal or supportive role, rather than that of conducting sap, and become the **heartwood**. The fibres towards the middle of the tree – but only roughly following the lines of the annual rings – clog as a result of chemical changes. Heartwood is darker,

other way and intricate patterns are produced, which are known as the **figure** of the timber. Because younger trees grow more quickly, the rings towards the centre of the trunk tend to be broader, growing tighter and narrower towards the outside as the tree reaches maturity.

In tropical climates, with no distinct seasons, there may be few or no visible rings at all, the trees growing continuously the whole year round.

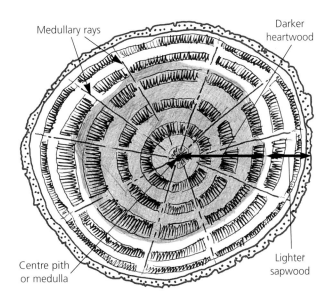

Fig 6.16 Some distinctive features of a tree's cross section

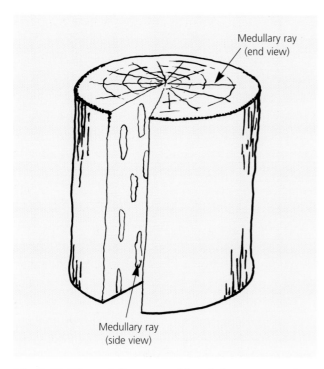

Fig 6.17 The medullary rays, although they appear as lines in a cross section, are actually sheets of tissue, conducting food and water across the tree

denser, more stable and generally more disease-resistant (Table 6.2), and as such it is the wood of choice for carvers. Sometimes, though, the heart of a tree is completely absent, leaving a surprisingly healthy tree consisting only of a ring of sapwood.

Fig 6.18 The medullary rays, often contributing much to the figure, are apparent as irregular flecks in this piece of oak fencing

	HEARTWOOD	SAPWOOD
Moisture	–	+
Weight	+	–
Density	+	–
Porosity	–	+
Stability	+	–
Disease resistance	+	–
Darkness	+	–

+ proportionally higher
– proportionally lower

Table 6.2 General characteristics of heartwood and sapwood

This **sapwood**, situated outside the heartwood, has the original qualities of the fibres laid down by the cambium. It is softer, lighter in weight and colour, still porous, and contains moisture or resins; it is more 'living', and is also more subject to disease, especially when the tree is dead. In most cases these qualities make sapwood unattractive, if not useless, to the carver.

HARDWOODS AND SOFTWOODS

There are two broad categories of tree: **hardwoods** and **softwoods**. These terms should not be confused with 'hard' wood and 'soft' wood, which are much looser terms to do with the actual physical density of the material.

HARDWOODS

Such trees might more properly be called broadleaf trees, and include oak, walnut, box and maple. They have broad leaves, and most are deciduous, the leaves changing colour and being shed in the winter. The timber tends to be close-grained with fine pores, making it harder, heavier and more durable than most softwoods.

112

SOFTWOODS

These trees might more properly be called conifers or needle-leaf trees; most of them are evergreen. Species include pines and firs, but also, despite their appearance, hemlock and yew. Their internal structure is recognizably different from that of the broadleaf trees, with large open fibres called *tracheids*, and a grain that is usually easy to split. Most splinter easily and are less durable than the hardwoods, although some, such as redwood, hemlock and yew, are very durable.

WOOD AS A MATERIAL

Although there are some sculptors who carve trees *in situ*, normally wood or timber is changed so drastically in making it fit for carving that it is easy to forget it once grew as a tree.

CONVERSION

This is the term used for reducing a whole tree into various useful pieces of wood. This is usually undertaken by timber yards, although carvers may do the work themselves. There are two reasons for converting trees into timber:

- to make the most economic and best use of the material

- to **season** or dry the wood (see pages 114–17).

Both converting and seasoning wood produce different qualities in the timber from those present in the original tree. These are qualities needed by carvers.

When trees are converted into timber, they can be sawn up in many ways. When wood is bought, any **nominal size** quoted will be the dimensions arising from the original sawing – rough and unplaned. Some allowance is usually left for shrinkage when the wood was cut. If you take a 2in (50mm) nominal board, it should be exactly this measurement – but may finish to only 1¾in (45mm) after planing. If you want to end up with a finished 2in (50mm) board you must start with a larger nominal size; this may be as much as 2½in (65mm), which is obviously

less economical. **Finish** or **finished** means the surfaces have been planed.

Sawing itself can be straight **through and through** (also called **plain-sawn**, **slash-sawn** or **slab-sawn**), where the tree is moved across a huge bandsaw blade which rips it into parallel boards (Fig 6.19). There is little wastage and wide boards result, so the wood tends to be cheaper. However, the figure is less interesting and the wood is less stable the further it is cut towards the sides of the tree, tending to move and warp.

Quarter-sawing is an alternative method, but is comparatively rare and costly. The tree is rotated in its presentation to the saw, producing radially cut planks – that is, they are sawn roughly in the direction of the medullary rays (Fig 6.20). This method is more wasteful and time-consuming, which is why it is more expensive. Cutting along the sheet-like medullary rays yields wood with the best figure and greatest stability; it shrinks less and more uniformly, tending to split and warp less.

A **flitch** or **slab** is timber, usually thick, which has the rounded sides of the tree still clearly visible.

After sawing, the wood will be sorted for quality and seasoned – an extremely important procedure for any woodworker.

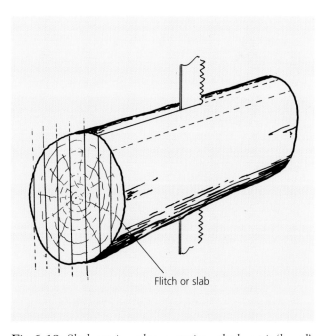

Flitch or slab

Fig 6.19 *Slash-sawing a log; sometimes the heart is 'boxed' or removed*

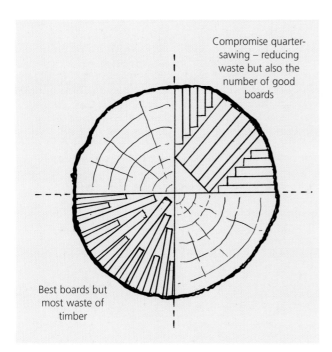

Fig 6.20 There are several ways of quarter-cutting a log – all aim to reveal the figure of the medullary rays in the most economic way

SEASONING

The fibres of a living tree, especially the sapwood, are full of water. This water is continually drawn through the fibres from the soil as the sun evaporates moisture from the leaves above. Once a tree is dead – whether still standing or cut as a log or as boards – the water will start to leave the wood by evaporation. If left long enough, an equilibrium will be reached: the amount of moisture in the wood balances the amount of water vapour in the surrounding air.

The effect of moisture in wood is a matter of everyday experience. In the winter, with damper atmospheres, wooden doors swell and stick and frames warp. In a dry summer gaps appear where once there was a neat fit, surfaces start to check or crack, and joints loosen. The shrinking and expanding of wood fibres according to their water content is the phenomenon that makes it appear to be 'alive', or to breathe.

Immediately a log or board is cut from a tree, it starts to lose water from the cut ends of the fibres (Fig 6.21) – to be replaced by air. Water is lost first and most quickly from between the cellular fibres,

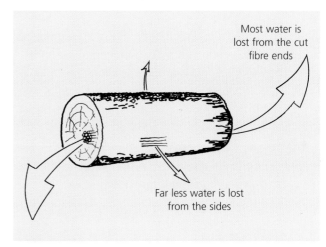

Fig 6.21 Relative water loss from a newly cut log

then more slowly from within the cells themselves. As the wood dries out it shrinks (Fig 6.22).

The outer sapwood has a much higher water content than the inner heartwood, and so shrinks more. This sets up stresses which are released as cracking or checking at the surface – at times quite severe splits arise as the medullary rays are torn apart. Terms like *shake*, *split* and *check* are freely used to mean the same event, that is the opening up of fibres to varying degrees through water loss and shrinkage stresses. Distortion and warping can also result from the different shrinking of heartwood and sapwood.

Water leaves through the cut ends of the fibres far more quickly than from the sides, which may still be covered in bark, so the ends of planks and logs shrink and split more than the more internal parts of the wood. Light shakes at the ends of the wood are to be expected, and must be allowed for when calculating requirements.

Eventually, as the wood dries, the stresses reach a new equilibrium and the wood settles down to a new shape. Seasoning is the attempt to control the drying process of wood so that the stresses are minimized, a level of moisture content equal to that of the surrounding air is arrived at, and the wood is as free from shakes as possible.

The **moisture content** is the weight of water in a piece of wood, measured as a percentage of the weight of the same wood completely dried. The moisture content needed by woodworkers will vary according to the average **relative humidity** in which they are

114

Fig 6.22 The wide gap shows how much the log has shrunk around its circumference since the segment was cut out of it. If it had not been cut, it would have split

SEASONED	UNSEASONED
Low moisture content	High moisture content
Lighter	Heavier
More stable	Less stable
More predictable	Less predictable
More disease-resistant	Less disease-resistant

Table 6.3 *Comparison of the properties of seasoned and unseasoned timber*

working, and the dryness of where the wood will eventually reside. The level can vary between about 9% and 14%.

Seasoning used always to be done in the air, but **air drying** has a measure of unpredictability. **Kiln drying** in special ovens allows more predictable behaviour in the wood.

Seasoned or dried wood has several advantages over **green** or wet wood. Seasoned wood is lighter in weight and harder than wet wood; it is more resistant to infection or woodworm; and it has arrived at a balance of internal stress, making it not only more stable, but a predictable size (Table 6.3).

Kiln-dried wood, as a result of the treatment itself, sometimes has different working properties to air-dried wood of the same species. For example, beech tends to become pinker in colour and more brittle to work if dried in a steam kiln.

The idea of balanced forces within a piece of timber is important. It is a mistake to think, just because a lump of wood has been seasoned or has been lying around for years, that it is completely inert.

Removing further material from the lump, or bringing it into a dry, heated workshop, will create new stresses. This is especially likely where there are both thick and thin parts in the same carving, or where both sapwood and heartwood are present. The balancing of these internal forces, or stresses, may well lead to checks appearing in the surface – or even outright splitting of the wood. Any joiner's shop will tell of beautiful, wide, seasoned boards that rip down the middle to produce two useless, banana-shaped pieces (Fig 6.23).

If a piece of wood splits, it is, to say the least, very frustrating. All that can be done is to minimize the risk right from the start. Kiln-drying is normally the task of specialized firms, as it is a fairly exact process involving special equipment. Air-drying wet wood is undertaken by many carvers, especially those who

Fig 6.23 Resawing a piece of wood releases stresses which may cause further distortion, despite any previous seasoning

have been given free wood. The main requirement is the correct storage conditions – features which are necessary for correct storage of wood anyway.

To air-dry wood successfully, the natural process of drying must be slowed down and made more even, giving a chance for the fibres to mould into a new shape. The following measures all help towards this end:

- It is best to fell a tree in the winter, when it contains least water. For some species, such as oak, elm, ash or chestnut, if the tree is already dead, leaving it in the ground a while with the bark on allows a little more water to drain away slowly. But some other species, such as sycamore and beech, start to rot immediately.

- Leaving wood to cure as a whole log creates the most drying problems. The figuring in a whole log is always the best, but the different shrinking of the heartwood and sapwood create more stress than most wood can stand without splitting. Elm is a wood that has an interlocking grain and is therefore often successfully dried as a whole log.

- Logs are best halved or quartered to relieve the stress between the heartwood and sapwood. Cut away the pith and the immediately adjoining **heart**. Medieval carvers used to carve wood wet, but halved and hollowed out at the back. This minimized and sometimes avoided splitting, and also accounts for the large numbers of wall-mounted, three-quarter-view carvings made in this period. Boards should be cut in uniform thickness.

- Leave the bark on, so slowing water loss from the sides.

- Seal the ends with melted paraffin wax, shellac, varnish or commercial end-sealer. Keep an eye on the ends – water is lost quickly here and splitting can happen rapidly. Reseal the ends if any signs of splitting occur.

- Store the wood off the ground **in stick**, with spacing battens to allow good air circulation (Fig 6.24). Keep it protected from rain, wind, frost, sunlight and dry atmospheres (such as

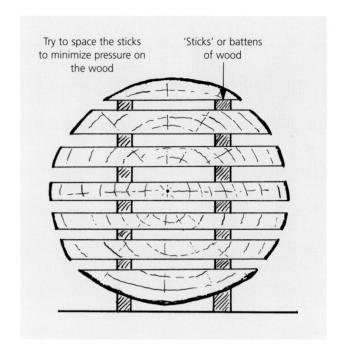

Fig 6.24 *A whole log stored in stick; the same principles apply to storing wood, as well as to drying it*

central heating). Mechanical restraint such as binding or weighting can also be used to 'coax' a board into shape.

- Some people like to store smaller pieces inside plastic bags to retard moisture loss – but keep an eye out for mould at warmer temperatures.

- It is always a good strategy to have the seasoned wood in the workshop for a while before use; or, ideally, leave it in the place where the carving will eventually reside. This gives it a chance to adjust and settle down. The dry atmosphere of central heating must be taken into account by carvers working at home.

The rule of thumb is that hardwoods need at least one year of drying for every inch (25mm) of thickness. So a 4in (100mm) slab or flitch really needs four years; but as the rate of drying varies between species a little sampling at an earlier stage will help assess how the drying is coming along. If you are planning to air-dry your own wood from scratch, you have to see the process as having a time pattern rather like making wine: laying down stocks at intervals for use in the future, with a little tasting now and then.

Using green or wet wood is a hazard that some carvers are willing to risk in order to achieve the size they want without having to laminate smaller pieces of wood. These gains are offset by the threat of splitting. Hollowing out has already been mentioned, as well as selecting woods such as elm where possible. Carving should be done as quickly as you can, with the wood still fresh from the tree and sealed, or kept under plastic wraps, at all other times. The more uniform the distribution of mass, the more evenly the wood will dry – so mixing a large bulk with thin sections is the most risky approach.

A chemical called polyethylene glycol (PEG) is available which replaces the water in timber. It is a messy process which involves soaking the wood in vats, and makes the timber subsequently unpleasant to work. It is used by some sculptors when they want to work in large single pieces of otherwise unstable material, but even this chemical is not a guarantee of complete success.

MOVEMENT

The seasonal movement of wood (seen in doors and windows) must be taken into account; to a large extent it follows a predictable pattern. The movement can be estimated by considering where in the tree the original piece of wood came from (Fig 6.25). As a general rule, a log shrinks:

- the least along its length

- the greatest around its circumference (i.e. tangentially)

- somewhere in between in a radial direction.

So, the movement will depend on the lie of the grain in a piece of wood – how the fibres relate to the tree. Combinations of these movements create the stresses which cause warping and twisting. Fig 6.26 shows how these principles work in practice, with pieces of wood taken from different parts of a tree.

As long as seasoned wood is free to 'breathe' – to expand and shrink freely – there is little problem. But when wood is glued up and no longer able to move independently, various stresses are again brought into play. Gluing up will be dealt with on pages 134–7.

A similar problem arises when a large, flat panel is clamped to the bench for carving. Even though seasoned wood may be glued up in such a way as to minimize warping, the side of the panel that is

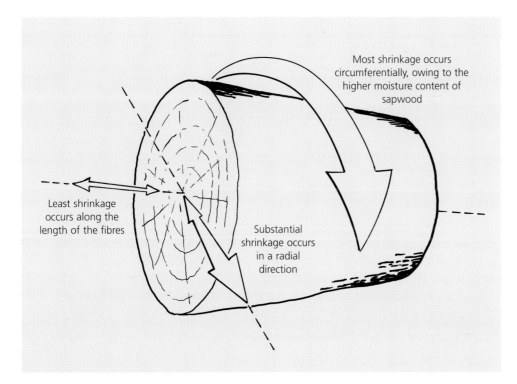

Most shrinkage occurs circumferentially, owing to the higher moisture content of sapwood

Least shrinkage occurs along the length of the fibres

Substantial shrinkage occurs in a radial direction

Fig 6.25 *Relative amounts of shrinkage in a newly cut log*

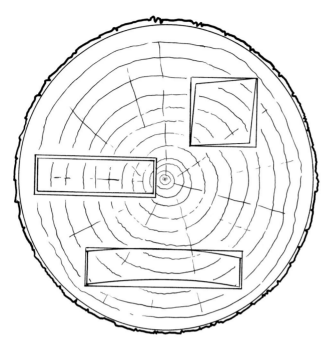

Fig 6.26 The outer sapwood shrinks more than the inner heartwood, and boards taken from different parts of a tree will change shape according to their relative position. The quarter-sawn board at left is the most stable

clamped to the bench is shut off from the atmosphere and no longer able to breathe. In dry air, the free surface can lose water and shrink quite quickly; when, after a few days, the work is unclamped, the panel may spring up at the ends (Fig 6.27). The side

towards the bench has a higher moisture content and is, by comparison, swollen. You can try wetting the drier surface and clamping the opposite side down, but sometimes the panel will not return to its original shape. When such a panel is not being carved, unclamp it and stand it up, perhaps even turn it over, so that air can circulate freely around it.

Defects

What carvers and sculptors want – or put up with – from their material is an individual matter: one carver's sense of defect is another's sense of strength or character (Fig 6.28). There are some sculptors who accept splits, knots, sappy wood or even woodworm as in some way the 'truth' of the material, although a consensus of most carvers would find these characteristics unacceptable and interfering with their vision.

The idea of a 'defect' implies some state of perfection against which the qualities of any single piece of wood can be measured. But as no such ideal exists, perhaps the best way of describing a defect is to say that it is some characteristic in a particular piece of wood that interferes with the intended design or execution of a work. Such a problem may not be present in another sample of the same species.

In this sense, almost any quality may be a defect at some time or other. But in practice there are some

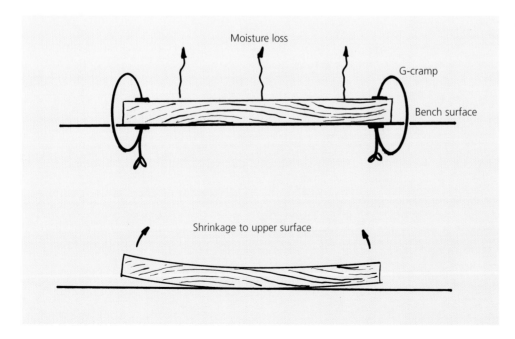

Fig 6.27 Take care not to keep a flat panel clamped to the bench for too long without allowing the underside to 'breathe'

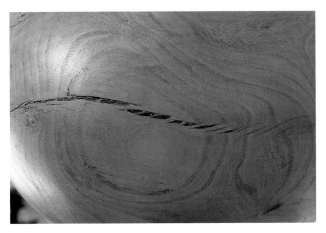

Fig 6.28 A particular pattern of shakes might be considered an interesting feature of some sculptures, rather than a 'fault' to be avoided

defects which most carvers avoid if at all possible. Sometimes defects reveal themselves as carving progresses; for example, what appeared to be a small knot on the surface can become a large hole full of decayed wood. The best that can be done is to learn to read the wood as accurately as possible and minimize the risks.

The two principal defects are splits and knots.

SPLITTING

This is a principal category of defect and a bane of all workers in wood. Splits can render a piece of wood useless. Although all precautions with seasoning may be taken, once carving has started, a new balancing of stresses may impinge on a weakness in the fibres and result in them opening up.

Other terms for the lengthwise parting of wood fibres are *cracks*, **checks** or **shakes**, all of which can be any size from a hairline surface check to splits right through from the outside to the heartwood (Fig 6.29). Although these terms are often used to mean the same thing, checks tend to be more surface phenomena (Fig 6.30), whereas shakes tend to be deeper, and splits disastrous (Fig 6.31).

Ring shakes involve separation between annual rings, and will usually be seen in the original log (Fig 6.32). Ring shakes may result from the impact of the tree on the ground as it is felled, or from excess bending of the tree in high winds. Substantial amounts of useful wood may still be available from a log with a ring shake, depending on its position and extent.

Heart shakes are splits radiating from the centre, often right across to the outside. Where the number

Fig 6.29 Parting of wood fibres along the length of the tree due to shrinkage stresses

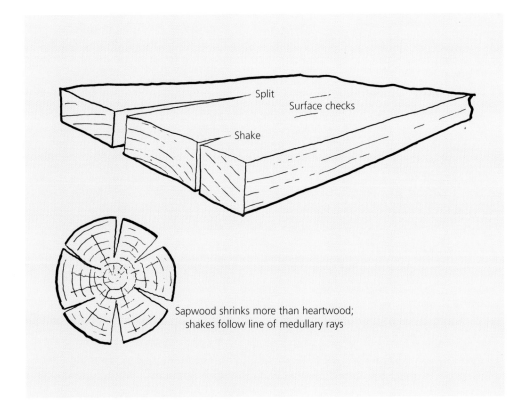

Split

Surface checks

Shake

Sapwood shrinks more than heartwood; shakes follow line of medullary rays

Fig 6.30 *Surface checking, following the medullary rays, may not penetrate very deeply; most of this piece is likely to be usable*

Fig 6.31 *With a split like this you have to accept that you now own two boards, not one*

of radiating splits is extensive, it is known as a **star shake** (Fig 6.33). Both heart and star shakes are thought to arise from the very heart of the tree as it starts to decay after reaching maturity, but probably high winds and sudden changes in temperature may be factors. Such defects can make a log unusable.

Splitting as the result of drying always starts from the outside of a log – or the equivalent place in a board – as the sapwood shrinks more than the heartwood.

If a split is present in the wood before the carving starts, it is often possible to redesign the work around it. Some of the elements can be shuffled around so as to cut out the split with the waste wood (Fig 6.34). There is great satisfaction to be had when you can do this – taking what looked like a forsaken piece of wood and redeeming it.

If a split occurs *after* carving there are a few options, depending on the extent of the damage:

- Ignore it and use the 'Well-it's-wood-isn't-it?' ploy when you come to sell the carving, which may involve using the 'truth to the materials' argument mentioned above. It may indeed be best to leave small surface checks, perhaps filling them with wax, along with the waxing of the rest of the carving (Fig 6.35). With large splits, though, no amount of idealism can prevent the gaping truth ruining the work.

Fig 6.32 *Ring shake in a board and in a log*

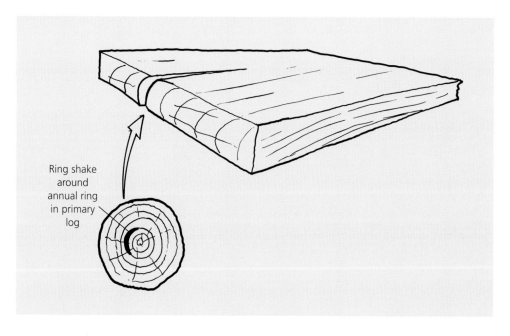

Ring shake around annual ring in primary log

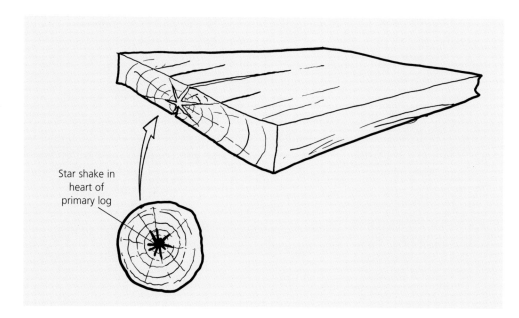

Fig 6.33 *Heart shake is a serious defect, usually affecting a large part of the log*

Star shake in heart of primary log

Fig 6.34 *Placing a design within a board to eliminate the unwanted defective wood may involve altering the design to fit*

Shake

Knot

Fig 6.35 *Surface checks in a whole-log elm sculpture. The smaller ones are filled with wax, which squeezes out or fails to fill, as the wood expands and contracts with the changing humidity of the seasons*

- See if there is yet scope for judicious fiddling with the design.

- A small element of the carving can be deliberately broken off at the split. This should leave a perfectly matching pair of surfaces to reglue, and the repair should be virtually invisible if carefully done and the surface recarved. Spring-wire C-clamps, made from old bed springs, can help with the gluing.

- Filling may be possible, either with slivers of matching wood (Fig 6.36), commercial filler, glue-and-sawdust mixture, or wax (Fig 6.37). Using wood to fill may be a problem if the carving later swells with a change in ambient moisture. The splits, originally releasing particular stresses, may want to close, thus exerting pressure on the inserts and causing new tensions and splits to appear elsewhere. Wood inserts can be a successful repair if the splits are small, but allow the wood to settle down adequately first. Wax and other fillers will be similarly squeezed out and drawn in as the wood swells and contracts.

Filling, like other repairs, can help a piece by preventing the eye from being continuously distracted by an obvious defect, but careful judgement is needed. If possible, assess the cause of splitting – perhaps your stock of wood is less dry than you thought it was.

Keeping carvings covered in plastic between carving sessions will prevent rapid drying and changes in stress.

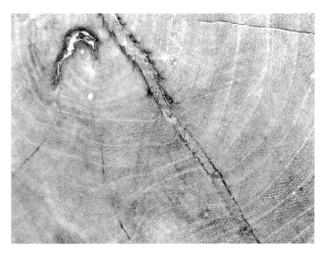

Fig 6.36 *Larger cracks filled with wedges. Even though the wood was carefully matched some 10 years previously, colour changes have made them more obvious; nevertheless they help the feel of the work when it is touched*

KNOTS

Knots can be a source of great beauty in work where the natural qualities of wood are being exploited. However, they can also be a distraction when the carving is more figurative – an awkwardly placed knot in a face, for example, may look like a disfigurement. As with splits, it is often possible to design around knots or place them in waste areas.

Knots can be exploited in ways that splits never can be, and may be 'live' or 'dead'. **Live knots** are still integrated with the surrounding wood fibres and arise from twigs of branches which were alive when the tree was felled. They sometimes mark a change in grain direction (as do **crotches** and other natural formations), allowing a weak part in some designs to acquire strength. Sometimes the grain is just awkward, but this can usually be dealt with by taking shallow cuts and working across the grain of the knot.

Dead knots are often loose in the timber and surrounded by an unsightly black or chalky ring (Fig 6.38). These knots are much older, being from branches that were dead before the tree was brought down. Such knots can often be knocked out and glued firmly back in again, but the different colour makes them very prominent.

One option may be to replace the dead knot with a live one, removed from another piece of the same timber by means of a plug-cutter (Figs 6.39–6.41). Try not to let the visible insert look too geometrical, though this may not be possible. A Dutchman is another possibility: a more lozenge-shaped insert, orientated along the grain and using carefully

Fig 6.37 *A collection of waxes in different colours, used for filling small defects in the wood surface*

Fig 6.38 *A typical dead knot*

Fig 6.40 *Close-up of the repair. The rotten dead knot was bored out, and a live knot inserted; the leaves were then adjusted to camouflage the circular pattern as well as possible*

matched wood. The insert need not be very deep, depending on how much overcarving needs to be done. Cut the insert with square walls first, and match the hole to it. A tighter fit is got if the Dutchman is well dried first, expanding when glued so as to tighten the joint. This sort of repair can be very effective, especially if the carving is worked over it.

Fig 6.39 *If you look carefully at the right-hand side of this carving, a small repair is visible where a black hole appeared at the point where it was hoped only a tiny knot would be*

Fig 6.41 *The back of the carving shows the other end of the knot. By hiding the main bulk of the knot at the back in this way, what proved to be an otherwise lovely piece of wood was redeemed*

Fig 6.42 Not knots, but hollow resin channels in a piece of jelutong. Many tropical hardwoods have such channels running deeply through them, and they are not necessarily apparent on the surface

Some woods, such as jelutong, may contain pockets of resin; these resemble dead knots in appearance, and can be treated in similar ways (Fig 6.42).

DECAY

The natural cycle for a dead tree is to rot down under the onslaught of weather, insects and fungi, gradually returning its constituents to the soil.

Foxing, a yellow-brown discoloration in timber, is one of the first signs of decay and is caused by fungus infestation. **Spalting** is a mottling and lining of the wood, and can be desirable when an interesting figure is required (Fig 6.43). Spalting also represents early decay, and may contain sapwood which has

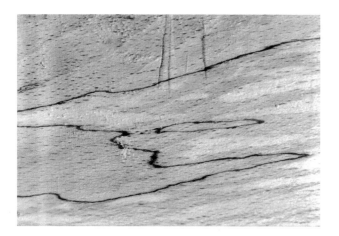

Fig 6.43 Spalted beech. Spalting usually reaches irregularly through the whole length of the piece of wood

Fig 6.44 A piece of limewood, showing the characteristic blue-grey stain or foxing caused by fungal infection

become spongy. The black lines themselves seem to be a damage-limitation response by the tree to the fungal infection. Limewood, one of the carver's favourites, is prone to bluish-grey streaks (Fig 6.44).

Wood decays most readily when:

- it is wetter than the surrounding air

- it is in contact with the soil

- it contains sapwood.

This means that, as with seasoning, wood is best stored in the dry and away from soil.

It is the chemical properties in timber which make it resistant to decay, as much as the physical ones. The chemical-rich heartwood is much more resistant to decay than sapwood. It is even, in some species, poisonous to insects and fungi. It is best not to use sapwood if it can be avoided.

WOODWORM

If you see the familiar hole, with a little sawdust plug, it means that the beetle has emerged from its pupa, strolled along the surface of the wood and probably laid its eggs close by (Fig 6.45). One hole represents lots of tunnels which were created when the previously laid eggs hatched into larvae – the 'worm' – and voraciously fed. Normally, as with most insects, woodworm activity is seasonal, but with more and more uniformity of temperature in houses, they can be active all the year round.

Fig 6.45 Anobium punctatum, *the common furniture beetle, varies in length from ⅒ to ¼in (2.5 to 6mm) and accounts for 75% of all woodworm damage in Britain. Larvae may bore around in the wood for up to 2 years, and infestation only becomes apparent when the beetle emerges, leaving a ¹⁄₁₆in (1.5mm) hole. After only 2 weeks as a beetle, a further 30 eggs may be laid*

There are several species of woodworm, some worse than others. From the biologist's point of view they are only doing their job of recycling dead wood; but from the carver's point of view, none of them is welcome.

Most woodworm prefer sapwood to heartwood, and moist wood to dry. So properly seasoned, good-quality timber is a good start to avoiding them. Also avoid leaving sapwood around the workshop.

Active woodworm holes have sawdust in them; old holes are dirty and empty (Fig 6.46). There are many colourless, proprietary agents available which can be used in a preventative way – always following the manufacturer's safety recommendations. Treat a finished piece of carving as a matter of course, before final polishing. Also treat the workshop. Filling the existing holes with wax may make new holes easier to spot.

STORAGE

The best way of keeping wood is as if it were being air-dried (see page 116). The points mentioned in that context also apply to the general storing of wood and should be referred to.

It is worth having timber in the workshop for some time before using it, whether it has been air- or kiln-dried, so as to allow it to acclimatize and settle down. Ideally the wood should be stored for a while where the carving will eventually reside, but this is not normally possible.

Beware of dry atmospheres such as those in centrally heated houses, where a lot of leisure carvers work. Keeping wood in a damp outhouse or garage, and then bringing it into a warm, very dry house is asking for trouble. Try to introduce what you need gradually – perhaps initially in a plastic bag – some time before you need it, and keep a close eye on it. Keep work covered in plastic between working sessions.

Fig 6.46 *Classic woodworm damage: the single surface holes lead to extensive tunnelling beneath. The absence of light-coloured dust suggests that these holes are not recent*

QUALITIES OF WOOD

Wood may be simply a vehicle to display the carving, as in the work of Grinling Gibbons where a figureless limewood supports the virtuosity of the designs. Conversely, the wood itself may be the source of inspiration – the sculpture a result of the carver's exploration of the material. Or there may be a point in between, where a type of wood is sought for qualities which work with a preconceived idea.

Whichever approach is taken, wood exhibits many properties that need to be considered in the carving design or as the carving is evolving. Not only do species differ in their characteristics, but individual trees and parts of the same tree differ as well. The qualities in any particular piece of wood depend on how the tree has grown. This is the same as saying that it depends on how the fibres were laid down, or the nature of the grain.

GRAIN

Grain refers to the layout of the hollow fibres in the tree. Originally, as annual rings, they conducted sap or water; later, clogged with chemicals, they performed a skeletal role. Grain fibres run the length of the tree and may be straight or twisted, bent or interlocking, or spiralling around the tree in a direction which changes every year.

Beginners find grain a little confusing at first – a little difficult to 'read'. One way to understand wood grain is by imagining the fibres as a bundle of straws. Think how you sharpen a pencil: the fibres in the pencil run parallel along its length. As you sharpen it with a knife, slicing off the end, you are working **with the grain** – the straws – the wood fibres – are pushed together and support each other, resulting in easy, clean cuts (Fig 6.47).

If you try to sharpen a pencil in the opposite direction to normal, the fibres catch and tear up, failing to support each other. You are pushing the straws apart by trying to cut **against the grain** (Fig 6.48). The expression 'against the grain' itself has the sense of going against the natural inclination of a thing. It *can* be done with a very sharp blade and taking shallow cuts; but the surface is never as good, and carvers only attempt this way if there is no alternative.

Cutting at right angles to the fibres is cutting **across the grain** (Fig 6.49). With sharp tools in some woods, this can be as clean as cutting with the grain.

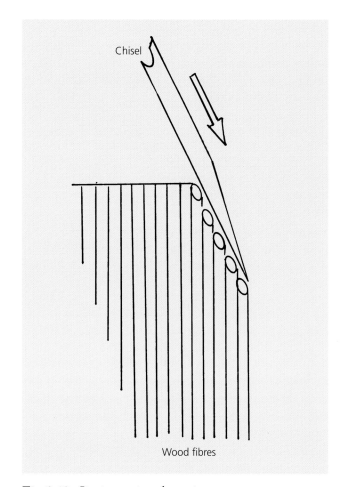

Fig 6.48 *Cutting against the grain*

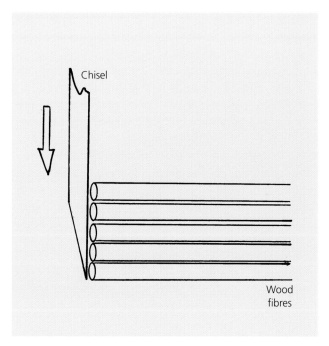

Fig 6.49 *Cutting across the grain*

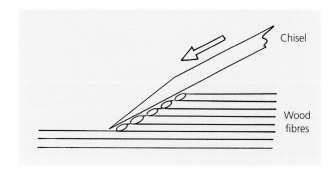

Fig 6.47 *Imagine the grain of wood as a bundle of straws: this figure shows cutting with the grain*

The grain, then, is the arrangement of fibres in a piece of wood – their direction in three dimensions. Recognizing the way the wood is modified by the lie of the grain – either by inspecting it visually in advance, or by reacting to how the wood is cutting – is a necessary skill of the carver; one only properly acquired through experience.

Carving with the grain gives the sweetest, cleanest cut; against the grain, the roughest. An experiment will further help beginners get used to the idea of grain. Using a V-tool or U-shaped gouge, cut an arcing groove in the surface of a small panel of wood, making the curve run through at least 90°. Examine the edges of the cut (Fig 6.50). At any point, one side of the groove will be shiny and the other rough, as the cut has been simultaneously with and against the lie of the fibres or the grain. Try with a sharp blade to clean the side of the groove *against* the grain. You may be successful, but not as successful as reversing the direction of the cut and taking a thin shaving with the grain.

A related term is **end grain**. Cutting across the grain reveals the hollow ends of the tube-like fibres: this is end grain (Fig 6.51). It is seen, for example, in the cross-section of the log, but is always present throughout any carving. By capillary action, end grain will soak up any finishing liquids (stains, oils, varnishes, etc.) far more than **side grain**, the walls of the fibres. Liquids pass *between* the fibres of side-grain, but not so much *into* them. Because of this different reaction to liquids, and the differing ways in which the surfaces reflect light, the end grain tends to have a darker, more matt appearance than side grain. This can be a problem, about which a little more will be said in Chapter 7 (see pages 138–9).

Besides the need to take grain into account while actually carving and in the finishing of a piece,

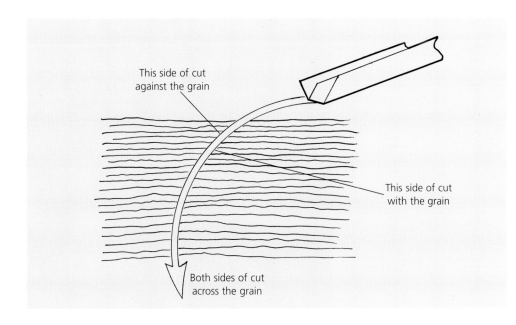

This side of cut against the grain

This side of cut with the grain

Both sides of cut across the grain

Fig 6.50 Using a V-groove to demonstrate how the direction of grain affects the surface of the cut

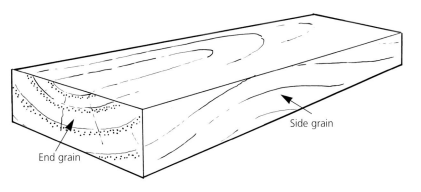

End grain

Side grain

Fig 6.51 End and side grain

grain must be considered in the design stage before any carving actually starts.

The maximum strength of wood is along the length of the fibres (**long grain**), and weakest where the fibres are shortest (**short grain** or **cross grain**). Where possible, this feature should be used to make any potentially delicate element in a carving as strong as possible: for example, by running the grain down the legs of a carved horse, or along fingers. If the grain ran in the opposite direction – across the legs – they would be significantly weaker. The short grain might not even survive the trauma of being carved.

Sometimes, if the grain can be used to strengthen one element in a carving, it is running in the wrong direction for another (Fig 6.52). Some options to deal with this problem are:

- Redesign the piece rather than risking breakage.

- Find some compromise in presenting the design to the wood, so lessening strength in one area to gain it in another.

- Find a crotched piece of wood, or a piece with an unusual run of the grain.

- Strengthen the design by 'tying' some other element to it. For example, a bird may be placed so as to touch a leaf or twig in a nonchalant way, which effectively acts as a support or brace. Some cunning is necessary to make such an artifice look unaffected (Fig 6.53).

- Glue on another piece of wood with grain going in the direction that is wanted. One very common place where this solution has been adopted, for centuries, is in the outstretched arms of a crucified Christ (or *corpus*). In such a body

Fig 6.53 *A detail of* St Joseph the Elder *by Hans Leinberger, c.1523. The depth to which wood has been removed around the book is at least 15in (380mm). This no doubt involved boring away at least some of the waste first, and a lot of cutting across the grain. The fingers are casually 'tied' to the book – beautifully supporting the otherwise weak cross grain*

Short grain across leg is weak

Long grain along the leg is strong

Fig 6.52 *This T'ang dynasty horse illustrates the problems of suiting the grain, with its longitudinal strength, to the carving*

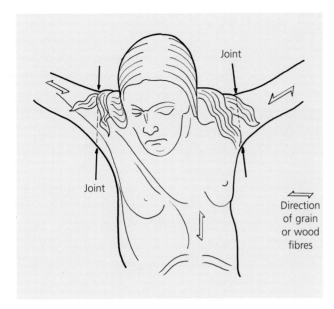

Fig 6.54 *A masterpiece such as the Gero Cross in Cologne Cathedral (970CE), which is nearly 6ft 2in (1.85m) high, must have separate arms. This is partly because no tree would match the size needed, partly for economy of material and partly for the strength gained by running the wood fibres along the arms. Careful jointing with dowels or a tenon is further obscured by the hair*

position, the grain of the arms is always at right angles to that of the body: one way long, the other short. The solution is to carve the arms, with lengthwise grain, separately from the body, joining them at the natural crease between the deltoid and biceps muscles, thus making the joint almost invisible (Fig 6.54).

- Use secret dowels and pin from behind.

- Accept the risk, but go carefully. The final piece will probably need some protection from handling or being touched. Viewers of carvings have strong tendencies to wiggle delicate bits to see how strong they are.

HARDNESS

Hardness depends on the relative air and chemical content of a piece of wood after it has been seasoned. Conductive sapwood has a lot of air, but while it is easy to cut in most species, it can be spongy and not take an edge. Heartwood, with a high chemical content, is much harder and denser. Some tropical woods, such as lignum vitae, are as hard as some kinds of stone.

Hardness also depends on the bonding of the wood fibres, giving rise to variations in flexibility, strength, and the ease with which the piece will split.

FIGURE

A cross section through a tree shows the cut ends of wood fibres laid down in annual rings. If the tree is cut in any other direction the grain of the annual rings forms a pattern – this is the figuring or **figure** of the wood.

Some woods, such as ebony, may have little or no visible figure at all; some, such as maple, have a slight, regular pattern; and yet others, like lacewood, are highly figured. English oak is prized for its silvery medullary rays (Fig 6.55); in bird's-eye maple it is the tiny knots which are the attraction. The figure is affected by how the tree has grown, from which part the wood has come, the presence of knots or burrs, and so on – making each piece unique.

Burrs or **burls** are the wart-like outgrowths seen in some species of tree, such as elm. They are like a benign tumour, with an excessive growth of numerous small twigs, possibly caused by viruses or trauma. The grain is completely haphazard within the burr, which can make for difficult shaping, although the final figuring is usually extraordinary.

Fig 6.55 *The 'silver rays' in quarter-sawn oak are a particularly prized form of figuring*

Along with figure there is the colour. This can vary greatly between heartwood and sapwood, as for example in yew; or there can be very little variation, as in ash. Colouring in wood ranges from black to white, red to yellow, and more or less any other colour as well.

How much figure or colour is wanted depends on the carver's design and intentions. Colour and figure need to match the subject of the carving. A face, normally of a uniform colour, would look strange if mottled by the use of a highly figured wood; or an otter may look best in brown or brown/red wood, rather than pale yellow.

TEXTURE

Wood is a very tactile material, attractive to the hand and feeling warm because of the insulating air within it. Woods with a more open grain, such as oak or ash, feel different from those such as box, with its tight grain and silky-smooth surface.

The openness of the grain is important when considering the amount of detail that is required in a particular carving. The more open the grain, the bolder and simpler the carving needs to be. The finest details need the tightest grain of wood (Fig 6.56). Comparing carvings from different periods in history will demonstrate this principle nicely. Different styles of carving are suited to different openness of wood grain – usually from a locally available timber. Compare carvings in, say, oak, lime or boxwood.

Fig 6.56 *Bland limewood, often being likened to cheese, will take finely detailed carving and not camouflage it with strong grain*

DURABILITY

Seasoned wood, kept dry and at an even temperature, will last far longer than most people believe is possible – witness woodcarvings found in Egyptian tombs. But this sort of case is the exception. Left to its own devices, wood follows the natural pattern of decaying, especially if left in damp conditions or in contact with the earth.

There are few woods which survive well outside. Frost, for one thing, will freeze the internal moisture and cause splitting. English oak has always been considered a very durable wood, and teak is selected for its natural protective oils – but even these will succumb to frost.

Decay can be delayed by treating outdoor woodcarvings, such as signboards, with one of the proprietary preservatives on the market, and by protecting the wood from direct confrontation with the elements. Linseed oil is a traditional preservative; thinned a little with turpentine and brushed on regularly, it tends to darken the wood considerably.

SUITABILITY OF DESIGN AND MATERIAL

Points have been made several times in this chapter about matching the material to the design of the carving. Gathering these points together as a series of questions, but not in any order of importance, will produce some helpful considerations and guidelines.

- How big will the work be? Will the wood need gluing up, or will the design fit into an available piece of timber?

- Does the carving depend on the light and shadow of a detailed design, the wood primarily being a vehicle for this; or is the wood figuring of primary importance, with a broader, more 'shaped' approach to the carving (Fig 6.57)?

- What is the relative cost and availability of the timber?

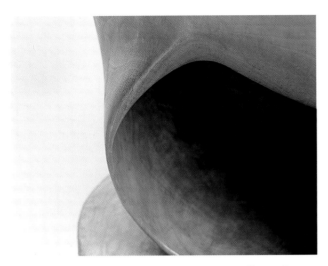

Fig 6.57 Simple, bold lines and planes are well suited to a wood such as elm

- Are you designing within your own capabilities as a carver?

- How appropriate are the figuring and colour of the wood to the design? Does the wood relate to the subject?

- How much detail needs to be held by the wood?

- How much strength is needed, and where? Is the work to be handled or not?

- Is a highly polished finish wanted, or some rougher texture?

- Is the carving to be eaten from? (A tight-grained and flavourless wood, such as sycamore, is needed in this case.)

- Is the finished work to reside outside or inside?

- Will the wood have any effect on your carving tools? (Some tropical woods contain calcium deposits which may blunt tool edges.)

A few woods, such as the rosewoods and cocobolo, are allergenic, and the dust of others, such as iroko, affects some people adversely.

In the past, generations of carvers would evolve designs that worked well with the local woods they, of necessity, had to use. They would select from among a few species which were known to 'work'. The wood itself was often painted or gilded; a 'natural' surface would have been considered unfinished. The idea of 'wood for wood's sake' is a new one.

Your own opinions about the use of any tropical hardwoods need to be considered, and perhaps enquiries made into the origins of the wood you want to use. Today the world, like the number of trees in it, is shrinking and many more woods are available and consumed by carvers. Never forget that wood is a 'renewable resource' only if it is replanted or encouraged to regenerate naturally.

CHOICE OF WOOD

There is very little wood that cannot be carved; it is doubtful if there is a timber out there that someone, at some time or other, has not had a go at carving.

Most trade carvers use a limited range of wood, perhaps half a dozen species. Instrument makers may only ever want to carve one species for one part of the instrument. Some sculptors make a point of working with as wide a range of wood as possible.

Although established carvers will know what woods they want, the approach taken here is intended for newcomers and is based on how we all acquire knowledge: from others and from our own experience. Some books on carving give great lists of woods, with statistical columns of comparable qualities. My view is that newcomers to carving have never found this approach particularly helpful. For a start, there is too much material (what does an 'average density of X' really mean, anyway?). Even within a species, there are trees and parts of trees deviating from the general characteristics. This is not to deny that knowledge of general characteristics is important or helpful.

Rather than give such lists of wood, another approach may be found more helpful to those starting woodcarving, and unsure about which wood to choose.

- Begin by not worrying too much; see yourself exploring wood in the same way you are exploring everything else: the carving tools, the designs and the techniques.

- In the beginning, when you are finding your way around tools, how they work and so on, find one or two species of famously carver-friendly wood. Use well-seasoned wood, with little figure – not too hard, nor too soft; clean and knot-free – on which to practise and experiment with the tools. Limewood, fruitwood such as pear, basswood (American lime) and walnut are examples. Avoid the pines and the oaks – extremes of soft and hard – to begin with.

- As you start becoming familiar with tools and handling them, and start to design and widen your ideas – look. Look at carvings in books and magazines with a magnifying glass. Best of all, examine carvings *in situ*. Look at old and contemporary work: both the design and the wood, and how the two aspects work together. Store up this information in your heart and mind. So many carvers have gone before you and have left an enormous resource of visible information for you to mull over. Meet other carvers, possibly in local carving clubs, and exchange ideas.

- Using what has been said in this chapter as a guide, and your increasing knowledge, start exploring species of wood, one by one, as you feel the need. Start collecting bits of wood wherever you find them until you have a small stock readily available for designs as they arise. Explore ways of dealing with defects and problems.

In this way knowledge grows slowly but surely into a natural appreciation of wood and its suitability for particular designs and uses.

SOURCES OF WOOD

Wood is technically the fibrous 'woody' matter which constitutes the bole, trunk, branches, twigs and even leaf veins of a tree. **Timber** is the term for this woody material in usable quantities, especially after conversion.

If you are not 'growing your own', there are two sources of wood for the carver:

'FREE' WOOD

It is not unusual for carvers to be given wood, as many people prefer to give it away rather than burn it. Logs will have to be converted and seasoned.

The wood in old and second-hand furniture tends to be dried out and more brittle than it was originally. Scrape off the varnish rather than sanding the wood.

For those inclined to sculpture, woodlands and driftwood from beaches need be their only source (Fig 6.58). All found wood should be washed with warm water, and a soft brush used to remove the dirt and salt. Be careful to dry the wood as slowly as possible.

Fig 6.58 *Some carvers only ever work with free 'natural' wood*

Other sources include beams from demolition sites, reclamation yards, railway sleepers (railroad ties) and so on.

BUYING WOOD

Wood is often bought by a carver to suit a particular design. Wood that is bought from a specialist supplier can be seen and inspected, some aspects of its quality are guaranteed, and there should be an assurance about its seasoning and moisture content.

Carving is labour-intensive, and the cost of the wood is usually only a small part of the overall cost of a project. Carvers, probably more than most woodworkers, can therefore afford to spend money on the right wood for a particular job. It is always a great shame to lose a carving – not to mention the time – by using inferior wood as a cheaper expedient.

There are quite a few timber yards today that advertise in woodworking magazines. Some make a point of serving the woodcarver or turner, and sell smaller, selected stuff; often the manager has a personal interest in the craft. Such firms often produce catalogues, and may have a mail-order service.

Check out all the local timber yards too. They vary tremendously in how helpful they are and what they stock. Most are reluctant to sell less than whole boards; nevertheless, as the definition of a 'board' can vary considerably, it is always worth asking what they have in stock. Clubbing together with other woodcarvers can be a useful approach.

SELECTING THE WOOD

It is always best to select the wood yourself, even if you are a newcomer to the job – you can see shakes and knots as well as the next person (Fig 6.59). Take along a block plane or spokeshave, as you will normally be allowed to clean a small area of a selected board for closer inspection. Do not leave the selection to someone who has no interest in what you are doing, but is only interested in selling you a lump of wood quickly, before their tea break. Try to find out their least busy time of day and enlist their help or interest.

Hardwoods in Britain are sold in cubic feet, with allowances made for the **waney edge**, bark and splits.

Fig 6.59 *A carefully selected stack of timber for a large carved panel*

This is a comparative measure to which all the odd sizes are converted for pricing. Although softwoods are now sold in metric sizes in the UK, metric hardwoods are some way off as yet.

One cubic foot could represent a board in any of the following shapes:

- 1in (25mm) thick x 12ft (3.6m) long x 12in (300mm) wide

- 2in (50mm) thick x 6ft (1.8m) long x 12in (300mm) wide

- 3in (75mm) thick x 3ft (0.9m) long x 12in (300mm) wide

- 4in (100mm) thick x 1ft 6in (0.45m) long x 12in (300mm) wide.

Remember that you may be dealing with nominal sizes, as sawn from the tree. Shrinkage should have been allowed for, but this needs checking, especially if an accurate planed dimension is needed. Wood may be warped, bent, etc. – another reason for seeing what you are buying.

As a last point, buy wood from properly managed, sustained sources. It can no longer be thought of as simply 'growing on trees'.

GLUING UP

FUNDAMENTALS

You might want to glue wood together for a variety of reasons:

- to arrive at the size of wood you need

- to get an appropriate direction of grain

- to economize on time and waste

- to avoid the instability inherent in a single, large piece of wood, which may contain a mixture of heartwood and sapwood.

So, gluing gives control over the following aspects:

- size

- stability

- grain direction

- waste.

Plain glued joints – which rely on the glue for strength, with no mechanical advantage from the shape of the joint – are usually all that is needed (Fig 6.60).

There are many excellent woodworking glues available today, often stronger than the wood itself, and easy to use. PVA (polyvinyl acetate) or 'white' glues are the most suitable for carvers, giving permanent and strong joints. Some of these glues are suitable for both indoor and outdoor use.

Urea-formaldehyde-based glues (Cascamite is an example) are excellent for outside use. To some degree they are space-filling, but with their brittle, crystalline nature they do tend to take the edge off carving tools, so they should be used with caution.

There are specialized glues which will stick wet wood with up to 25% moisture content. An example is Balcotan, which is used in boat building – it actually reacts with the water in the wood. This is more expensive than white glue, and can be used if there is any doubt about the dryness of the timber.

All glues have an 'open time' when the joint can be adjusted. They then pass through a curing

Fig 6.60 *If you look carefully you can see the join. In fact there are a total of six joints in the oak making up this king's head, but the careful colour and grain matching, and the overcarving, will render them more or less invisible*

stage, during which time the joint should be clamped and rendered immovable. At some point the jointed wood can safely be handled, with the final, fully cured strength developing later. Details of these times and stages, the optimum drying conditions, and the shelf-life of the glue, will appear on the container.

Glues work by:

- chemically bonding to the fibres of the wood

- soaking between the fibres and setting around them.

Consider the following points before gluing:

- With the exception of the specialist glue mentioned above, glues are susceptible to the surrounding temperature and moisture. Always read the information on the bottle or pack.

- Gluing fibres end to end forms a very weak joint that needs dowelling or strengthening in some way. Fibres glued side to side produce the strongest bond.

- The more closely the two surfaces fit, the stronger the joint. It is worth taking that extra bit of trouble over preparing the surfaces. Once carved, a joint which has 'sprung' can be very difficult to reglue or clamp up.

- The harder or denser the wood, the greater the pressure of clamping that is needed to get the glue to penetrate the fibres.

- Glue will not penetrate naturally oily woods (such as teak or pitch pine) particularly well, as most glues are water-based. The surfaces to be glued need washing several times with methanol (methylated spirits, denatured alcohol) beforehand, and the corner of a chisel can be used to raise small 'keys' of grain.

CONTROLLING MOVEMENT

When two pieces of wood are glued together, either face to face or edge to edge, they continue to 'move' as separate items. It is important to consider how any piece of wood will perform in the context of the whole; how the movement can be minimized, or one movement made to compensate for another.

The best solution is to use quarter-sawn boards, but these are not necessarily available. Problems may arise in the following situations:

- when different species of wood are used, which shrink and expand by differing amounts

- when grain runs in different directions, so movements are working against each other (Fig 6.61)

- when different cuts from the same tree are used, for example mixing slash-sawn with quarter-sawn wood (Fig 6.62)

- when the moisture content differs between the pieces of wood, with one being less seasoned than the other.

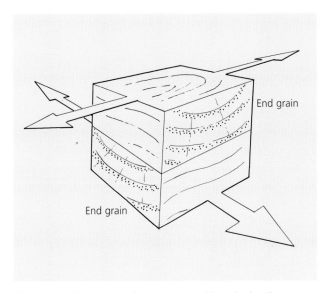

Fig 6.61 *The principal movements of boards that have been glued with fibres running in contrary directions will be antagonistic*

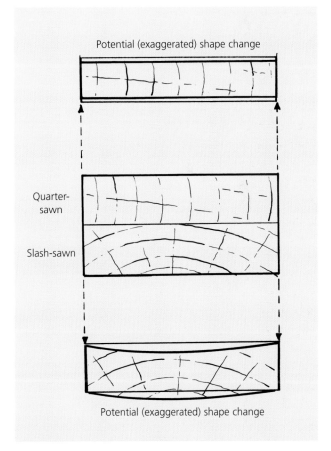

Fig 6.62 *A joint using different cuts from the tree may give rise to stress problems because the individual pieces move differently*

TYPES OF JOINT

The plain glued joints that carvers use take the following forms:

EDGE TO EDGE

This sort of joint is used in panels. It may be **rubbed** – in which case one piece is left perched neatly on top of the other – or clamped, using sash cramps to pull the joint tight. 'Rubbing' is literally that: air and excess glue are squeezed out by rubbing one piece of wood against the other until the joint is felt to stick, which is when the glue starts to be absorbed.

Arrange the grain so that each plank warps or moves in the opposite direction to the one next to it (Fig 6.63). The movement between boards is mutually compensating. Sometimes a wide plank is split into narrow ones to avoid excess movement and give the panel greater overall stability.

FACE TO FACE

This sort of joint is used to create a solid bulk of wood. For example, a block 10in (250mm) thick can be laminated from five 2in (50mm) boards. Again, allow for movement; but this time the movement needs to be complementary (Fig 6.64). The clamping pressure needed is much greater than for edge joints, as it is spread over a wider surface and a certain amount of pressure is always needed to force the glue between fibres (Fig 6.65). The more open the grain, the more easily the glue will penetrate. In this sort

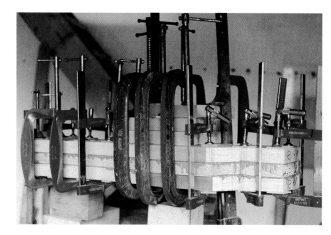

Fig 6.65 Gluing boards face to face requires large pressures to ensure that the glue penetrates the wood fibres sufficiently

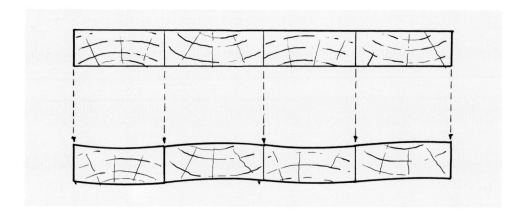

Fig 6.63 Gluing boards edge to edge with grain directions alternated to allow compensatory movement

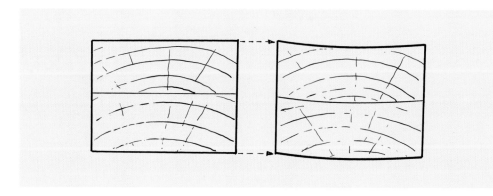

Fig 6.64 Boards glued face to face must move in the same direction

of clamping, with wide surfaces, there is more risk of using too few clamps than too many.

FLATS

Flats are small surfaces on a carving to which a carver sticks extra pieces of wood, building out a certain section for effect. In these cases, offcuts from the original wood are kept and the grain closely matched. A rubbed joint may be all that is necessary. Small C-clamps made from bedspring coils are also helpful.

END GRAIN

Where end grain needs to be fixed to side grain, for example in a crucifix or a bird's wing, dowels, dowel screws or some type of mortise and tenon joint is needed to achieve mechanical strength.

BASIC PROCEDURES

- Always do a dry run to check the equipment, the set-up, and the order of doing things.

- Check the matching of grain, not only from the point of view of movement but also for colour, figure, etc. Unless it is a feature, the joint should be as neat and invisible as possible (Fig 6.66). Take enough time over this, as gluing is difficult to undo. A thicker glue line is a weaker one – the more closely the fibres are in contact, the better.

Fig 6.66 *Careful grain-matching should make the joints almost invisible once they have been carved over*

- Design the carving so as to put the glue line where it is least noticeable: in a shadow or groove, and not, for example, down the centre of a face.

- Remember that a glue line cut at right angles only shows as a hair line; whereas if the glue line is cut along its length to any extent, a thicker line appears.

- Enough even pressure is needed to squeeze the glue out all around the glue line, but excessive pressure will squeeze out too much glue, leaving the joint dry.

- Wipe away excess glue with a damp cloth to allow the glue line full access to the air.

- Store the glue in the right conditions according to the maker's recommendations. Some glues have a limited shelf life.

SUMMARY

This chapter sets down some basic information that carvers need to know about their material. But how much do carvers really need to know about wood?

One answer to this question is that it is not possible to know too much about the material you are working in – but it is possible to know too little. The consequences of knowing too little will be some adverse effect on a carving: the wood splitting through inadequate seasoning; a disastrous result from staining; the wood failing to meet the needs of the design, and breaking; or the shadows of the form being camouflaged by an uncontrolled grain.

Knowledge will reduce the risk of meeting these hazards. And knowledge best comes with the natural flow of experience, which hopefully is enjoyable and the result of exploration and challenge.

CHAPTER SEVEN

FINISHING

AIMS

- To look at why surface applications are used, and at some of their effects

- To describe some basic, straightforward and reliable finishes, applicable to most carvings

- To suggest some alternative areas for experimentation

In this context 'finishing' refers to the surface treatment of a carving, after all toolwork or sanding has been completed. There is not the space in this book to deal with finishing in detail; this would need a book in itself. For example, gilding – a traditional complement to carved work – is a craft in its own right (Figs 7.1 and 7.2).

As a preliminary point, experimentation is very important. The final appearance of a carving will depend on a combination of:

- the surface texture of the carving

- the colour and quality of the wood itself

- the type of finish that has been applied.

Leaving the wood surface straight from the chisel or sanding it are only two of the options available to the experimenting carver or sculptor (Figs 7.3 and 7.4). Before applying a finish, consider using the following: texturing with wire brushes; burning and brushing; frosting or using rotary burrs; inlaying other materials. There are many possibilities to be consciously explored.

The natural colours of some species of wood will combine with that of the applied finish to affect the final colour of the carving. There are many different finishes that can be used to achieve the effect the carver wants, from simple waxes to chemicals and colours. Always try the finish out on some hidden part first to avoid unexpected results.

The surface of the wood reflects light (Fig 7.5), so whatever effect the wood surface has been given prior

Fig 7.1 *Gilded robes in a relief carving by Veit Stoss in the Lorenzkirche, Nürnberg, Germany (c.1517). Extravagant use of gold has turned the wood surface into a swirling field of energy*

Fig 7.2 *A little gold can go a long way: part of* The Assumption *by the brothers Asam, completed in 1750 in the Rohr Abbey Church, Bavaria. The* theatrum sacrum *is evoked by the richness of surface and colour as much as the subject. Before Protestant times, little wood was left unpainted in churches*

to the finish will affect how the light is reflected. This in turn will alter the appearance of the finish. For example, all woods tend to darken when oils and polishes are applied, and porous end grain will darken more than less absorbent side grain. The final cut of a sharp chisel closes the pores and smooths the surface of the wood; this has a different effect on finishes, compared with sanding.

Fig 7.4 *Detail of a headboard in limewood. In this sort of work, where a smooth, polished finish is needed, sandpaper is used to remove tool marks from the surface*

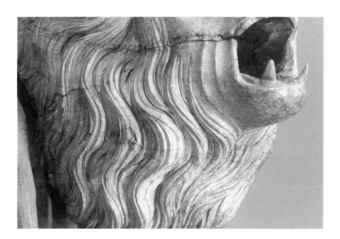

Fig 7.3 *The lion's mane from* Death Astride a Lion, *carved for a bell tower in southern Germany in about 1400. Vigorous use of gouge and V-tool leaves a surface texture which needs no finish to enliven it. A split to the side of the mouth has been repaired with wooden inserts and overcarved; a plugged knot hole has been filled poorly at a later date*

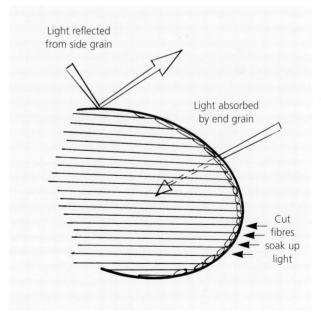

Fig 7.5 *The cut of the fibres in the wood affects the absorption of finishes and how the carving appears after their application*

REASONS FOR FINISHING

Woodcarvings from the earliest known onwards were **polychromed** – that is, coloured or painted to look lifelike. The wood itself was only a supporting medium for the coloured skin of 'reality' (Fig 7.6). Even Greek marble sculpture was polychromed in this way.

During the middle ages, woodcarvers began to leave their work uncoloured, perhaps only burnishing it with a handful of shavings or a tool handle; sometimes sharkskin was used. Both Grinling Gibbons and Tilman Riemenschneider of Würzburg used simple varnishes to seal what was otherwise the natural appearance of the wood. The woods used were plain, and a foil for decorative and detailed carving. Since that time, many have thought that carvings need no

Fig 7.7 Jennifer Rung, Sielunpeili (The Mirror of the Soul), 25 x 15in (630 x 380mm). Carved in burled birch and finished in mixed water stains, sanded back to allow the natural wood to show through, followed by coats of shellac and beeswax. There is a dreamlike quality to the twelve eyes carved into the wood; a thirteenth takes the form of a mirror, in which to view yourself

Fig 7.6 Back of Der Englische Gruß *(The Angelic Salutation) by Veit Stoss in the Lorenzkirche, Nürnberg, Germany (c.1517). The wood is subservient to the colour as Stoss tries to make his subjects real; this is very different from the majority of modern carving, which leaves the wood uncoloured*

more additional polish than that coming from use and handling – and, indeed, one way of finishing is not to 'finish' at all.

Today, there is a further change of taste and appreciation, with a greater variety of interesting and exotic woods available to be carved – some particularly prized for their beauty and figuring – as well as an abundance of new finishing agents. Many carvings are enhanced or even 'made' by the finish. It is rare now to find a carving that has not been treated in some way (Figs 7.7 and 7.8).

There are three principal reasons for finishing:

PROTECTING

By filling the pores between the wood fibres, the wood is protected from picking up dirt and grease, especially that acquired through handling. The patina left from either of these sources may leave naked wood looking dull and grubby. Often the same areas of a carving are fingered repeatedly, so that the colour begins to appear irregular in a way that detracts from the overall appearance.

Protection may include a prophylactic treatment against woodworm .

Fig 7.8 Judith Nicoll, Barn Owl, life-size. Carved in Louisiana tupelo, following detailed research, with measurements and colours taken from preserved skins. Each wing is carved separately so that the grain runs down the thin, contoured flight feathers. The feathers are textured with knives and rotary tools, burnt with a fine pyrography nib and then painted with acrylics. The mouse is carved from jelutong, with fish backbones for whiskers and a brass tail. For any wildlife carving to have such an impact requires from the carver a strong sense of dynamic form and narrative, and an extraordinarily painstaking attention to details and finish

SEALING

Sealing wood inhibits or slows down the transfer of moisture between its surface and the air. Centrally heated houses can be very dry, and workshops damp. The woodcarving, if sealed, remains in a fairly well-controlled environment and is not so vulnerable to ambient moisture changes.

ENHANCING

Whether the finish is a simple application of a sealer or the sandblasting, burning and colour-staining used on some sculptures, the finish itself must enhance the work. To put it another way: if the finish detracts from the appearance of the carving, there is no point in using it.

A carving which has taken days, weeks, even months to complete may be ruined in a few minutes by applying the wrong finish. Many a carver, having been impatient to finish a job, has regretted not making a few experiments on similar waste wood first.

SOME SIMPLE FINISHES

The following basic treatments, while not particularly adventurous, have been used successfully by myself for many years. They may be all that your carvings ever need.

Lacquers or varnishes that produce a synthetic, glossy appearance cannot be recommended for woodcarvings – except occasionally as a special effect (Figs 7.9 and 7.10).

Fig 7.9 Snail in butternut, width 15in (380mm). The 'hill' is the original wood, just waxed. The shell is bleached, sealed with a matt (flat) acrylic varnish and clear wax. The snail itself is finished with washes of watercolour greens, rubbed back and gloss-varnished

Fig 7.10 *Detail of the snail's head. The surface is punched all over to get the texture – notice that the eyestalks are left smooth for contrast. It's the gloss varnish which does the trick: snails are slimy*

Remember that all toolwork or sanding needs to be completed *thoroughly* before finishing. Oils and (especially) stains will make any torn grain, sanding scratches, cutting faults, tool or file marks stand out.

SHELLAC

Shellac is made from lac, a resinous substance exuded by an insect (*Coccus lacca*) in the course of laying its eggs. It is collected, crushed, melted, filtered and sold in flakes. The shellac is then dissolved in methylated spirits (denatured alcohol) to make the usable liquid. Shellac can be bought already made up. Button polish, white polish and sanding sealer are all based on shellac. It is used in the French-polishing of furniture – which is not our concern here.

Shellac dries quickly on the wood as the alcohol evaporates, without raising the grain fibres. Working with it needs an efficient speed. There is a choice between natural shellac, which is orange or brown, and clear, transparent shellac which has been bleached. The choice will depend on the lightness or darkness of the wood. Brown shellac will enrich the darker woods.

APPLYING SHELLAC

1. Make sure the wood is completely dry before applying the shellac.

2. Apply the liquid with a brush, which has to be cleaned with methylated spirits (denatured alcohol). As shellac dries quickly, work systematically with the grain, keeping a 'live edge' into which subsequent brush strokes can be worked.

3. Several thin coats are better than one thick one, leaving 30 to 60 minutes between coats. When dry, the shellac can be lightly cut back with the finest wire wool (no. 0000). Brush or vacuum the dust off carefully; do not blow.

Shellac will seal wood after oiling or prior to waxing. It cannot be mixed with water, nor is it waterproof; water will stain it.

OIL

Oil finishes look best on hardwoods. **Linseed oil** is the most common oil used in this context. It dries in contact with the air in the wood to form a skin; it may react with the chemicals in the wood as well – usually to the benefit of the appearance. Oils will not raise the wood grain.

One disadvantage of oil is that it makes any figuring more prominent, compared to, say, a simple wax finish. Limewood, for example, may look streaky. I would strongly advise testing the finish beforehand on waste wood.

Linseed oil comes in a raw or boiled state. The boiled oil is thicker, penetrates more slowly and dries faster than raw linseed oil. To make the application of these oils easier and to get them to penetrate the wood quicker, they need diluting with pure turpentine. Dilute three parts raw linseed oil with about one part turpentine; dilute boiled linseed oil with equal parts of turpentine. Keep these drying oils in sealed jars to prevent them forming a skin.

APPLYING LINSEED OIL

1. Apply the diluted oil – fairly warm if possible – with a soft brush on to the clean, dry, bare wood and allow it to soak in. A safe way to warm it is by placing the oil bottle in a bowl of hot water for a few minutes.

2 Keep brushing on the oil until it starts to remain on the surface. Leave for 10 minutes and then wipe off the excess with a cloth. Do not allow oil to stand in pools.

0 After several coats the oil will penetrate less and less as the wood becomes saturated. Wipe off the excess and, taking a clothes brush, vigorously brush the surface. As the oil dries, brush regularly to bring up the polished sheen. Keep a brush especially for burnishing oiled finishes.

One method used by some carvers is to submerge the carving completely in linseed oil, which may then be heated up slowly to assist the oil's penetration into the wood. When bubbles no longer arise from the carving it is considered saturated and should be removed and thoroughly wiped off. This is perhaps useful for smaller carvings.

It is worth mentioning a few other oils:

Tung oil (China wood oil) is a natural oil, more expensive than linseed but more water- and heat-resistant; it can be used instead of linseed oil.

Teak oil is a blend of natural oils and solvents developed originally for teakwood, and is light brown in colour. It dries quicker than linseed oil but added pigments will affect the end grain of lighter woods, making them look grubby and oily.

Danish oil contains resin-based hardeners that make the oil go off quickly to form a hard shell that is resistant to wear. It cannot be applied to a waxed surface (as linseed oil can) to freshen it up. Like teak oil, it may affect the end grain of lighter woods.

Walnut oil is used for carved vessels and other food containers, as it is an edible oil that dries with a nutty aroma.

After oiling as described above, a coat or two of shellac will seal the surface further, prior to waxing. Shellac is not affected by oil as it is by water. The advantage of sealing in the oil is that the carving can then be handled and the surface kept clean. The oil continues to dry and 'cure' with the air in the wood itself.

WAXES

There are three sorts of waxes, depending on their origin:

- mineral, e.g. benzene or paraffin wax
- vegetable, e.g. carnauba wax
- animal, e.g. beeswax.

White **paraffin wax** can be used where a completely bland or clear finish is needed, although beeswax is also available in a bleached form. Mineral wax brushed on to the ends of timber will inhibit the drying process, in which case it can be dissolved in white spirit (mineral spirit). A little mineral wax added to beeswax will make the beeswax harder.

Silicon waxes, made into commercial polishes with all sorts of additives, cannot be recommended.

Carnauba wax comes from a Brazilian palm. It dries to a very hard finish and, again, a little added to beeswax will give a tougher finish. Carnauba is too hard and brittle to use on its own.

Beeswax is a well-tried finish for carvings, although it is maintained by some museums that this

Fig 7.11 *Pure beeswax and turpentine are the only ingredients needed for a basic wax polish. Once mixed to the desired consistency, keep it sealed from the air to prevent the turpentine evaporating*

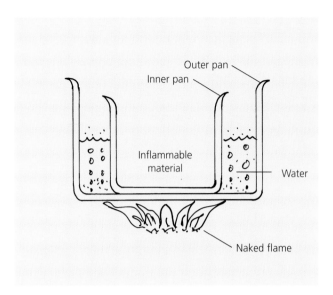

Fig 7.12 A double boiler prevents inflammable substances overheating and igniting on a naked flame

wax (and its vehicle, turpentine) oxidizes with air over time, to the actual detriment of the wood. It is the principal wax for finishing carvings, and can also be used to repair small surface checks. It is a soft, yellow wax which melts at a low temperature; it does not seal the pores well, and tends to pick up dirt and show water marks. Bare wood should therefore always be sealed before waxing, and the wax left to dry thoroughly before handling.

Beeswax needs to be dissolved in pure turpentine to make it soft enough to apply; as the turpentine evaporates, so the wax is left to harden (Fig 7.11).

MAKING BEESWAX POLISH

Heat is needed to dissolve the wax properly and, as turpentine is very flammable, *wax polish must always be made up in a double boiler – not over direct heat or a naked flame*. A double boiler consists of a container with the inflammable substances to be warmed or mixed, placed inside another container with heated water (Fig 7.12). Although called a 'boiler', the water will not necessarily be boiling; with beeswax it need only be hot to very hot. The outside, heated container will obviously be a metal pan, but the inner vessel can be polythene or plastic. This system of heating ensures that the turpentine never rises to a flash temperature and is safely placed to warm up and mix with the beeswax.

Method

❶ Grate up the beeswax and spread it out evenly on the bottom of the inner container. Adding about 5% carnauba wax to the beeswax greatly increases its hardness and resistance to dirt.

❷ Pour in the pure turpentine until the wax is just submerged.

❸ Warm up the mixture in the double boiler on the stove, with the windows open, or simply add boiling water to the outer container. Stir as the wax melts to a creamy paste.

❹ Take a little out and allow it to cool; examine the consistency. Add more turpentine for a thinner consistency, more wax for a thicker consistency.

❺ If your beeswax is from a beekeeper, unrefined (the wax, not the beekeeper), pass the melted wax through muslin to remove impurities.

❻ Store in an airtight container.

APPLYING BEESWAX POLISH

❶ Apply the creamy wax to the carving with a soft brush, after sealing with oil or shellac. Work it well into the corners but prevent them filling or clogging – once the wax is dry these are difficult to clean out. A toothbrush is useful for small details (Fig 7.13).

Fig 7.13 It is a good idea to keep separate brushes for polishing oil or wax finishes. Keep another brush entirely for brushing bare wood

② Use a soft brush, such as a clothes brush, to burnish the surface vigorously – it is a good idea to keep a brush especially for this purpose. The waxed wood will remain sticky for some time and should not be handled.

③ After 24 hours a second coat can be applied with clean, fine (no. 0000) wire wool, which cuts back the first coat.

④ After another 24 hours, brush the carving again and allow the wax to dry. The carving can then be polished with a cotton cloth.

COLOUR

The use of pigments in the form of stains and dyes to add colour to all, or part, of a carving, is a subject that needs more space to cover than is available here. However, a few notes may be a helpful start to an exploration of stains or dyes.

The terms **stain** and **dye** are to all intents synonymous for carvers (though a distinction is sometimes made between stains, consisting of a suspension of solid pigments which sits on top of the wood, and dyes, consisting of fully dissolved material which penetrates the wood). Stains can be bought already made up or in powder form, in a huge variety of colours. Clothes dyes, watercolours and oil paints also work on wood. Improvised dyes made from household materials can be surprisingly effective (Figs 7.14 and 7.15).

There are three main types of stain, depending on the medium which carries the pigment: water-based, oil based and spirit-based stains. The same medium is also used if any further dilution is required.

Fig 7.14 Buddha sculpture in English oak, height 30in (760mm). The wood was reclaimed and badly stained with blue in parts in the robes, making particularly unpleasant multicoloured joints. I bleached the blue from the wood and stained the robes with… coffee. The face and body, hands and feet were just waxed

Fig 7.15 Head of the previous sculpture. Coffee gives just the right tone for oak, put on in many diluted coats to achieve the depth of colour I wanted, with Danish oil and wax to finish

WATER-BASED STAINS

Water-based stains have the pigments dissolved in water; their characteristics include:

- good penetration into the wood

- quick drying by evaporation, with a risk of tide marks or overlap marks

- compatibility with further finishes (but sealing is needed first)

- a tendency to raise the wood grain; this makes them most suitable for sanded carvings, which need dampening first with clean water, then drying and resanding.

OIL-BASED STAINS

These have their pigments dissolved in linseed oil and turpentine; their characteristics include:

- poorer penetration into the wood compared to water-based stains

- longer drying times, so there is no danger of tide marks or overlap marks.

- Sealing with shellac or wax is needed – but be warned that not all finishes are accepted, so some trials will be necessary.

- They do not raise the wood grain, which makes them suitable for carvings that are not going to be sanded.

SPIRIT-BASED STAINS

Spirit-based stains have the pigments dissolved in methanol; their characteristics include:

- poor penetration

- very quick drying, so overlap marks are easily created; the drying can be slowed by adding a little shellac-based polish.

- After sealing, further finishes can be applied.

- They do not raise the grain, so they are suitable for carvings left from the chisel.

The colour of the wood itself will affect the final colour of the stain: stains appear darker:

- when wet

- on a rough surface

- on end grain.

So work the colour in thin coats, allowing the wood to dry in between, so you can see what is happening. Do test some spare wood first, as stains are very difficult to remove (Fig 7.16).

Wood can be bleached before colouring to remove natural colour and strong figuring. The 'two-part' bleaches are strongest, but need great care in use.

Fig 7.16 A 'colour stick' on which several different dilutions of the same dye have been tested

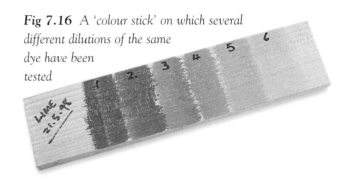

Fig 7.17 A detail of The Banquet at Simon's *by Riemenschneider (1490–2). Note the subtly stained background in the windows which, together with the sketch lines of the V-tool around the outside, adds to the depth of relief. It is not known to what extent the equivalent of sandpaper was available at this time, but it is thought that materials such as sharkskin might have been used to smooth over already well-flattened surfaces*

Fig 7.18 *For a* trompe-l'œil *carving like my life-size lobster, it might be more appropriate to stain the subject and leave the background plain. A red dye was used, followed by wax, and a little gilt wax for highlights*

Staining some parts of a carving only – for example, backgrounds – while leaving other parts natural wood, can look very interesting (Figs 7.17 and 7.18).

FUMING

Fuming is an old method of darkening oak that depends on this wood's ability to react with ammonia. Originally done by hanging the wood in stables to react with horse urine, or painting with the same, today fuming is undertaken in a tightly enclosed space with a discreet bowl of ammonia accompanying the carving (Fig 7.19). Start with a piece of waste wood, testing various quantities of diluted ammonia and varying lengths of time.

SAFETY

The shellac, oil and wax finishes and stains discussed above are safe enough if due care is taken. Use common sense and proceed conscientiously.

- Follow all instructions and advice on packages, especially with bleaches and other caustic finishes. Some firms produce leaflets and guidelines for using their products.

- Use and store turpentine, spirit- and oil-based stains, as well as all other finishes, in well-ventilated areas.

- Keep containers closed when not in use; keep them away from children, and away from heat and naked flames.

- All brushes should be cleaned properly, and used rags sealed in plastic bags and disposed of away from the workshop. It is not unknown for rags in some circumstances to spontaneously combust.

- Avoid inhaling the vapours, or allowing vapours to contact skin and eyes. If contact is made with the eyes, irrigate them fully with lots of fresh water and seek medical advice if necessary.

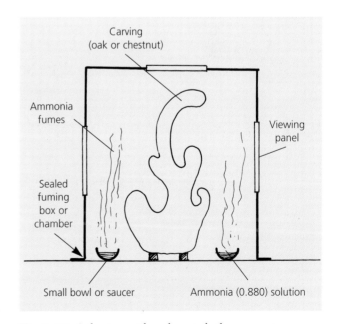

Fig 7.19 *A fuming cupboard controls the ammonia vapours in contact with the carving*

CHAPTER EIGHT

RESEARCH AND DESIGN

AIMS

- To encourage the use of drawing, clay modelling and other forms of preliminary study, which will help you to work better in the craft even though they are not acts of carving in themselves

RESEARCH

When carving something which is intended to represent something else, adequate research is essential: partly for the belief and appreciation of the viewer, but also to help you plan the process of carving itself (Fig 8.1). It is difficult to carve wood which has already been carved away.

Fig 8.1 *To visualize clearly what you want to carve, it helps to have lots of information: photographs, sketches and working drawings – even the original (or parts of it), where possible. The next stage might be a model*

Say, for instance, the carving is to be of a squirrel. Few people can sit down and draw a convincing squirrel in three dimensions, let alone carve one. Our brains recognize the real world by the smallest of clues – a bushy tail may be all you need to identify a squirrel as it disappears up a tree – but much more information is needed to carve one (or even catch one). And how much more information is needed for a complicated subject such as *The Death of the Great Northumbrian Hero, Siward*?

Research means looking at squirrels (or whatever) as closely as possible. Look at them in life, in books; handle a squirrel if possible; look at how other artists have dealt with this and similar subjects; draw them and model them – anything to understand the subject better. This is particularly important with wildlife carvings – what looks like an interesting line to the carver may be a shootable condition to a horse fancier.

DRAWING

I have come across many woodcarving students who think drawing (and modelling for that matter) is a waste of time, saying, 'Well, it's not *carving*, is it?' I counter this attitude with three thoughts.

The first is a question: Where does a woodcarving start? Certainly not when the gouge bites the wood. A woodcarving starts with an idea. And between this idea and the final result lies a lot of work: catching the idea, working it out, planning the project (Fig 8.2). Drawing is indispensable for saving time and effort, and preventing mistakes.

The second is that carving, whether relief or sculpture in the round, is about light and shadow (Fig 8.3). In turn, this is as much about the nature of seeing itself as about carving. We understand about a three-dimensional form because of the lights and shadows, and we understand a relief carving because

of the outline. Drawing helps you see this world of form more clearly.

Thirdly, what if you have limited time and opportunity to carve? The chances are you will still have no problem finding moments to put pencil to paper and draw. Without doubt, drawing (and modelling) is the most important thing to practice, outside of carving itself, for developing your carving skills.

Unfortunately, drawing fills many carving students with dread. Perhaps you recognize this in yourself. You see yourself as 'inartistic'; you have never been taught, or forgot whatever you learned at school. More than likely, you have a wrong view of what it is that you need to achieve *as a carver*. We are not talking gallery-standard, accomplished fine art; for

Fig 8.2 *Detail from the Marienaltar in Creglingen, southern Germany, carved by Tilman Riemenschneider between 1505 and 1510. Onlookers who have never tried to carve wood often fail to appreciate the background of draughtsmanship and (usually) modelling that makes such work exude confidence*

Fig 8.3 *The play of light and shade brings life to the billowing cloak of the risen Christ in this detail from Riemenschneider's* Crucifixion *altar at Detwang, near Rothenburg on the Tauber*

woodcarving this is not necessary. Our drawings are a means to an end – the woodcarving – and the act of drawing itself is a means to a parallel end – becoming a better woodcarver.

Differentiate, too, between 'drawing' and 'sketching'. 'Sketching' is much quicker and looser; 'drawing' more finished and studied. One woodcarving may need only a few sketched lines in order to begin. Another may require sketches to be followed up with a well-structured, shaded drawing, complete with most of the details. In the case of a carving in the round, the project may require all this *and* a model before you are really ready to start. And, yes, this all takes time. But you will work with more confidence, and more quickly in the long run; and the results are likely to be more successful.

So, for the purposes of woodcarving, drawing is a means to an end. If you could just go straight into a carving successfully without a drawing, all very well. But that would be unusual, even for experienced carvers; and a habit of drawing can help your carving ability in many other ways. Let us just go over the many additional advantages it has for the woodcarver; then I will give you some idea how to go about it.

WHY DRAW?

To help catch, generate and firm up ideas

Even simple cartoon-like drawings, with a few additional comments and thoughts, can provide a useful notebook for an uninspired day. Repeated thumbnail sketches can quickly work an idea into a woodcarving, show you what will work and what won't, and demonstrate the very comforting fact that there are always endless design possibilities for every seminal idea.

To help predict potential problems

At least as many carvings fail through a lack of research and preliminary work – such as drawing provides – as through lack of skill. Many inexperienced carvers start projects before they are ready: their ideas are not firm enough, they have inadequate knowledge of their subject, or they have not thought through the strengths and weaknesses of the wood, the direction of the fibres that will be needed or the lie of the grain.

To allow you to take measurements or cross sections

Drawing is the obvious way to assess what materials you need for a particular woodcarving; or, to put it another way, how the design may fit the wood to hand (Fig 8.4).

As an aid to visualizing during the carving process

Sketches, drawings and notes are essential for beginning work, but also to keep you on the straight and narrow while you are working. What exactly had you in mind? What did this object look like? Is there scope to change your mind in mid-carving?

Fig 8.4 *A full-size working drawing, like this one of an eagle lectern, allows you to estimate materials and plan joints with accuracy. Note the extensive cutting and pasting that is sometimes needed until everything is 'just right'*

To communicate to others what you have in mind

Convincing potential clients that you can satisfy them with a great woodcarving might mean providing sketches of alternatives, finished drawings, and a model. Remember: you have to convince yourself first.

A word of warning: a two-dimensional drawing is not a three-dimensional carving. As the depth of a carving increases, so more of the object appears. And, unlike a drawing, real life doesn't have lines around its hard and soft edges; it changes continuously with our viewpoint. You may need a second drawing to the side or back, and a top view as well, before you are really confident that you know what you are doing.

If you still approach drawing with trepidation, remember that:

- Anyone who is 'artistic' enough to carve is artistic enough to draw – enough, at least, to back up their carving in the ways I have just described. I have never met anyone who cannot draw to this modest extent.

- For us woodcarvers, the baseline is that drawings are a means to an end; they are not woodcarvings. You are not drawing for a gallery.

- The more you draw, the better you will get, and the better you will carve; and the more you carve, the better you will draw. Such is the transfer of skills.

MATERIALS

It really can be just a doodle on the back of a napkin. Forget the computer; you just need a low-tech pencil and paper. These days nothing beats a photocopier for enlarging drawings to a particular size. And, if you want symmetry, or to clean up your efforts, you will find a light box useful. Alternatively, you can tape your drawing to the window, and a fresh piece of paper over it, which is a good trick for reversing a drawing anyway. Another good reversing trick is to draw on tracing paper; you can photocopy from both sides if necessary.

PENCILS

Get a small range from hard to soft. In UK nomenclature, choose these three as a minimum: HB ('normal' medium softness), 2H (hard, giving a light line) and 2B (soft, a dark line). These will give you plenty of shading options (Fig 8.5).

Fig 8.5 *Basic drawing tools – cheap, low-tech, transportable and blissfully repairable: hard, medium and soft pencils and an eraser*

PAPER

Choose a paper with some 'tooth' – that is, some roughness to the surface. A slightly rough surface grips the pencil as it passes across and gives it, and your hand muscles, something to work against; the lines are sweeter and there is more potential for light and dark. A surface with little or no tooth, such as smooth printer or copier paper, is very slippery, less pleasant, and makes it less easy to control the pencil. Paper needn't be from an art shop: for lots of rough sketches a good, cheap option is a roll of wall-lining paper.

ERASERS

It isn't 'cheating' to use an eraser, just another means to an end. If you begin with light lines first and then add and overlay with darker ones, you'll find you won't need to rely on the eraser.

ALTERNATIVES

Most of my drawing is done with pencil on paper, but of course there is nothing to stop you working with pens, felt-tips, wax crayons or whatever you like.

If you are into bolder, simpler, more sculptural forms, you may find that charcoal or very thick waxy pencils allow you to work more fluently; or that lines come more freely with chalk on a blackboard.

GETTING STARTED

LINES

First: relax! Most newcomers are very tense and expect too much. Relax your mind as well as your muscles, keeping your fingers and drawing arm firm but loose. This should be fun; kids love it.

If you have never drawn before, practice making lots of repeat curves and S-shapes, using fingers, wrist and arm – smooth and relaxed.

Hold pencils lightly, use your wrist – you can pivot on the small wrist bones for curves – and keep fingers flexible.

Work very lightly with the hard pencil (2H) to begin with. Strengthen and concentrate your lines (HB, then 2B) when their position seems right. Use an eraser if you have to, but rub lightly.

SHADING

Think what you are doing when you are shading: you are adding shadow. As shadows depend on the direction from which the light falls, you must bear in mind the light source. So (unless you are drawing a real object from the life) decide on an imaginary light source and visualize the logical effect this would have. If your light is coming from the top right, for example, then all the raised parts of the carving should cast a shadow to the left and below. Keep shading (2B) basic and simple: lines, cross-hatching and dots. You are trying to help yourself visualize the three-dimensional form, not to produce a work of art. Put in faint, experimental shadows at first, using either logic or observation of your model, then, as you did with the lines, selectively darken them.

ERASING

If your drawing looks a mess, you can trace off the successful lines – a light box makes this easier, if you have one – and restart. Or stick a piece of paper over an unsatisfactory area and redraw – none of this is 'cheating'.

TYPES OF DRAWING

The following notes apply just as much to drawing something in front of you as something from your imagination. I tend to use, broadly speaking, three types of drawing. I might use all three in sequence, or I might stop once I have achieved what I need.

THUMBNAILING

It doesn't matter whether you are working from your imagination, using a photograph from a book or copying a real-life subject in front to you – as with carving itself, don't try to start with the finished product. Start loose, end firm; sneak up on your final working drawing. Don't expect to arrive without many steps in between.

Begin with a few small sketches of about matchbox size. I might do many of these; they give me a feel for the object and are a quick way of generating lots of alternatives. The proportions of your 'matchboxes' should correspond to those of the object in front of you or of the available wood. The limited room inside the box will force you to keep matters simple. Place the main lines – both outlines and internal lines – and the main shapes and shadows. If you find the thumbnail getting fussy or overworked, outline another box to the side and begin another. Number the sequence so you can track changes.

Rough out many thumbnails until the idea or design begins to look about right. Indeed, it is not unusual to end up with a choice of several alternative approaches, which may generate further carvings.

FIRMING SKETCHES

The thumbnails should at least get you moving in the right direction, and you can return to them at any time. Increase the size, ideally to full and certainly to scale, for the next stage. You can draw a grid over the thumbnail to help you enlarge it. Firm up lines and shadows so that the result begins to look like a drawing from which you can work.

Use the hard pencil first to make light lines, blocking out the main proportions, outlines, flows and rhythms. Don't put in details; this stage is not unlike bosting in. When you feel your lines are in the right places, start strengthening them and adding shadows.

If you want to check proportions, use the same method as 'real' artists. Hold your pencil in line with the object, close one eye and mark its total height along the pencil with your thumb. Transfer this length to a side part of the paper as a datum. If you repeat this looking at another part of the subject, your thumb mark will be in proportion to this line and can be used to guide the drawing. Always extend your thumb and pencil the same distance from your eyes.

Ask yourself what you need to know for your carving. Will your drawing tell you what you need to know in a few months' time? Write notes to yourself on the drawing to remind you.

WORKING DRAWINGS

Although they may still look sketch-like, working drawings are the ones that allow you to begin carving with confidence. They will probably be full size – at least to scale – with plenty of information, perhaps including notes and side sketches (Figs 8.6–8.8). This is the drawing you might present to a customer to explain and illustrate your intentions.

You may not need to go this far to begin with, but the point is that if you are not confident in what you are doing then you probably need to think it through more: get more information, make a few more sketches, and so on.

Figs 8.6–8.8 Details of the working drawing for the eagle lectern (see Fig 8.4)

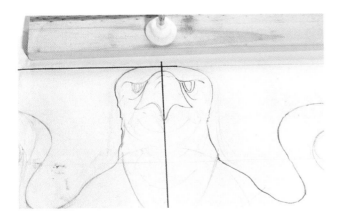

Fig 8.6 The eagle's head. I could measure up the wood and probably bandsaw from the firm outlines, which are a little oversize to give some room for working out inner details as the carving proceeds

Fig 8.7 The eagle's feet are only sketched in. I am not quite sure of their form yet; I will almost certainly need a clay model when I get to that stage

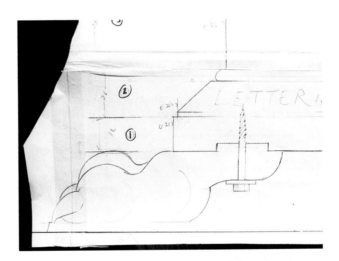

Fig 8.8 Carving will start with the feet of the pedestal. There are measurements and notes, and a good enough profile to start a carving or an interim model. Note that the method of attachment has already been planned

PHOTOGRAPHS

Photographing a subject, or model, as the basis for a carving is a quick way of rendering an exact pose. It helps with problems of **foreshortening** and suits those who really cannot make headway with their drawing. If possible, though, use it in conjunction with active sketching.

A photocopy of the print can be enlarged and transferred to the wood ready for bandsawing. A slide can be enlarged and projected straight on to a panel surface or on to drawing paper hung on the wall.

Photograph the many carvings and sculptures that appear all over our cities. These architectural decorations and patterns will develop your eye for form, interest and beauty. Don't forget to build up a portfolio of your own work as well.

THE 'MORGUE'

This is a term used by some graphic designers for a reference collection of cuttings, pictures and information filed in scrapbooks, folders or drawers.

Built up over years, the morgue is browsed through for inspiration, and studied when a problem needs solving. For example – and this is probably where the term originated – if you are interested in the human body, then gathering pictures from magazines, photographs, anything that depicts heads, hands, eyes, poses, action, old and young, male and female, will soon build up an invaluable source of reference.

PLASTER CASTS

Sometimes it is possible to take a simple plaster cast of a carving, or part of a carving – to record it, study it and perhaps even copy it. Low-relief carving works best, as there are problems in taking a cast from undercut work.

Push a malleable modelling material (such as warmed Plasticine) on to the wood, allow it to cool, and lift it off. Being oil-based, it usually comes away cleanly without leaving a residue on finished work. Carefully build up the sides of your cast so that it forms a container, and pour in plaster of Paris. When this has cooled, the modelling material should again peel away easily. Care needs to be taken to prevent distortion. Dry the plaster well in a warm place before varnishing it.

Different plasters are worth investigating. Some, like dental plaster, will take fine details; some new types dry extremely hard.

CLAY MODELLING

Many adults are nervous of clay. In some ways this is surprising, as most of us had experience of playing with clay and making things with it – even eating the stuff – as children. Perhaps, as adults, we fear that a return to clay will find us lacking any improvement in creativity over the intervening years. Many students also avoid modelling simply because it is not woodcarving. I think these people simply misunderstand the use to which modelling is put by woodcarvers, and its many very definite advantages at all levels.

It is unusual to find an experienced carver starting a complicated woodcarving, particularly in the round, without *some* model in clay or other material, even if it is only a crude proportional sketch; and before the model there will have been drawings. Such carvers understand that modelling, like drawing, is one of the means to their end: a better carving, and ultimately a better woodcarver (Figs 8.9 and 8.10).

Fig 8.9 *This is quite a well worked-out model in self-hardening Nuclay, good enough indeed to consider casting from it; I got very absorbed in the work and subject matter, the proportions and appearance*

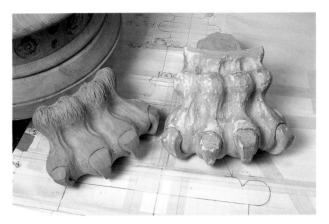

Fig 8.11 *Three stages in creating the foot of the eagle lectern: the working drawing, the clay model and the finished foot*

Fig 8.10 *Although careful measuring allowed me to get close to the model, there are many differences; features characteristic of carving include tool marks, tighter changes of plane, etc.*

Why model?

For a woodcarver, a model serves many purposes:

Pinning down an idea

Sometimes pencil and paper are simply not enough. Even though it is usual to start with a sketch (Fig 8.11), when you feel comfortable with clay you can catch an inspiration directly, missing out the drawing stage altogether.

Exploring an idea three-dimensionally

A drawing has one viewpoint; a model can have them all. So for a complicated carving, as opposed to a simple relief, modelling will help you work the idea through and firm it up.

Solving problems

The model lets you study the potential carving from all directions. It helps, for example, in looking for the best use of grain direction to accord strength to likely weak parts of the design.

Measuring wood dimensions

You will need to know not only what size block to dig out from your wood store, but also whether it needs joining up and, importantly, where to site the joints.

Planning the initial roughing out

A model should always be to scale. This being so, you can assess what waste wood can safely be bandsawn from the block. Perhaps more vitally, a model will help you decide what wood to *leave*.

Reference

As the carving proceeds you may forget some of what you had in mind, so the model functions at all times as an *aide-mémoire*.

Saving time

I find that modelling and drawing always save me carving time in the long run – if only by avoiding mistakes – and the results are always better for it.

Gaining confidence

Modelling helps develop your three-dimensional eye, your sense of 'sculptural form', and your understanding of the effects of light and shadow.

Note that the model does *not* serve as an exact pattern for the carving. As we shall see, it is not a good idea just to make a clay model and copy it in wood.

Modelling, to the level we woodcarvers need, is not particularly difficult (much easier than carving!), and quite fun if you relax. To start at the beginning: just as an understanding of wood and its structure leads to an appreciation of the best way of carving it, so an understanding of clay as a material helps to explain how it may best be handled and modelled.

CLAY

Clay is refined mud, simply that, very common and cheap. Shop-bought clay is cleaned and purified, but you may even be able to dig up your own. Because clay originally comes from decomposed rock, broken up and subject to chemical and temperature changes over millennia, it is found in various particle (grit) sizes, in a range of colours, and with various chemical additions. Potters are, of course, very interested in these matters, and there are huge numbers of recognized varieties. Some are better than others for modelling.

Clay consists of particles of silica, which are sticky in the presence of water. In effect the particles are glued together by water adhesion. It is the presence of this water that renders all clay sticky and **plastic** (pliant or modellable). Plasticity is the property of a material which permits its shaping and allows it to retain this shaped form until otherwise manipulated.

Our everyday experience of mud or clay is that it becomes a rock-like lump if it loses the water. Put back a little water and the softness and plasticity return – you can shape the clay with your fingers. Put enough water back and you can make mud pies, even mud soup. Water is therefore one of the keys to understanding and using clay. Here are some principles which modellers need to know:

- You must adjust the water content of the clay to get the right plasticity, the right working properties, the correct hardness or softness for your purpose. (The less water, the drier and more leather-like the clay becomes; the more water, the more muddy or sloppy the clay.)

- Clay models must be prevented from drying out; they will readily crack and fall apart if they do.

- Clay has to be stored *damp*.

- Exercising the clay alters the relationship between the silica particles and the water. Kneading, stretching and folding clay like bread improve workability. You should always knead clay well before using it – the more the better. Keep worked (*tempered*) clay for re-use in a separate bin from the unworked material.

- The water makes the clay sticky. A certain amount of moistness is necessary to get a good bond when you add clay to clay; if in doubt, wet the surfaces.

I would add two more principles to give a fuller picture of this material:

- Clay has no strength of its own, no grain like wood. It is self-supporting in compact shapes, reliefs, etc., but once above a certain size or extension, gravity will take hold and the clay will slump. This is why you may need an internal skeleton or **armature** to hold parts up.

- Clay is homogeneous and solid; push it in one place and the mass must move to another. We will come back to this when we discuss modelling.

BUYING AND STORING CLAY

You can model in any type of clay, but the best would have an even consistency and not be too smooth (unless you are doing a small or very detailed model). A little fine **grog** (ground-up fired clay) adds 'bite'. Colour varies, but is functionally unimportant: 'ball' clays are blue-black, and terracotta is red-brown.

If you buy clay from a sculptors' supplier, a good type is bound to be specified. If you go to a potter, ask for something that will model well, hold together and have good plasticity; you are not interested in its firing qualities. In both cases you may well get samples to try.

Big blocks of clay can be cut into smaller ones with a length of piano wire, handled at both ends. These should be cling-wrapped or bagged in plastic, then stored in airtight plastic buckets and tubs.

Clay must be kept moist. If it dries out, break it up, add water and leave. Once it has crumbled down to mud, allow the water to evaporate, then beat and knead the clay and you find it as good as new – so clay models are endlessly re-usable.

When the time comes to use your clay:

- It should be soft enough to be easily rolled out or moulded by your thumb. It takes a little practice to appreciate what constitutes the correct pliability.

- If the clay is too soft (wet) you will need to spread it out and dry it, or add drier clay.

- If too hard, push in a few holes with your fingers, fill them with water and re-knead; or leave overnight wrapped in wet cloths.

ALTERNATIVES TO CLAY

In addition to clay I use:

Nuclay
A clay containing fine glass fibres. It works similarly to normal clay, but the fibre content strongly resists cracking. This means that you can allow your models to dry out, and even harden them with PVA or a special hardener.

Synthetic modelling materials
The oil-based, non-drying, clean modelling clays, used widely in schools and by well-known animators, are often referred to in Britain by the proprietary term Plasticine. Temperature is very important: the material loses workability far more quickly than normal clay when it grows cold. I warm mine in an oven and keep excess wrapped in tin foil until I use it.

There are many modelling materials sold in art shops, including hardening clays that can be rasped or filed but not re-used. They are all very expensive compared with clay; this matters more as your model gets larger.

TOOLS AND EQUIPMENT

What you need will depend on the scale and detail to which you are working. A lot can be done by improvising with what is to hand.

MODELLING TOOLS
Your hands are your most important tools for modelling. See any additional tools as extensions of your fingers and thumbs: work out what you want to do, then you will see what you need.

You can buy sets of modelling tools or make your own from wood – preferably smooth, and naturally oily if possible (Fig 8.12). Modelling tools that have serrated edges are also useful, for scraping back clay (Fig 8.13). Clean the tools after use and rub them with linseed oil.

Fig 8.12 A selection of modelling tools, mostly home-made in smooth, dense hardwoods

Fig 8.13 Some of these metal tools have toothed edges for scraping

As you model you will build up a collection of tools made from bottle tops, old toothbrushes, perspex, metal, whatever.

CUTTING CLAY

Obviously, clay is added to build up a form, but you can also cut it away. Wire (cheese or piano) is best to slice clay; it is hard work with a knife.

For removing smaller amounts, you can make your own tools, but I found it simpler to buy a couple of different-sized cutting tools, which are wire loops on handles. The loops may be serrated for additional scraping (Fig 8.14).

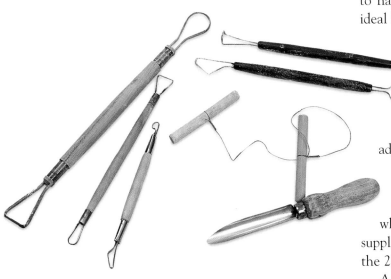

Fig 8.14 *Tools for cutting and removing clay include a fine wire with handles each end, stout wire loops in wooden handles, and a half-round tool for making holes*

WATER

You will need a little pot with a small sponge for wetting surfaces, a plant mister or spray with which to moisten the model and prevent it drying out while you work, and some damp rags to cover the clay model between sessions.

BRUSHES

These are used for consolidating and smoothing over surfaces, and for wetting the surface of one piece of clay before adding it to another.

MODELLING STANDS

To model a relief carving you only need a board; plywood is best. There is no need to treat it, but you may want to put a simple frame round the edge to represent the wood thickness.

Some modellers like to work a relief vertically for the benefits of perspective. For this you could use the 'Deckchair' carving stand described in my *Elements of Woodcarving* (pages 20–1). To prevent the clay slipping under its own weight, some 'butterflies' – little crosses of wood tied with wire – or something similar can be screwed into the plywood, using rust-proof brass screws.

For small models, a piece of plywood (if you need to nail on armature wire) or old roofing slate is an ideal base on which to work.

Modelling in the round is much easier if you have a revolving turntable: you can get at all parts easily and see the effect of light and shadow. You can make your own quite simply for a smaller model; or, if you have some adjustable device to hold woodcarvings, you may be able to adapt that. Once you appreciate the value of modelling you might want to think of investing in a small rotating modelling stand, which you can buy from sculptors' or potters' suppliers (Fig 8.15). Mine has been invaluable over the 20 years I have had it.

A full-size modelling stand, at which you can work upright, might be a luxury, or it might be just the job for the type, quality or amount of modelling you will be doing. As always with equipment, start simply and add to it on the basis of need.

Fig 8.15 *This table-top modelling stand is equally useful with clay or with synthetic modelling materials*

ARMATURES

An armature is anything that you put inside a part of the model to prevent it slumping with gravity. This may be a full wire and wood skeleton, or just a sliver of bamboo expediently pushed in.

Make armatures from materials that will not rust: wood, galvanized or plastic-coated garden wire, brass or zinc-plated screws, for example. Spaces in the model can be filled with damp rags or newspaper to conserve clay.

Since the armature is on the inside, you do need to plan ahead to avoid having a wire sticking through the clay, for example – though for a working sketch model this may not actually be a problem (Fig 8.16). Usually such planning is based on preliminary sketches.

Fig 8.16 You can see the armature wires protruding from the beak and tail in this small model of a bird

BASIC MODELLING

Many books are available to give you advice on keeping, storing and working clay. Relax, be patient, and enjoy what you are doing – don't take your modelling too seriously. As with every skill, practice and experience help the most.

Have tools and materials ready; think about whether you need an armature, and make one if you do; and knead some clay well to begin with. Figs 8.17–8.22 show the basic techniques.

You will learn best just by getting stuck in. As you do, here are some essential points and guidelines:

- Work to scale – failing to do so is a wasted opportunity.

- Remember too that you must 'think wood' even as you model clay: pay attention to grain direction, strength and so on.

Fig 8.17 Cutting lumps from a block of clay with thin wire is the easiest way to remove what you need

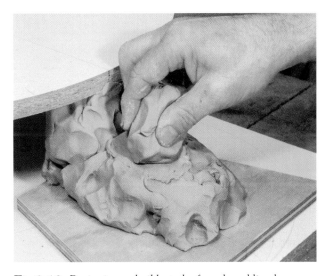

Fig 8.18 Beginning to build up the form by adding large pieces of clay

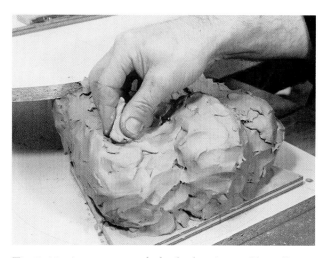

Fig 8.19 *As you approach the final surface, add smaller and smaller pieces*

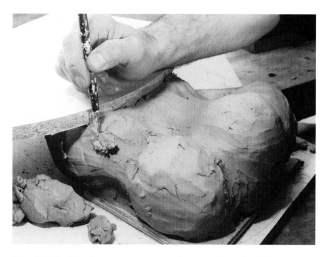

Fig 8.20 *Cutting away excess clay to refine the shape*

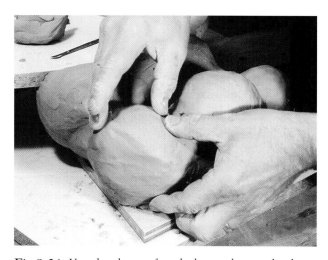

Fig 8.21 *Your hands are often the best tool to get the shape you want*

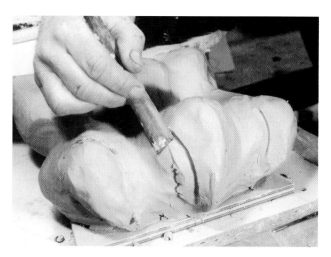

Fig 8.22 *At some point, modelling tools take over from the fingers to create the subtler forms and details. You can see now that this is the model for the lectern foot, shown complete in Fig 8.11*

- Your model must be built from the inside out, adding mass. This is the opposite of carving. Build up main masses first, then add smaller lumps in the directions you want to go; towards the end you will be adding very small pieces.

- Start with large lumps of clay. Put your modelling tools aside for the moment and just use your fingers. Smear together at the joins to avoid air bubbles; this will make your model stronger.

- After the main masses are in place, allow the clay to stiffen a little; then start adding smaller pieces to refine the shape.

- Only then do you start thinking of details. Just like carving, if the underlying form is right then the details will just fall into place.

- If you just push into the clay in one place, it will simply push out in another. Add and subtract, rather than pushing.

- Don't go straight for a complicated design until you have built up your confidence and competence – you will only be disappointed. Begin practising with simple shapes, perhaps even just a part of what you eventually want.

- You may have to attempt several models before you get it right. Cut back if you have to, with wire tools, to where you last 'had it right'. To add a new piece, roughen and wet both surfaces and rub them together a bit to close the joint.

- Keep the clay damp as you work with an occasional mist of water from the spray, and consolidate the surface with a soft, wet brush.

- When you have finished a session, cover the model with wet cloths and polythene to keep it moist. If there is a danger that this would damage the detail, make a polythene 'tent' and include a bowl of water to keep up the moisture inside.

Do keep in mind that for a woodcarver, your model has a job to do. So unless you want to keep your model – perhaps casting it in plaster – there is no need to go for an exact, beautiful finish. Stop when the job is done – when you have the idea of your carving fixed and clear in your mind, and you have enough information to make your measurements, and so on.

Even if your model is a disaster and you discard it after the modelling session, the making of it will have made you study your subject more closely. This must be of benefit; the model will still have gone a long way towards achieving its purpose.

HOW TO USE THE MODEL WHILE YOU ARE CARVING

Clay models and woodcarvings are different beasts. The two approaches and processes are distinct, and the difference is reflected in the result. For this reason alone, I would never advocate making a model just to copy it in wood. I think it is possible to strike a creative balance. When I have a model, I reckon that I look and calculate from it during the first third of the carving process. Somewhere around the bosting-in stage I find myself paying less and less attention to the model and becoming more absorbed in the carving; the carving has taken over. I then put the model by, and might never look at it again. This I recommend as an approach. It keeps the integrity of the carving while using the model to advantage (Fig 8.23).

Fig 8.23 *Another example of a clay model in which ideas have been worked through, and the derived carving, which is clearly not just a copy*

TRANSFERRING WORK TO THE SOLID

Tracing paper and carbon paper are two well-tried methods for transferring drawings. Standing a sheet of plate glass in front of a clay model and drawing its profile with a chinagraph pencil – while moving the eye-line to avoid distortion – is a way of capturing an outline for small three-dimensional work; another way is to use a try square to trace the shape on to a flat surface (Fig 8.24). This outline can then be cut out on the bandsaw.

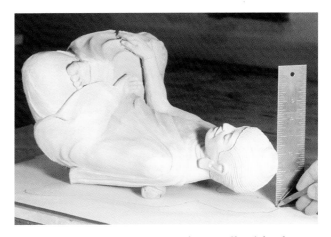

Fig 8.24 *Using a try square to take a profile of the clay model for the carving in Fig 8.10. The time taken up in making the model is justified by the ease with which the wood dimensions and the placing of the joints can be calculated, which allows accurate bandsawing*

SOME PARTING CUTS

I said at the beginning of Volume 1 that this book (and, even though it is now two volumes, it is still one book to me) does not contain carving projects. Its purpose is not to tell you how to carve but to give you that indispensable background knowledge needed to carve well – information only sparsely treated elsewhere.

If you think about it, the cutting edge of the carving tool is the interface, the meeting point, between you and the wood. On the other side of this place of contact is your material: wood. On this side is you: your talents, desires and energy. Carvers absorbed in their work know that the somewhat clichéd expression about tools being an 'extension of your hand' is, nonetheless, true.

Over and over again, when I ask woodcarving students what they want to learn, what usually comes first to their minds and lips is 'tools', 'sharpening' and 'wood' – things which feel like primary hurdles. I am convinced that the material in this book will contribute to answering these questions; and, despite the size of these two volumes, I know the answer to be plain and readily acquired.

But, once over these hurdles, what about learning to *carve* with the tools? Putting to one side the practical advice and projects in my other books, what can the beginner do about developing carving skills? What's the best approach?

I often use the analogy of learning to play the guitar when I'm talking about learning to carve: acquiring your carving tools is like buying your guitar – and of course you want to buy the best, and make sure the guitar is made properly. Sharpening your carving tools is like tuning your guitar: without this,

no matter what tune you want to play, it won't sound very good! But what next?

No embryonic classical guitarist in their right mind would think that they could sit down to play a Rodrigo guitar concerto straight away. A beginner would expect to practise – consistently, regularly, intelligently – and to invest time. They would start small, with easy finger exercises, repeated again and again, gradually increasing challenges as they become proficient. And, if they know about concert performers, they also know that the best continue such 'practice' forever. They would also listen carefully to other guitarists and to old and new renditions of fine guitar playing; would watch live performers closely, seek out the techniques and 'tricks' whereby the masters produced such sounds.

This is how you learn any skill, and surely carving is no different. Small steps, big walk; absorbing and being inspired; confidence begets competence.

And at the end of the day, it is the woodcarving that remains. The viewer will not see the tools, or the sharpening stones. They will forget the original tree from which this last fruit was carved. They won't hear the banging of the mallet, the intakes of breath, the curses of struggle, the cries of delight. They probably won't appreciate the investment of time, and money, and practice.

My last thought is always to keep this in mind: all these things – including this book – are a means to that creative end: the final carving. At the same time, there is great joy to be had in the travelling, the process of learning and acquiring skills, even if you never get very far. This is what makes woodcarving one of the greatest of crafts.

Detail from the centre of Lord Strathcona's Horse (Royal Canadians) trophy carved for HRH the Prince of Wales. Nose to tail, the beaver is 3in (75mm) long

A GLOSSARY OF
WOODCARVING TERMS

adze an axe-like tool whose straight or curved cutting edge is at right angles to the axis of the handle.

air drying the traditional method of seasoning timber by leaving it to dry in the open air.

allongee chisel or **gouge** one whose blade splays outwards all the way from the shoulder to the cutting edge.

angle grinder a hand-held power tool with a cutting or abrasive disc whose axis is at right angles to that of the body of the tool.

annealing removing the hardness from a piece of metal by heating and allowing to cool slowly.

annual rings the successive layers of wood produced each year by the growing tree, appearing as concentric rings in a whole log or as roughly parallel lines in a sawn board. Each ring consists of both **springwood** and **summerwood**.

applied carving relief carving which is made separately and subsequently attached to a background, rather than being carved *in situ*.

Arkansas the name given to the harder grades of novaculite sharpening stone. The different grades are, in decreasing order of hardness: black, translucent (the most useful to the woodcarver), hard white, soft white.

armature an internal framework or skeleton, usually of wire, to support a model made of clay or similar material.

back the convex side of a gouge blade.

backbent see **bent tools**.

backeroni a carving tool, now rarely used, which resembles a **fluteroni** with the central part of the blade cambered upwards.

background the plane against which the whole subject, especially of a relief carving, is placed; compare **ground**.

backsaw any saw which has a stiffening spine of steel or brass; usually classified as tenon, dovetail and gents' saws, in decreasing order of size.

bandsaw a stationary workshop machine in which a continuous, flexible saw blade passes over two large-diameter wheels or three smaller ones.

bark the protective outer layer of a tree, almost impervious to water.

bast a spongy layer immediately beneath the bark, which transports sap downwards.

bead either a semicircular moulding, or a short segment of one carved into a hemispherical shape. When bead mouldings are grouped or clustered together in a parallel series, they are called **reeds**.

beeswax a natural wax which, when mixed with turpentine, can be used as a wood finish and as a filler for small cracks.

belt and disc sander a sanding machine with both an abrasive disc and an abrasive belt.

belt grinder a bench grinder fitted with an abrasive belt instead of a wheel.

benchplate my preferred term for a polycrystalline diamond lapping plate or sharpening stone, which is generally much thinner than a conventional benchstone.

benchstone a flat-topped rectangular sharpening stone, used for sharpening chisels and the convex sides of gouges.

benchstrop a flat strop for use on chisels and the outside bevels of gouges.

bent tools chisels or gouges which have a curve or crank along their length, giving them a greater facility for getting into recesses. **Longbent** (**salmon**, **sowback**, **curved**) tools are bent along the whole blade length for shallower recesses; **shortbent** (**frontbent**, **spoon**, **spoonbit**) tools have a long, straight shank and a tight crank at the end for getting into deeper hollows; **backbent** gouges are reversed shortbents for use when the tool is to be presented to the wood 'upside down'. **Shortbent skew chisels** come in left- and right-handed pairs. A **knuckle gouge** is a frontbent gouge with an unusually sharp bend.

bevel the wedge of metal between the cutting edge and the heel of a carving tool. It is normally flat, with an angle of about 20°.

bit the cutting part of a drill, flexible-shaft machine or other rotary tool.

black Arkansas the hardest grade of novaculite sharpening stone, too hard to be of much use to the carver.

blade the cutting part of a carving tool; sometimes the term refers only to the part below the shoulder, and sometimes to everything except the handle.

block plane a small plane with its blade set at a comparatively low angle.

blueing a bluish discoloration indicating loss of temper in a tool blade, caused by overheating when grinding the blade.

bolster another name for **shoulder**.

bosting another word for the roughing-out or 'sketching' stage of carving, where the underlying forms and flow of a subject are established.

bowsaw a saw with a narrow blade strained in a wooden frame, for cutting curves in comparatively thick material.

buffing wheel another name for a **honing wheel**.

bullnosed another term for **nosed**.

burl or **burr** (1) wood with irregular, highly convoluted grain, taken from a growth on the side of the trunk or from near the root.

burr (2) another name for **wire edge.**

button another name for **snib**.

cambium the layer of growing cells in a tree, between bast and wood.

candle a margin of highly polished metal on an otherwise dull bevel, when the edge of the bevel has been stropped and the rest only honed.

cannel the concave side of a gouge blade; see also **in-cannel** and **out-cannel**.

Carborundum vitrified silicon carbide, used to make artificial sharpening stones.

carnauba wax a hard-drying vegetable wax which can be mixed with beeswax to make a durable wood finish.

carver pattern handle the common barrel-shaped or cigar-shaped handle used on both carving tools and carpentry chisels.

C-clamp the American term for **G-clamp**.

ceramic stone a man-made sharpening stone in which alumina (synthetic sapphire) is the abrasive.

channel the concave side of a gouge blade.

check a crack in wood, especially a minor one occurring during the drying process.

China wood oil another name for **tung oil**.

chip carving a style of decorative carving consisting of geometric motifs incised in the surface of the wood, usually with knives; in some styles, a V-tool or a veiner may be used as well.

chisel a carving (or carpentry) tool with a straight cutting edge, as opposed to a **gouge**, which has a curved cutting edge. Carvers often use the term loosely to refer to both chisels and gouges.

chops (singular and plural) a wooden vice. The type used by carvers for holding work in the round is similar in shape to a metalworker's vice, and sits on top of the bench surface.

combination stone a benchstone which is coarse on one side and fine on the other.

concave hollow (like 'caves').

conversion the process of reducing a tree into usable pieces for woodworking.

convex rounded.

coping saw a saw with a very narrow blade strained in a metal frame, for cutting curves in thin material.

corner chisel another name for the **skew chisel**.

corner grounder another name for the shortbent corner chisel; see **bent tools**.

crosscut saw one whose teeth are shaped for cutting across the grain.

cross grain (1) another term for **short grain**; (2) grain which changes direction, making the wood awkward or unpredictable to work.

crotch the Y-shaped formation where a tree trunk divides into two, or where a major branch divides from the trunk; the wood often has attractively convoluted grain.

curved gouge another name for a longbent gouge; see **bent tools.**

cutting angle the angle at which the blade approaches the wood.

cutting disc any of the various types of circular cutter designed for use in an angle grinder.

cutting edge the extreme edge of a cutting tool, invisible to the naked eye, which leaves the final cut surface.

cutting profile the longitudinal section through the cutting edge of a tool.

Danish oil a commercial oil finish containing hardening agents.

dead knot see **knot**.

devil stone another word for a **dressing stone**.

diamond stone any sharpening device, made in the form of a benchstone or slipstone, which uses artificial diamond as an abrasive.

die grinder a portable power tool, larger and less safe to use than a micromotor, consisting of a hand-held motor unit which accepts a range of rotary cutters and abrading tools.

dog a name used for various simple work-holding devices, such as a metal staple used to clamp boards together, a wooden or metal peg inserted into a bench top to restrain the workpiece, or a **snib**.

dogleg chisel a chisel with a sharply cranked end, for undercutting or working in tight recesses.

double-cut file one with two opposed rows of ridges across the blade, giving a comparatively fast cut.

dress to flatten the surface of a used sharpening stone or grinding wheel.

dressing stone a stone used to dress the surface of a grinding wheel.

dressing wheel a specialized tool for dressing the surface of a grinding wheel.

dry grinder a fast-running grinder which does not use water for lubrication.

dummy mallet a compact, heavy mallet with a soft iron head, used chiefly by stonecarvers. It should only be used with tools which have an end ferrule.

Dutchman a lozenge-shaped patch used to fill a blemish in the wood surface.

dye a preparation for colouring wood, especially one which penetrates well below the surface.

earlywood another term for **springwood.**

end ferrule a ferrule fitted to the top end of a tool handle.

end grain the surface of a piece of wood which shows the cut ends of the fibres.

eye a circular or drop-shaped recess which is a feature of some kinds of ornamental foliage carving.

eye punch a punch for forming eyes in foliage.

eye tool a small semicircular gouge, suitable for forming eyes in foliage.

face the concave side of a gouge blade. Also, the upper surface of the shoulder or bolster where it butts against the handle.

fence a slim wooden batten screwed to the work surface to prevent the workpiece from moving.

ferrule a metal hoop which is fitted tightly over the lower end of a tool handle, and occasionally the upper end also, to resist splitting of the wood.

figure any decorative pattern formed in the wood by the configuration of the grain, medullary rays and other natural features.

file an abrading tool whose cutting action is produced by parallel grooves or ridges in the surface, rather than separate teeth.

file card a fine wire brush for cleaning files.

finished size the dimensions of a piece of wood after planing or sanding.

firmer or **firmer chisel** another name for the woodcarver's chisel, bevelled on both sides; also the usual name for the general-purpose carpentry chisel, bevelled on one side only.

fishtail chisel or **gouge** one with a short, strongly splayed blade at the end of a narrow, straight shank.

flat a small flat surface on a carving to which an additional piece can be glued to increase the depth of relief.

flat gouge one with the shallowest sweep available (no. 3 in the Sheffield List); gouges become 'flatter' as their depth of cut decreases in proportion to their width. Amongst other uses, flat gouges are particularly effective in smoothing off surfaces to a finish.

flexible-shaft machine a power tool in which a flexible shaft runs from a motor unit to a handpiece which accepts various rotary cutters and abrading tools.

flitch a board, usually a thick one, on which the rounded sides of the tree are still visible.

flute a deep channel, groups of which may be gathered together in furniture legs, etc. The same term is sometimes used to denote the concave side of a gouge blade.

fluter or **fluting tool** a deep or U-shaped gouge, used for running deep channels, sometimes as an alternative to the V-tool. It is used in a different manner from arc-based gouges because of its straight sides.

fluteroni a carving tool, now rarely used, resembling a **macaroni** but with rounded corners and outward-leaning sides.

foot chisel a variant of the **dogleg chisel**, with 90° bends.

foreshortening the art of representing an object (in painting or relief) shorter than its natural length so that it appears to project towards or recede from the viewer.

forge to shape (heated metal) by hammering.

foxing a yellow-brown discoloration in timber, caused by fungal infection.

fretsaw a saw with an exceptionally fine blade strained in a metal frame, for making curved or enclosed cuts in very thin material.

frontbent see **bent tools**

froster or **frosting tool** a punch which creates a pattern of small, regularly spaced indentations.

fuller the convex or male former used in forging the sweep of a gouge.

G-clamp or **G-cramp** a metal clamp consisting of a C-shaped frame with a screw passing through one end of it; the term is sometimes applied also to quick-action clamps shaped like the letter F.

gouge a tool which differs from a chisel in having a cutting edge which is curved in cross section.

grain the arrangement of the longitudinal fibres in the wood. To work **with the grain** is to cut in the direction in which the fibres support one another and so resist tearing; it is easy to achieve a good finish this way. Cutting the opposite way, **against the grain**, encourages tearing and splitting of the wood. Cutting **across the grain**, at right angles to the fibres, can produce a clean finish with well-sharpened tools.

green (of wood) not seasoned.

grinder or **bench grinder** a machine for grinding metal, fitted with revolving abrasive wheels; uses include the grinding of tool edges as a preliminary stage of sharpening.

grinding wheel or **grindstone** the abrasive wheel fitted to a bench grinder.

grit the texture or degree of coarseness of an abrasive.

grog fired clay, ground up small and added to soft clay to improve its consistency.

ground differentiate this from **background**. A ground is the plane from which any part of the design is raised; so the main part of any carved feature forms a ground for the smaller details carved within it. A ground is 'enclosed' if there is no free side from which to gain access.

grounding or **grounding out** the process whereby a ground or background is reduced to a specified level. It usually involves a rapid lowering stage followed by levelling to finish off the surface.

grounding tool or **grounder** a shortbent flat carving tool (see **bent tools**) for finishing enclosed grounds in relief carving. In the past flat chisels were often used, at a time when a lot of grounds in low-relief furniture carving were punched or matted over (see **punch**), so that the torn grain left by the digging-in of chisel corners could be disguised. Today the tool of choice is more likely to be a gouge of no. 3 (flattest) sweep, which will leave a smooth, flat ground while keeping corners clear.

hand router a tool of the plane family, in which the blade reaches down below the sole of the tool in order to level the bottom of a recess.

hardening increasing the hardness of steel by heating it to a critical temperature and then quenching it.

hardwood wood from a broadleaved tree, which is generally, but not always, harder than **softwood**.

heart the central part of the heartwood, particularly prone to checking and therefore often removed (*boxed*) before seasoning.

heart shake see **shake**.

heartwood the denser, harder, more durable wood from near the centre of the trunk.

heel the corner where the bevel meets the back of the blade proper. It should be polished so that it burnishes the facet after the cut.

high-carbon steel steel containing a certain proportion of carbon (typically between 0.5 and 1.5%), used for making cutting tools which require a very sharp edge.

high relief a style of carving where the background is relatively deep compared with the width of the subject; as with **low relief**, the term does not refer simply to the measured depth. As a high relief gets deeper, so the subject approaches the full three dimensions.

high-speed steel (HSS) a steel which retains its hardness at high temperatures; it is widely used for woodturning tools but not, at present, for carving tools.

holdfast an L-shaped clamp which can be passed through a hole in the bench top to secure a workpiece well away from the edge of the bench.

hollow the concave side of a gouge blade.

hollow grinding grinding the bevel of a tool on the edge of a grinding wheel so as to make the surface of the bevel concave.

hone to sharpen a blade by abrading it on a stone.

honing stone any kind of stone used for sharpening.

honing wheel a wheel of fibrous material, impregnated with an abrasive compound, fitted to a machine of bench-grinder type and used to hone tool edges.

hook knife a tool resembling a **sloyd knife**, but with the blade strongly curved to permit hollowing cuts.

hoop a less common word for **ferrule**.

horse a workbench or work-holding device designed for sitting on.

in-cannel the concave side of a gouge blade. An **in-cannel gouge** has a sharpening bevel on the concave side only.

inside the concave side of a gouge blade.

in stick (of boards undergoing seasoning) stacked with sticks or battens between to allow air to flow around them.

keel the junction between the two bevels of a V-tool.

keyhole saw a saw with a short, narrow blade (which often retracts into the handle), for making enclosed cuts.

kiln drying the modern method of seasoning timber in a heated chamber, allowing a precise, predetermined moisture content to be achieved.

knot a rounded or elongated patch of cross-grained wood, formed by a branch around which the trunk has continued to grow. It may be regarded as a blemish or as a 'feature', depending on how the wood is to be used. **Live knots**, arising from healthy branches, are firmly attached to the surrounding wood. **Dead knots**, formed by diseased or broken branches, tend to be loose and discoloured; they may fall out, leaving a **knot hole**.

knuckle gouge see **bent tools**.

lap to flatten a metal component, or the surface of a sharpening stone, by abrading on a very flat surface.

lapping plate a thin, flat plate of polycrystalline diamond abrasive, intended for flattening benchstones, but also suitable for sharpening tools.

latewood another term for **summerwood**.

line of light another term for **white line**.

lining in outlining the subject prior to waste removal, normally with a V-tool or fluter. 'Outlining' is a good alternative, although the 'outline' is usually taken to be the principal one surrounding the whole subject.

linseed oil a vegetable oil used as a wood finish in its own right and as a constituent of other finishes. **Boiled** oil contains drying agents and dries more quickly and thoroughly than **raw** oil.

live knot see **knot**.

London pattern handle the common type of chisel handle which is mainly cylindrical (or octagonal, in the case of the London pattern octagon handle), with a waisted section near the ferrule.

longbent see **bent tools**.

long grain the arrangement of the wood fibres parallel to the length of the workpiece, resulting in maximum strength.

long-pod tool a term sometimes used to describe a tool intermediate between an **allongee** and a true **fishtail**.

low relief a shallow, but arbitrary, depth of carving. It is defined not so much by the actual physical depth of the background as by the relationship of this depth to the size of the subject. The depth of the subject is considerably less than it would be if carved in the round.

macaroni tool a carving tool, now rarely used, whose cross section is a flat-bottomed channel.

medium-pod tool a term sometimes used to describe a tool intermediate between an **allongee** and a true **fishtail**.

medulla the technical term for **pith**.

medullary rays sheets of tissue formed at right angles to the annual rings of a tree. In some species (notably oak) they form attractive figure on the radial surfaces of the wood.

micromotor a power tool, smaller and safer to use than a die grinder, consisting of a hand-held motor unit which accepts various rotary cutters and abrading tools.

Microplane a trade name for a rasp-like tool with many small blades of surgical steel.

microtool a name sometimes given to small versions of ordinary woodcarving tools; also an alternative name for **micromotor**.

modelling the stage in which secondary and further forms are carved, after the principal underlying forms have been established and before proceeding to detailing; also, the making of a preliminary model in clay or other plastic material.

moisture content the ratio of the weight of moisture currently in a piece of wood to the weight of the wood when completely dry, expressed as a percentage.

monocrystalline diamond an artificial diamond which resembles natural diamond and is widely used in the manufacture of diamond sharpening stones.

mop a polishing wheel made of fabric, for use in a grinder or similar machine.

motorized carver another name for the **reciprocal carver**.

mouse-tail file a small, tapered round file.

mouth the concave side of a gouge blade.

needle file a very fine file, available in a range of shapes.

nominal size the size to which wood is sawn at a sawmill, and on which the price of the wood is calculated. The actual *usable* size of the wood will be reduced by subsequent planing or other treatment.

nosed (of a cutting edge) rounded in plan view, so that the central part projects forward of the corners.

novaculite the hard, fine-grained, natural stone from which Washita and Arkansas sharpening stones are made.

oilstone any sharpening stone which is designed to be used with oil.

old woman's tooth a common name for the simplest kind of **hand router**.

out-cannel the convex side of a gouge blade. An **out-cannel gouge** has its principal or only sharpening bevel on the convex side.

outside the convex side of a gouge blade.

overall bevel angle the total angle between the bevels on the front and back of the blade.

padsaw another name for the **keyhole saw**.

palm mallet a commercial name for a shock-absorbing pad worn to protect the palm when using it to strike a tool handle.

paraffin wax a colourless wax which can be used as a clear wood finish.

parting tool an alternative name for the **V-tool**, which points to one of its principal functions: that of separating one part from another.

patera (plural **paterae**) a decorative rosette.

pierced relief relief carving in which the background is cut away, either completely or in parts.

pith or **medulla** the central part of a tree trunk, representing the position of the original seedling; a point of weakness in the timber, best avoided by the woodworker.

plain-sawn (of timber) converted by the **through-and-through** method.

plastic (of a material such as clay) able to be moulded into shape, and to retain the shape to which it has been moulded.

polishing stone a very fine sharpening stone – typically a waterstone of 6000 grit or finer – used to put the final polish on a cutting edge as an alternative to stropping.

polishing wheel another name for a **honing wheel**.

polychrome finished in a variety of colours, using painting, staining or gilding.

polycrystalline diamond an artificial diamond composed of multifaceted crystals, used in the manufacture of diamond benchplates.

power or **reciprocal chisel** alternative terms for **reciprocal carver**.

punch a small bar of metal with the end shaped for indenting wood, used either for cleaning and levelling the bottom of a small hole, for example, or for decorating a surface.

quarter-sawing the method of converting timber by sawing along the radius of the log, producing planks whose annular rings are perpendicular to the sawn surface; the resulting boards are stable and often attractively figured, but wastage is considerable.

quench to cool (heat-treated steel) rapidly by immersion in water or oil.

quick gouge one with a deep sweep (no. 8 or 9 in the Sheffield List); gouges become 'quicker' as their depth of cut increases relative to their width. The quickest gouge 'proper' (as opposed to U-gouges, which must be used in a different manner) has a semicircular sweep. Quick gouges remove wood quickly, and so help in the roughing-out stages of a carving, as well as serving to set in tight curves.

rasp an abrading tool resembling a file, but with individual teeth standing out from the surface.

rat-tail file a tapered round file.

reciprocal carver or **chisel** a power tool in which a motor unit is connected to a chisel- or gouge-like blade, either directly or via a flexible shaft.

reed see **bead**.

relative humidity the ratio between the amount of moisture actually present in the air at a given moment and the maximum amount of moisture which the air could hold at the same temperature, expressed as a percentage.

relief carving lies in its own world, somewhere between painting and sculpture. The depth dimension is compressed, and subjects are usually related to a virtual (original) surface plane and set against a background plane. See **low relief** and **high relief**.

reverse the convex side of a gouge blade.

riffler a paddle-like rasp, usually double-ended, available in many different shapes.

ring shake see **shake**.

ripsaw a saw whose teeth are shaped for cutting along the grain (**ripping**).

rocking cut a short **sweep cut**, one of the principal techniques of woodcarving. The handle of the gouge is given a twist (rotated) as it is pushed forward, so the chip is sliced out. This gives much cleaner cutting than simply pushing the tool straight ahead.

router a versatile power tool which consists of a motor unit mounted vertically over a flat base, and able to accept a wide range of rotating cutters. See also **hand router**.

rubbed joint a glued joint in which the components are rubbed together to exclude air and excess glue; clamping may not be necessary.

salmon-bend gouge another name for a longbent gouge; see **bent tools.**

sapwood the softer, less dense, less durable wood from near the outside of the trunk.

sash clamp or **cramp** a long clamp consisting of a pair of jaws, one of them fitted with a screw, which can be moved to different positions along a metal or wooden bar.

saw rasp an unusual type of rasp in which saw-like blades replace the customary teeth.

scorp a tool resembling a drawknife, with the blade sharply curved, sometimes into a complete circle.

scraper a smoothing tool consisting of a flat steel blade with a burred cutting edge, used by itself or mounted in some kind of holder.

scratch stock a tool for forming mouldings in wood, comprising a shaped scraper blade mounted in a guide.

scrollsaw a motorized fretsaw.

sculpture a term of wide interpretation. I use it to mean carving which is fully three-dimensional ('in the round'), as compared with relief carving, where the depth dimension is less than in reality.

seasoning the process of reducing the moisture content of wood before working it, in order to reduce the likelihood of warping, shrinkage or cracking in the finished product.

secondary bevel a narrow bevel on the extreme edge of a cutting tool, at a steeper angle than the main grinding bevel.

self-jigging (of a tool such as a paring chisel) designed to guide itself in a consistent direction, usually so as to cut in a straight line.

set to form the bevel of a chisel or gouge by grinding, in preparation for sharpening the edge; also, the angle to which the bevel is ground.

setting in precisely shaping the outline of a subject with vertical cuts.

shake a crack or split in wood, especially a major one caused by disease or trauma to the tree. **Ring shake** occurs between annual rings. **Heart shake** radiates outwards from the centre of the log; very extensive heart shake is known as **star shake**.

shank the upper part of the blade of a carving tool, adjacent to the shoulder.

shaper tool an alternative name for the **Surform**.

shaping the preliminary stage of sharpening, in which the shape of the cutting edge and bevel are established.

Sheffield List a numbering system for identifying the different types of woodcarving tools, devised in the late nineteenth century and first used in a trade catalogue known as the *Sheffield Illustrated List*.

shellac a natural resin used in the manufacture of French polish and certain other wood finishes.

shortbent see **bent tools**.

short grain the arrangement of the wood fibres across the width of the workpiece, rather than along its length, resulting in structural weakness.

short-pod tool a term sometimes used to describe a tool intermediate between an **allongee** and a true **fishtail.**

shoulder (or **bolster**) the prominent lump of metal between the blade and the tang of a chisel or gouge, which prevents the tang penetrating and splitting the handle.

side chisel a specialized chisel whose blade bends sideways through 90° to reach otherwise inaccessible places.

side grain any surface of a piece of wood which is roughly parallel to the axis of the growing tree, and shows the side walls of the cells rather than their cut ends.

single-cut file one with a single row of ridges across the blade, giving a comparatively slow cut.

skew or **skewed chisel** a chisel whose edge is ground obliquely, rather than perpendicular to the axis of the blade, so that one corner forms an acute angle and the other is obtuse.

slab another name for **flitch**.

slab-sawn or **slash-sawn** (of timber) converted by the **through-and-through** method.

slicing cut the gouge is given a sideways movement as it is pushed forwards. This may involve simply 'drifting' to the side – sometimes called 'sliding' – or rotating the handle a little (see **rocking**), or both. It can be done to the left or the right and is particularly effective with flatter gouges. See **sweep cut**.

slip or **slipstone** a small, shaped stone for working the insides of gouges or V-tools.

slipstrop a shaped strop, used like a slipstone on the inner bevels of gouges or V-tools.

sloyd knife a non-folding knife with a stout, leaf-shaped blade; the name comes from a Swedish word for 'handcraft'.

smoothing plane a general-purpose plane, typically about 9–10in (230–255mm) long.

snib a small wooden catch screwed to the bench top to hold down a thin workpiece.

socketed chisel or **gouge** one in which the handle fits into a conical socket forged on the upper end of the blade, instead of a tang; modern Western carving tools are rarely of this type.

softwood wood from a conifer, which is generally, but not always, softer than **hardwood**.

sowback gouge another name for a longbent gouge; see **bent tools.**

spade tool a term sometimes used to describe **fishtail** tools, or those intermediate between true fishtail and **allongee**.

spalting a fungal discoloration of wood, often (in beech, for example) forming brown areas attractively outlined with narrow black lines.

spokeshave a tool of the plane family with a very short body and handles either side, used mainly for shaping curved edges.

spoon or **spoonbit chisel** or **gouge** another term for a shortbent chisel or gouge; see **bent tools**.

springwood or **earlywood** wood formed in the spring, when the tree (in temperate regions) is growing at its fastest; less dense and lighter in colour than **summerwood.**

stain a pigmented preparation for colouring wood, especially one which does not deeply penetrate the surface.

star shake see **shake.**

stitching the process of forming teeth on a rasp.

stone (verb) to sharpen a blade by abrading it on a stone.

stone file a narrow, parallel-sided slipstone with a square, triangular or round section.

stop a less common word for **shoulder** or **bolster.**

stop cut a short, stabbed cut which limits the extent to which wood fibres may tear up during a subsequent cut. A saw cut may also be used as a stop cut sometimes, to prevent wood splitting along the grain (see Volume 2, Fig 2.5).

straight chisel or **gouge** one with an unbent, parallel-sided blade.

strop a strip of leather, dressed with a fine abrasive, used for the final honing and polishing of the cutting edge.

summerwood or **latewood** wood formed in the summer, when the tree (in temperate regions) is growing slowly; denser and darker in colour than **springwood.**

Surform trade name for a rasp-like tool with teeth stamped from sheet steel.

swage block the concave or female former used in forging the sweep of a gouge.

swan-necked gouge another name for a longbent gouge; see **bent tools.**

sweep the curvature of a gouge in cross section, when this is an arc of a circle. Gouges are identified by the amount of curvature, from **flat** (almost, but definitely not, a chisel) to **deep** (or **quick**, the quickest being a semicircle), with a range of sweeps in between.

sweep cut (or **sweeping cut**) a slicing cut with an emphasis on rotating the gouge by the handle so that the cutting edge tracks along the sweep. It is particularly used with deeper (but not U-shaped) gouges, which can make full use of their perfectly shaped sweeps to set in clean outlines.

tang the sharp upper end of a carving tool's blade, which fits into, and should be in line with, the handle.

tang ferrule a ferrule fitted to the tang end of a tool handle.

teak oil a commercial mixture of natural oils, solvents and colouring matter, used as a finish on dark woods.

temper the degree of hardness or brittleness left in a piece of steel by the tempering process.

tempering reducing the brittleness of hardened steel by reheating it to a critical temperature (much lower than the hardening temperature) and then quenching it.

tempering colours the distinctive spectrum of colours formed on steel during the tempering process, which the tool manufacturer may or may not remove by polishing.

throat the amount of space available between the blade and the frame of a bandsaw or scrollsaw, which determines how far from the edge of the wood the machine can cut.

through-and-through the method of sawing a tree trunk into flat boards by means of parallel cuts, resulting in minimal wastage but comparatively unstable boards.

ticketing the process of sharpening a scraper by burnishing the wire edge.

timber strictly speaking, that part of the wood of a tree which is suitable to be used by a woodworker; but the term is often used as a synonym for **wood.**

tpi teeth per inch (25mm) – a measurement of the coarseness or fineness of saw teeth. The teeth are counted inclusively: for example, 4 tpi means that tooth 1 is on the zero mark of the rule and tooth 4 is on the 1in mark.

trench tool or **trenching tool** less common names for the **macaroni tool.**

tung oil a vegetable oil which forms a more durable wood finish than linseed oil.

undercutting cutting away from behind an upstanding edge, particularly in a relief carving, to increase the sense of thinness or relief.

U-shaped gouge or **U-tool** a gouge whose section is deeper than a semicircle; usually nos. 10 and 11 in the Sheffield List.

veiner or **veining tool** a small (⅛in (3mm) or less) deep or U-shaped gouge.

V-tool or **V-chisel** a carving tool with a blade of V-shaped cross section, sometimes also called a **parting tool.**

walnut oil an edible oil which can be used as a finish on wooden items, including those used to hold food.

waney edge an uneven edge in a sawn board, comprising the original outer surface of the tree.

Washita the softest grade of natural novaculite sharpening stone.

wasting removing unwanted wood so as to approach the surface form or outline of a subject.

waterstone a natural or artificial sharpening stone designed to be used with water rather than oil, and typically faster-cutting than an oilstone.

wet grinder a slow-running grinder which uses water for lubrication.

whet to sharpen a blade by abrading it on a stone.

whetstone any kind of stone used for sharpening.

white Arkansas the name given to the medium grades of novaculite sharpening stones. The three recognized grades, in descending order of hardness, are: translucent, hard white, soft white. The translucent is recommended for bringing carving tools to their final edge.

white line the light reflected from the thick edge of an unsharpened or partly sharpened tool, which helps to show which parts of the edge need further grinding or honing.

winged (of a cutting edge) having corners which project forward of the central part.

wing parting tool a variant of the **V-tool** in which the two halves of the blade are curved outwards, rather than flat.

wire edge a feather-edge of metal protruding beyond the true cutting edge of a tool, which is formed during the grinding or honing process and must be removed before true sharpness can be achieved.

wood strictly speaking, all the fibrous material contained in a tree, whether usable by a woodworker or not.

woodcarving tool in this book, the term refers specifically to the various kinds of chisel and gouge which are designed expressly for woodcarving.

PHOTOGRAPHIC CREDITS

Photographs in this book are by Chris Skarbon, © GMC Publications Ltd, with the following exceptions:

Chris Pye: Figs 1.1–1.4, 1.15, 1.18–1.21, 1.23, 1.25–1.27, 1.32, 1.33, 1.39, 1.43, 1.58, 1.70, 2.2–2.4, 2.7–2.14, 2.17–2.21, 2.25, 3.13, 3.25, 4.8, 4.48, 5.1, 5.7–5.9, 6.2–6.6, 6.14, 6.18, 6.30, 6.31, 6.36, 6.43, 6.53, 6.56, 6.58, 6.59, 6.65, 7.1–7.4, 7.6, 7.9, 7.10, 7.14, 7.15, 7.17, 8.1–8.3, 8.5–8.10, 8.16–8.24

Tony Masero: page v

GMC Publications/Terry Porter/Mark Baker: Fig 2.1

Hegner UK: Fig 2.6

BriMarc Associates: Figs 2.15, 2.16, 2.27, 2.28

Craft Supplies Ltd: Figs 2.24, 2.26

Veritas Tools Inc.: Figs 4.14, 4.15

GMC Publications/Anthony Bailey: Fig 6.46

Jennifer Rung: Fig 7.7

Judith Nicoll: Fig 7.8

Daniel Pye: page 163

The author and publishers wish to thank the above individuals and companies for their kind assistance.

METRIC CONVERSION TABLE

INCHES TO MILLIMETRES					
inches	mm	inches	mm	inches	mm
⅛	3	9	229	30	762
¼	6	10	254	31	787
⅜	10	11	279	32	813
½	13	12	305	33	838
⅝	16	13	330	34	864
¾	19	14	356	35	889
⅞	22	15	381	36	914
1	25	16	406	37	940
1¼	32	17	432	38	965
1½	38	18	457	39	991
1¾	44	19	483	40	1016
2	51	20	508	41	1041
2½	64	21	533	42	1067
3	76	22	559	43	1092
3½	89	23	584	44	1118
4	102	24	610	45	1143
4½	114	25	635	46	1168
5	127	26	660	47	1194
6	152	27	686	48	1219
7	178	28	711	49	1245
8	203	29	737	50	1270

ABOUT THE AUTHOR

Chris Pye has been carving professionally for over 25 years, and owes his formative start to the master carver Gino Masero. His work is done mainly to commission, with clients including HRH the Prince of Wales, and ranges from architectural mouldings to figure carving, furniture to lettering, bedheads to fireplaces. Individual pieces include his own expressionist carving and abstract sculpture.

He has taught local and residential woodcarving classes in England for many years, and is also a member of the faculty at the Center for Furniture Craftsmanship (http://www.woodschool.org) in Maine, USA, where he runs carving courses each year.

He is the author of *Woodcarving Tools, Materials & Equipment* (1994), of which the present book is a revised edition; *Carving on Turning* (1995); *Lettercarving in Wood: A Practical Course* (1997); *Relief Carving in Wood: A Practical Introduction* (1998); and *Elements of Woodcarving* (2000). All of these are published by GMC Publications. He has also written extensively about woodcarving for several magazines.

Chris Pye has written and runs a website (http://www.chrispye-woodcarving.com) dedicated to the teaching, learning and love of woodcarving, from which he edits the interactive journal *Slipstones*.

He lives in rural Herefordshire with his wife Karin Vogel, a psychotherapist, and son Finian. His older son Daniel has a degree in art and plays guitar in the rock band Manchild. When not carving, teaching or writing, Chris Pye's other interests include painting, biking and tae kwon do. A Buddhist for many years, he was ordained into the Western Buddhist Order in 1990. This approach to being deeply affects his outlook and attitudes to life and work.

Chris Pye
The Poplars
Ewyas Harold
Hereford HR2 0HU

Email: chrispye@woodcarver.f9.co.uk

INDEX